Relationships for Aid

Relationships for Aid

Edited by Rosalind Eyben

London • Sterling, VA

First published by Earthscan in the UK and USA in 2006

ISBN-10:   1-84407-280-0   paperback
ISBN-13:   978-1-84407-280-4   paperback
ISBN-10:   1-84407-279-7   hardback
ISBN-13:   978-1-84407-279-8   hardback

Typesetting by JS Typesetting Ltd, Porthcawl, Mid Glamorgan
Printed and bound in the UK by Cromwell Press, Trowbridge
Cover design by Ruth Bateson

For a full list of publications please contact:

Earthscan
8–12 Camden High Street
London, NW1 0JH, UK
Tel: +44 (0)20 7387 8558
Fax: +44 (0)20 7387 8998
Email: earthinfo@earthscan.co.uk
Web: **www.earthscan.co.uk**

22883 Quicksilver Drive, Sterling, VA 20166-2012, USA

Earthscan is an imprint of James and James (Science Publishers) Ltd and publishes in
association with the International Institute for Environment and Development

A catalogue record for this book is available from the British Library

Library of Congress Cataloging-in-Publication Data

Relationships for aid / edited by Rosalind Eyben.
     p. cm.
   ISBN-13: 978-1-84407-279-8 (hardback)
   ISBN-10: 1-84407-279-7 (hardback)
   ISBN-13: 978-1-84407-280-4 (pbk.)
   ISBN-10: 1-84407-280-0 (pbk.)
   1. Economic assistance–Developing countries. 2. Poverty–Developing
countries. I. Eyben, Rosalind.
   HC60.R455 2006
   338.910091724′4–dc22

                                        2005036147

Printed on totally chlorine-free paper from well-managed sustainable forests

Contents

List of Figures and Boxes

Figures

Boxes

List of Contributors

Seema Arora-Jonsson received her doctorate from the Swedish University of Agricultural Sciences for the dissertation *Unsettling the Order: Gendered Subjects and Grassroots Activism* (2005). She is concerned with questions of participatory research and reflexivity, and built up her research around processes of co-operative enquiry. At present, she is working at the Collegium for Development Studies at Uppsala University, Sweden.

Robert Chambers is a research associate in the Participation Group at the Institute of Development Studies (IDS), Sussex, UK. His development work has been mainly in East Africa and South Asia. His current interests include participatory methodologies, institutional learning and change, and knowledge in development. His most recent books are *Participatory Workshops* (Earthscan, 2002) and *Ideas for Development* (Earthscan, 2005).

Andrea Cornwall is research fellow with the Participation Group at IDS, Sussex. She has worked extensively on participation and is the author of *Beneficiary, Consumer, Citizen: Perspectives on Participation for Poverty Reduction* (Sida, 2000) and co-editor of *Pathways to Participation* (with Garett Pratt, IT Publications, 2003).

Rosalind David is an independent consultant based in New Zealand. She has over 15 years of experience in international development work at grassroots, policy and management levels. Her last post was joint head of impact assessment at ActionAid. Rosalind has also worked for Oxfam-GB, SOS Sahel and as a consultant to UK, European and New Zealand aid agencies. She has particular expertise in implementing effective monitoring, evaluation and impact assessment systems.

Rosalind Eyben is a social scientist with a career in international development policy and practice, including in Africa, India and most recently Latin America. She resigned from the UK Department for International Development (DFID) in 2002 to become a fellow at IDS at the University of Sussex, where she convenes the Power, Participation and Change programme that supported the production of this book. Current interests include rights-based approaches, women's empowerment, the politics of policy-making, organizational learning and change, and the sociology of donor–recipient relations.

Irene Guijt is an independent adviser and researcher focusing on learning processes and systems (including monitoring and evaluation) in rural development and natural resource management, particularly where this involves collective action. She is completing her PhD on the contribution of monitoring to trigger learning in participatory rural resource management. Key publications include *Participatory Learning and Action: A Trainer's Guide* (1995, with Jules N. Pretty, John Thompson and Ian Scoones, International Institute for Environment and Development, London) and *The Myth of Community: Gender Issues in Participatory Development* (1998, with M. K. Shah, Intermediate Development Technology Group Publishing, London).

Renwick Irvine has been working in the education and development field for six years. He has experience in Guatemala, Mexico and Argentina with a variety of non-governmental organizations (NGOs). He has also worked and undertaken research in India and Pakistan. In 2004, he completed an MPhil in development studies from IDS. Currently, he is an education adviser for DFID based in Rwanda and covering Burundi.

Antonella Mancini has over ten years' experience of international development work at grassroots, policy development and management levels. Much of her experience has been gained during her time with ActionAid (AA) International's impact assessment unit, working with teams and staff across AA's programmes to encourage participatory planning, monitoring and learning approaches that help to strengthen citizen voice and action in decision-making, policy processes and transforming power relations. Antonella supported the introduction of the Accountability, Learning and Planning System (ALPS) into AA's country programmes and led the consultation and initial drafting process for the revisions to ALPS in early 2005. Antonella now works as an independent consultant.

Katherine Pasteur is a researcher and project manager at IDS, UK. She is a specialist in rural livelihoods, but has had a strong, ongoing interest in process issues such as organizational learning and change, knowledge management and monitoring and evaluation. She has been involved in work to facilitate reflection and improved implementation in these areas, principally with donor agencies, including the DFID.

Patta Scott-Villiers is a researcher at IDS and has spent most of her career working in East Africa on a variety of aid programmes, focusing, in particular, on the relationships between poor people, aid agencies, governments and other authorities. She is now based in Ethiopia working on the capabilities of pastoralists to negotiate with and influence global, national and local institutions.

Cathy Shutt is a development practitioner who has had ten years of experience working with development organizations in South-East Asia. She is currently a

DPhil student at IDS researching the operation of power in relationships between Cambodian NGOs and their funding 'partners'.

Fiona Wilson is professor of International Development Studies at Roskilde University, Denmark. In her research, she has explored processes of change in Andean Peru from the 19th century to the present day, as well as gender–class relations in Mexico's clothing industry. In the past, she worked with the Copenhagen-based NGO International Work Group for Indigenous Affairs.

Preface and Acknowledgements

This book challenges some of the assumptions about the practice of aid. It argues that if donors are to achieve their aims of contributing to the reduction of global poverty, they need to invest as much or more time in their relationships up, down and across the aid chain as they currently spend in managing their money. It means that staff in international development agencies, individually and collectively, will have to learn to change their behaviour, both with their own colleagues and with those with whom they interact at global and local levels. It means asking who we are and why we understand the world in a certain way because of our identity. How does that understanding have an impact on our behaviour and on our relations with others?

My interest in relationships for aid began when I was working in London as chief social development adviser in the UK Department for International Development (DFID). I left that post to lead a team of practitioners in DFID's small country office in Bolivia. We wanted to make a difference with a limited budget. We learned that our major aid instrument was ourselves: our country team that had a balance of highly motivated nationally and internationally recruited professionals working at the same level. We developed tools to contribute rapidly and flexibly with small amounts of money to support our partners' innovative efforts. We sought to understand the processes of social change by engaging with local researchers and through regular contact with the reality of poor people's lives. We took risks and recorded our errors, trying to learn from our mistakes. Above all, we sought to establish relations of trust and mutual respect with a diversity of partners, not trying to do things by ourselves but with others. I learned that aid agencies can make a difference not only through formally defined projects and programmes for spending money related to objectives, but also through the relationships and influence that they have on others, the values they represent and spread, and how the worth of their activities is judged by others.

When I started working at the Institute of Development Studies (IDS) in 2002, after two and a half years in Bolivia, I discovered and joined a group of colleagues who had already established a collaborative programme of work with interested practitioners in the Swedish International Development Agency (Sida), ActionAid (AA) and DFID, who through learning and innovation were exploring how to make sense of their aid relationships. This book is a fruit of that collaboration.

It would be impossible to name all the very many friends and colleagues whose ideas and encouragement have inspired me to produce this book. However, from my time in Bolivia I should mention Rosario León, whose deep experience and insights into the way aid works on local realities continue to challenge my preconceptions, as well as Liz Ditchburn, an exemplar of innovative aid practice built on trust, honesty and constant learning.

I am most grateful to Alan Fowler for reviewing a full first draft and for his advice and feedback on the book's overall structure and contents. Robert Chambers, Andrea Cornwall, Irene Guijt, Itil Asmon, Jethro Pettit and Fiona Wilson were enormously helpful and encouraging at various stages of preparation. I would also like to thank all the contributors for their ideas, enthusiasm and interest, and for delivering their chapters on time.

Finally, as convenor of the IDS Power, Participation and Change programme that is funded by DFID, Sida and the Swiss Agency for Development and Cooperation (SDC), I gratefully acknowledge our donors' support to this programme, of which this book is one of the products.

Rosalind Eyben
March 2006

List of Acronyms and Abbreviations

AA	ActionAid
AIDS	acquired immune deficiency syndrome
ALPS	Accountability, Learning and Planning System
APRA	Alianza Popular Revolucionaria Americana
APSO	Agency for Personal Service Overseas
BMZ	Bundesministerium für wirtschaftliche Zusammenarbeit und Entwicklung (Germany Ministry for Development Cooperation)
BP	British Petroleum
BTOR	Back to Office Report
CBO	community-based organization
CENDHRRA	Centre for the Development of Human Resources in Rural Areas (the Philippines)
CEO	chief executive officer
CIDA	Canadian International Development Agency
CIES	Economic and Social Research Consortium
CITE	Comité Intersectoral de Trabajadores Estatales (Peru)
DFID	UK Department for International Development
DO	development organization
EC	European Commission
EDP	Exposure and Dialogue Programme
FO	facilitating organization
FONCODES	National Fund for Compensation and Social Development in Peru
ForoSalud	Foro de la Sociedad Civil en Salud (Peru)
FPT	*Fighting Poverty Together* (ActionAid report)
GRIP	Grass Roots Immersion Programme (World Bank)
GTZ	Gesellschaft für Technische Zusammenarbeit (German Development Agency)
HIV	human immunodeficiency virus
HR/OD	human resource and organizational development
IAS	Indian Administrative Service
IAU	Impact Assessment Unit
IDO	international donor organization

IDS	Institute of Development Studies (UK)
INGO	international non-governmental organization
LDO	local development organization
MDG	Millennium Development Goal
Minsa	Ministerio de Salud (Peru)
MIS	Management Information System
MRTA	Movimiento Revolucionario Tupac Amaru
NEPAD	New Partnership for Africa's Development
NGO	non-governmental organization
OECD	Organisation for Economic Co-operation and Development
OVI	Objectively Verifiable Indicator
PPA	Programme Partnership Agreement
PRA	participatory rural appraisal
PRRP	participatory review and reflection process
RBA	rights-based approach
RBM	results-based management
SDC	Swiss Agency for Development and Cooperation
SEWA	Self-Employed Women's Association (India)
Sida	Swedish International Development Agency
TCO	technical cooperation officer
UK	United Kingdom
UNDP	United Nations Development Programme
US	United States
USAID	US Agency for International Development
VIP	Village Immersion Programme
WIEGO	Women in Informal Employment Globalizing and Organizing

Introduction

Rosalind Eyben

Relationships: A new perspective on international aid

This book is concerned with four linked factors of significance to international aid. The first is that the quality of relationships within and between organizations in the web of aid is crucial for organizational performance. We explore how reflective practice can enhance that quality. A second factor is unequal power relations. The potential for aid relationships to support progressive social change is limited by the operations of power within and between aid organizations, something that remains largely unnamed and unchallenged, thus constraining transformative learning. The third factor also related to power is weak mutual accountability within the web of aid that prejudices the quality of relationships and hinders learning. The final factor concerns the mindset of many aid practitioners whose understandings of social change are based on the premise that society is a predictable machine. The illusion of being in control leads to the neglect of relationships that would privilege different perspectives and offer new answers to managing the turbulent political environment of which donors are part, and contribute towards creating.

This introduction aims to consider these factors as they relate to the context of international aid in the mid 2000s, as well as to describe the book's origins and to identify its cross-cutting themes.

The aid web

In exploring aid relationships, it is not helpful to think of binaries: donors, on the one hand, and recipients on the other. Most organizations are both receivers and givers of money designated as 'aid'. Money moves along a chain of organizational relationships from taxpayers in Organisation for Economic Co-operation and Development (OECD) countries through their ministries of finance who, with the mandate of the legislature, pass the money onto their own official aid agencies, who, in turn, disburse part of it to non-governmental organizations (NGOs) in their own country for onward transmission to NGOs in 'recipient countries'. Of the rest, some goes directly to governments and NGOs in these countries and the remainder to 'multilateral' organizations, such as the World Bank, the European Commission or the United Nations Development Programme (UNDP), who, in turn, pass it along to recipient country governments and NGOs. However, this description can be unhelpful to understanding relationships if we focus too much on the concept of chain. It risks ignoring the diversity and complexity of networks and connections of power between the plethora of organizations that constitute the international aid system. Thus, I prefer the idea of a web.

Until recently, and with some notable exceptions (Fowler, 2000; Pomerantz, 2004), surprisingly little attention has been paid to the workings of the relationships within this web, or to the contradictions that play out in everyday practice, leading to questions such as:

- What relationships should international aid agencies prioritize in their work and what criteria should they use to guide that choice?
- How can and should aid agency staff respond to conflict and contestation within a recipient country? Whose voice and knowledge count in the decisions they make?
- How should financial management and reporting procedures be revised to optimize a concern for quality relationships in aid?

These were timely questions to pose in 2005, the year international aid moved up the agenda when leaders of the Group of 8 (G8) committed a doubling of aid expenditure within five years. They made a renewed pledge to achieving the Millennium Development Goals (MDGs) – for example, in relation to improvements in health and access to education. The assumed fears of taxpayers were soothed by stressing that money would not be misspent, and that a performance-oriented, results-based approach would deliver the desired outcomes. That same year and along the same lines, the report of the Commission for Africa noted that greater harmonization in donor procedures and alignment with the recipients' budgetary processes, combined with the better policies and institutions in recipient countries, would be the principal means for meeting the MDGs.

The commission echoed the OECD Paris Declaration on Aid earlier in that year, which also emphasized principles of mutual responsibility and partnership. However, in both cases there was little consideration as to how donors should change to live up to these principles. There has been little public discussion of what we have learned from psychology: that, ultimately, the only people we can change are ourselves (Harris, 1969) and that in order to be part of the solution, donors must recognize that they are part of the problem. This is the challenge that this book takes up. We aim to contribute not only to aid effectiveness, but also to wider learning by governments and civil society in OECD countries.

Learning to change

Under pressure from developing country governments and from constituencies for change in their own countries, donor governments are recognizing that aid is not enough to secure poverty reduction. For example, the Make Poverty History campaign has focused the attention of the public on the glaring injustice of international trade regimes constructed through historically generated unequal relations of power that aid by itself cannot redress. In its new global development policy, Sweden has committed itself to government policy coherence in which trade policy does not, for example, undermine the efforts of Swedish aid to reduce global poverty. Underpinned by a rights-based approach in which the rights and interests of poor people are central to policy, this commitment reveals difficult issues concerning the legitimacy of action, the practice of power and lines of accountability. Sweden and other donors with similar policies will experience a number of paradoxes embedded in contested understandings of state sovereignty and global rights and responsibilities.

Identifying these and other dilemmas – and finding timely responses – can help international aid to better support rather than undermine efforts towards greater global equity and social justice. This book suggests that exploring and responding to such dilemmas requires an ongoing process of *reflective practice* throughout the web of aid relationships – from prime ministers to those working at the front line in community-based organizations (CBOs). At its simplest, reflective practice[1] – a term made popular by Schön (1983) – is the ability to be aware of the dynamics of our social and professional environments, reflecting on how these shape our own behaviour and the impact that this has on other people. It means looking at one's own practice with a view to understanding and then potentially transforming it – and thus, in the context of this book, learning to change and improve the quality of our relationships with others.

Current concerns about extremism and global insecurity make the cultivation of reflective practice ever more urgent. It can encourage donor governments to appreciate how their behaviour in one arena impacts negatively upon the quality of their relationship in another. For example, observing how young men in northern Nigeria wear Osama t-shirts and perceive UK government intervention in Iraq as an unjust and illegal use of force, Sarah Ladbury noted that the best intentions of aid practice are undermined by how these citizens in an aid-recipient country view UK government behaviour overall.[2]

By late 2005, security was beginning to replace the MDGs as the focus of international aid policy. This newer concern revealed more clearly the political tensions and ambiguities in aid relationships and thus challenged the conventional approach to aid that sees development as primarily a technical matter of investment and growth. Opportunities would be missed if donor governments were to pursue their security concerns through a non-reflective imposition of their 'technical' ways of doing things, particularly in what they labelled 'fragile states'. Such an imposition would be likely to encourage resistance to the aid agenda. On the other hand, donor governments' interest in deepening democracy to combat global insecurity offers opportunities if donors can focus on changing their own behaviour as fundamentally necessary to supporting progressive change in other countries. The case studies in this book reveal the possibilities for donor reflective practice that can significantly support aspirations for a more just, secure and peaceful world.

Aid through the lens of complexity and power

Our focus on relationships draws on thinking from a wider body of current research and practice that looks at social and organizational change through the lens of complexity (see Chapter 2). The premise of complexity theory, as it relates to understanding how history happens, is that change is emergent. Organized efforts to direct change confront the impossibility of our ever understanding the totality of what is happening in a pattern of systemic relationships that is in constant flux. Composed of innumerable patterns of relationships continuously shaped and reformed through interaction with each other, new processes are constantly being generated that, in turn, may affect (loop back) and change those processes already in existence. Thus, we cannot predict all the effects that any of our actions may have on processes of change or, indeed, on ourselves as initiators of the action. Small 'butterfly' actions may have a major impact, and apparently significant actions may have very little.

Complexity theory posits that self-organizing sets of relationships through networks rather than hierarchical structures are a key element in societal change (De Landa, 2000).[3] This challenges a bureaucratic ideology that ignores the dynamics of relations which shape people's behaviour and that sees the world in terms of bounded units of control, an ideology that the contributors to this book argue prevents the learning necessary to respond to the complex and dynamic environments in which aid agencies operate – arguments initially developed in the predecessor to this volume, *Inclusive Aid* (Groves and Hinton, 2004).

Inclusive Aid was the product of a workshop held in 2001 when a group of practitioners and academics met at the Institute of Development Studies (IDS) in Sussex to consider the interplay of power, procedures and relationships in international aid. By linking 'power' with 'relationships', the workshop organizers were revealing the contradictions in the vogue for partnerships – fundamental incongruities and tensions that officialdom was ignoring in its enthusiasm for promoting 'country-led' policies. 'Power' was a particularly daring word to introduce in a consideration of aid practice.

When I asked permission from my managers in the Department for International Development (DFID) to leave my post in Bolivia for a week to participate in the workshop, I decided not to provide them with its exact title, fearful that 'power' might confirm their belief in my dangerous radicalism and dissuade them of the utility of my participation. Putting 'power' into the title of the workshop made it for me both a subversive and an empowering occasion. Because naming it reveals its existence, donors and recipients are still adverse to perceiving *power* as fundamental to the multiple sets of relationships that shape development practice. Very recently, a DFID employee volunteered to me: 'Power is at the heart of what we do; but it is an invisible word.'

While the 'P' word then and now is definitely still not on the official agenda of bilateral and multilateral aid agencies, power has been extensively examined and deconstructed during the previous decade of critical and theoretical literature on development (see, for example, Ferguson, 1990; Crush, 1995; Cooper and Packard, 1997). However, although this literature provided a welcome and needed critique of the concept of 'development', most staff in aid agencies (including me) were unfamiliar with it. In any case, its largely post-modernist perspective offered little help for those, such as the workshop participants, seeking to improve development aid. We were committed to a modernist project, sustained by a firm belief that humanity can intentionally and effectively organize itself for greater global justice and equity. How, then, were we to square the circle: to find a bridge between these two worlds to challenge and transform practice? The editors of *Inclusive Aid* suggested that what is needed are:

> ... *flexible, innovative procedures, multiple lines of accountability and the development of skills for relationship-building such as language and cultural understanding. Internally, there is a need for new organizational norms based on learning, growth and mutual respect, and where teamwork and initiative are valued over hierarchy and control.* (Groves and Hinton, 2004, p6)

Some participants at the workshop decided to explore how these new organizational norms were emerging in aid agencies.

Origins of this book

As a direct result of the workshop, IDS developed a collaborative programme of work with the Swedish International Development Agency (Sida), ActionAid and DFID to explore understandings of learning and innovative practices in relation to notions of participation and accountability.

These three aid organizations – two government agencies and an international NGO – are very different from each other, a reflection of their histories, ways of working and sources of funding. Sida is a government agency with semi-autonomous status from the Ministry of Foreign Affairs, to whom it reports and from whom it receives its funds. Swedish development cooperation started some 40 years ago during the United Nations Development Decade with a strong vision of solidarity in struggles for social justice in the developing world. Sida staff saw themselves as grassroots workers supporting radical agendas for change, rather than bureaucrats. Swedish aid has always had poverty reduction and human rights objectives.

DFID, on the other hand, initially called the Ministry of Overseas Development when established at the same time as Sida, is the direct lineal descendant of the former Colonial Office from whom it evolved. British aid tends to concentrate in its former colonies. Many of DFID's ways of workings and hierarchical form of organization are rooted in its identity as a ministry, receiving its funds from the UK Treasury and reporting directly to the UK Parliament on policy and programme implementation. Since 1997, British aid has had an overarching goal of poverty reduction.

Over 30 years old and, until recently, with its head office in London (now in Johannesburg), ActionAid is a registered charity committed to fighting poverty and is largely dependent upon voluntary donations linked to child sponsorship. Working in over 40 different developing countries, it employs about 2000 people, roughly equivalent to DFID and slightly more than Sida. Unlike the two government organizations, 90 per cent of its staff come from the countries where it is working, although recently DFID has tended to follow this trend.

Findings from this collaboration were published in an IDS series, *Lessons for Change*. Sida staff worked to explore understandings and practices of participation across the agency. Arora-Jonsson, Cornwall and others helped them to experiment with participatory learning groups (see Chapter 4). Pasteur and Scott-Villiers worked with DFID's rural livelihoods department and country offices in Uganda and Brazil to explore the importance of learning about relationships in two very different but highly aid-dependent countries where DFID exerts considerable influence, and one where its role is, arguably, very peripheral (see Chapter 5). Learning in ActionAid centred on institutionalizing a radical organization-wide approach to the Accountability, Learning and Planning System (ALPS). David, Mancini and Guijt discuss how the new system prioritizes accountability to poor people and partners, and consider its potential for revolutionizing how the organization works (see Chapter 7).

In support of the collaboration with DFID's rural livelihoods department, Pasteur undertook a review of the existing literature on organizational learning and its relevance for development practice (see Chapter 1). Given the wide range of literature relating to learning in the public, NGO and private sectors, and the huge array of definitions and perspectives, her aim was to develop focused and clear analysis of the type of learning appropriate to the context within which DFID collaborators were aiming to influence country-level policy by building effective relationships with partners; demonstrating alternatives through project and advisory work; and trying to build local ownership for these initiatives in order to influence longer-term change.

The network expanded to include others in sharing examples of practice and in pushing the theoretical frontiers. In 2003, soon after joining IDS, I began to explore accountability, learning and relationships within bureaucratic modes of organization (see Chapter 2). Meanwhile, although DFID staff in Peru had not consciously engaged with complexity theory, they responded to the potential that self-organizing networks represented for aid practice. They invested far more energy and resources in supporting relationships and social processes both within and outside the state administration than in formal institutions, and their emphasis was other than securing technical and measurable outcomes. Wilson and Eyben were among a bigger team invited to document this experience (see Chapter 6). Concurrently within IDS, we had began to explore, with the German Exposure and Dialogue Programme, the significance of 'immersions' in enabling staff in aid agencies to learn experientially and to reflect on the lives of the poor for whom their organizations exist (see Chapter 3). Finally, in terms of chronology, Shutt used current research and past professional practice to explore how donors' financial rules and procedures can distort and seriously damage the recipients' efforts to pursue the social justice goals that it shares with its partners (see Chapter 8).

This is how the collaborative learning programme evolved to include new themes and partners. The book's structure does not follow that chronological trajectory. Following this Introduction, two theoretical chapters help to frame our understanding of aid relations. After this, case studies follow that are sequenced to move from exploring personal change through relation-based learning, to organizational change through collective learning processes within aid agencies, to studies of the challenges of learning not only within, but also between, organizations in the aid web.

Written from various perspectives within the world of aid – practice, research and facilitation – a significant feature is the authors' ability to locate themselves in their stories as participant observers and actors, struggling with complexity, ambiguity and doubt. Practitioners have become researchers and *vice versa*. These changes in perspectives provide opportunities for empathetic learning; for those of us who went through these transitions, we remember how the world looked to us when *we* were in *their* shoes. Such learning is a crucial step to strengthening relationships for a reformed international aid practice. The exchange of ideas, ways of knowing and interrogation of shared values that are continuously evolving within the web of relationships in which all the book's contributors are variously located have shaped the chapters' analytical and reflective approaches to the three themes of power, learning and accountability. These are now briefly explored in the remainder of this chapter.

Relational notions of power

The meaning that any one of us gives to *power* depends upon why we are interested in it and what we want to get out of it. Interest and motivation are shaped by our education, our personal experience and by how we understand ourselves in relation to the world (our politics and values). The particular context of our interest and motivation also shapes the content that we give to the concept. I think about power differently when considering the invasion of Iraq than when wondering why my grandson has me pick up, for the nth time, the spoon he has dropped on the floor.[4]

The case studies in this book approach power in a variety of ways. One of these is a typology of processes in which A gets B to do something, as, for example, in the visible, hidden and invisible types of power discussed by Pasteur in Chapter 1. Another is an understanding of power as producing an effect. We know that power is operating when we spot resistance. Eyben (Chapters 2) and Shutt (Chapter 8) discuss this with reference to resistance learning and 'the weapons of the weak'. Other contributors sometimes understand power as relational and sometimes as a resource that can be divided up. For example, David, Mancini and Guijt (Chapter 7) suggest that ActionAid's internationalization should be understood as part of an attempt to distribute power more equitably within the organization and, in the longer haul, between ActionAid and poor people. ActionAid is relatively unusual in exploring the implications and meanings of power for its practice. Yet, it is only beginning to understand the implications of understanding power as a relational process that defines boundaries and creates meanings.

Can other aid agencies follow ActionAid's example and seek to break free of their own past and get to grips with power as a fundamental issue to partnerships for social justice? As Chapter 7 shows, such an effort is difficult, costly, needs time and brings its own ongoing challenges, as well as achievements. Those involved have learned that it means addressing relations of power within, as well as between, organizations. The top leadership in ActionAid – management and board – not only supported the change, but also enthusiastically promoted it. In contrast, the other case studies in this volume that relate to Sida and DFID are accounts of energetic and committed individuals and limited networks, tolerated but hardly supported by senior management.

Relational notions of power challenge the idea of objective value-free knowledge because such knowledge – how we understand and describe the world – is contingent upon our time and place, and the relations with others that shape our lives and identity. Pasteur (Chapter 1) describes this in relation to Flood's four windows of learning, one window of which is power that determines legitimate knowledge. Hence, aid agencies develop and deploy instruments and procedures that reflect and reproduce certain ways of understanding the world – thus excluding other ways. Examples discussed in this book are the Country Assistance Plan (Chapter 6) and the Programme Partnership Agreement (Chapter 7).

The obligatory inclusion of the logframe by many bilateral and multilateral aid agencies is another example. Its imposition can lead to 'regressive learning', discussed by Shutt (Chapter 8). 'Regressive learning' occurs when a recipient organization 'learns the ropes' and changes its own values and ways of working so as to respond to the requirements of the financing organization. However, while learning to comply, the organization might also learn to resist. The DFID office in Peru conducted a logframe for their Country Assistance Plan; but their approach to knowledge in designing a rights-based approach was very different. Thus, they appeared to be compliant, while resisting, protecting their core area of work,[5] as I discuss in Chapter 2.

Similarly, ActionAid staff were not prepared to play the compliance game, but vocally objected to the DFID imposition of a logframe in their Programme Partnership Agreement. As a matter of principle, they objected to conforming to 'normal practice' that defines clear objectives and outcomes. These different reactions to the standardized ways of constructing knowledge and framing problems in aid practice indicate the potential for reflective practitioners to explore the circumstance in which others in the web react as they do to the way in which relationships are understood and constructed by the donor. Several contributions to this book demonstrate that it is learning through *these* relationships that supports and strengthens such reflective practice.

Learning through relationships

The presence of power can make learning through relationships difficult. Guijt (Chapter 7) observes that, despite considerable achievements, ActionAid still has to consolidate and fully implement processes for organization-wide horizontal learning from local field offices, as well as from national offices. Who does and does not learn complements Pasteur's question in Chapter 1 about who decides what is knowledge. In both cases, we cannot separate the process of learning from the sets of relationships in which such learning takes place. This is why several contributors emphasize the importance of workshops, meetings, retreats and even email discussion or online communities of practice 'as spaces and opportunities for improved learning through dialogue and enquiry' (see Chapter 2).

 While Pasteur touches on personal critical reflection for transformative learning, her emphasis here, as with Scott-Villiers (Chapter 5), is largely on the challenges at the organizational level. This is because the content of individual professional learning is generated from the organizational context in which it takes place, as well as from the narratives that are chosen by the organization to communicate learning – discussed by Irvine and his co-authors in relation to the wider significance of feedback from personal experiences of immersions in Chapter 3.

 An experiment to encourage Sida staff to learn differently through a cooperative enquiry process that became a site for collective learning and reflection through action is the subject of Chapter 4. Arora-Jonsson and Cornwall describe an event for Sida bureaucrats that, through changing the familiar context and narrative, offered an opportunity to learn something different about the way in which they worked with each other. Yet, while some embraced this chance to reflect on their own histories with Sida and what 'participation' has come to mean to them, the different environment created by this event was disconcerting to others. It led to 'a sort of understanding, but it seemed intangible' (see Chapter 4). The authors note that because, when learning about relationships, people are dealing with issues that *are* less tangible, experiences and concepts will often be shared through stories and anecdote, involving high levels of ambiguity as well as emotion. A relationship is a process, not a thing. It is characterized by conversations, assumptions and the power relations between the parties.

 Sida's learning group's problem was how to translate this new understanding of relationships back into the conventional world of aid practice in which activities are designed to lead to clearly determined outcomes. Nevertheless, argue the authors, this kind of 'counter-cultural' experience offers the chance for the development of new capabilities and new ways of relating within the organization – and from that to new ways of relating and understanding in the wider world of aid practice.

Chapter 4 and Chapter 3 on immersions provide examples of learning activities for reflective practice. Unless its own staff members explore how the way they learn shapes their attitudes and behaviour, an aid agency may find that its efforts to support capacity development in recipient organizations will come to naught. Everyone will see that the agency is not practising what it preaches. In Chapter 7, David, Mancini and Guijt comment that organizational change is often sought through altering an organization's mechanics and structures, the easiest things to change, with too little attention paid to principles and behaviour, which play a more important role in shaping relations with others. This is why ActionAid's new ALPS process emphasized values and principles.

Learning through relationships poses yet a further challenge – that of 'making the covert visible', something that Sida staff feared might undermine the prospect of their learning group being taken seriously by colleagues and managers, as well as exposing the tactics they used to navigate their way within the strictures of bureaucracy. Power operates through what is not said. Current power relations in the world of international aid could be described as 'knowing what not to know'[6] – being aware of elephants in the room and colluding to pretend that they are not there. For example, in Chapter 8 Shutt notes that 'regressive' or compliant learning takes place within a context of broader complicity in which all parties to the relationship 'know' that there is a discrepancy between the organization's financial situation presented in annual accounts and the reality of everyday life; but such knowledge is covert. The fear of what happens if the shared secret is revealed may be one reason why aid staff are largely reluctant to explore the everyday life which immersions offer them (Chapter 3).

It is one thing to recognize the benefits of learning through relationships, but it is another to translate that recognition into practical tools and processes. Pasteur and Scott-Villiers (Chapter 5) point out that there are numerous books advising on the subject; but the practice is far from simple. One recent suggestion is that more face-to-face visits between donor and recipient organizations foster more open dialogue and improve upward and downward accountability by making monitoring and accountability more rigorous and meaningful (Mawdsley et al, 2005).

One of the simplest things to do is for agency staff to spend some time with the end users of aid, seeking their hospitality in their homes in villages or urban slums. Irvine and his co-authors (Chapter 3) argue that the efficacy of immersions is a more profound understanding of the reality of the lives of people living in poverty. This can contribute to rethinking policy and practice. On the other hand, we are warned that immersions only have this impact if individuals are emotionally and intellectually prepared, and if their organizations are capable of responding to the experiential learning that immersions offer. Immersions are uncomfortable because they challenge assumptions. Efforts to look at the world from someone else's perspective can be deeply disconcerting and possibly painful if it includes seeking feedback on one's values, attitudes and behaviour from those with whom we work.

Building relationships in which the national government has primary ownership appears central to the approach of DFID and other official donors as they move towards budget support and policy influencing (see Chapter 5). However, this same switch has also led to staff spending much less time interacting with the beneficiaries of their organization's efforts (see Chapters 3 and 4). This, at best, limits their circle of potential relations and, at worst, results in increasing time being spent in improving the way in which the recipient government manages its finances to the detriment of learning why spending this extra money does not necessarily lead to the desired change.

Conversely, as DFID in Peru argued, a small budget does not necessarily constitute a major constraint to making a difference. It was *how* the money was spent that mattered. DFID's partners commented that what they appreciated from the relationship with DFID was not the money, but the intellectual input and the accompaniment (see Chapter 6). Perhaps, significantly, the cases from DFID where relationship-building rather than money management is a primary concern – for example, in Peru and in Brazil (Chapter 5) – are those where the organization's annual expenditure is small. In Uganda, on the other hand, DFID's country office appeared less interested (Chapter 5). This may be because Uganda is highly aid-dependent and DFID has a big budget to spend. Pasteur and Scott-Villiers believed that it was the lessons from the Uganda experiment that made the organizational learning partnership more successful in its subsequent engagement with DFID's office in Brazil; but there may be another reason. In non-aid dependent Brazil, DFID was a small player with a little budget and may therefore have decided that it needed to invest more in relationships if it were to make a difference.

Understanding relationships and making the most of them requires what has been termed 'emotional intelligence' (Goleman, 2001). Pasteur and Scott-Villiers consider its importance for organizational learning in Chapter 5. In Chapter 8, Shutt looks at what happens in the absence of emotional intelligence and describes the stress we cause to others when we fail to empathize with their situation – for example, when they are at the receiving end of a more powerful organization's inflexible procedural requirements. She argues that lack of emotional intelligence by donors has a negative emotional impact on staff in recipient organizations and hinders their learning to develop mutual accountability.

The challenges of accountability

A key aspect of learning in relationships, argue Pasteur and Scott-Villiers (Chapter 5), is developing self-awareness and a sound understanding of the power, position and biases that one holds in relation to others. Is it possible to shape accountability in a similar fashion?

In conventional aid practice, accountability is conceptualized in terms of good governance and refers to holding organizations and individuals within them responsible for their performance in relation to their commitments. Thus, one definition of accountability is 'the obligation of power-holders to account for or take responsibility for their actions and choices. "Power-holders" refers to those who hold political, financial or other forms of power' (Johnson, 2005, p3). ActionAid has introduced this notion of accountability within their own practice, and from such an understanding come ideas of vertical accountability in which the ability to hold power-holders to account depends upon the relations within a hierarchy of power. This model informs the principles of ALPS (see Chapter 7).

ActionAid's efforts are part of a growing movement, particularly in the field of non-governmental practice that seeks to tackle the current accountability practices of international aid agencies, which, it is argued, impede democratic decision-making, prevent learning and breed waste and corruption.[7] Here the emphasis is on an accountability that requires civil society organizations to be inclusive in their engagement with stakeholders, and transparent and open in their public reporting. This agenda is driven by a concern to be accountable to both voluntary givers in the North and end-users or beneficiaries in the South.

In the world of official aid practice, accountability has also become an increasingly prominent issue for many of the same reasons, while particularly driven by a concern to justify an increase in financial aid. Thus, at the Monterrey Conference on Financing for Development, the 'international community' concluded that there were the makings of a new development partnership based on a framework of mutual accountability between developed and developing countries. Monterrey recipients pledged to practise good government and donors pledged to provide sufficient resources (IMF, 2002). Compared with domestic line departments, such as health or education, foreign aid agencies are unusual in the sense that their intended beneficiaries are neither citizens nor residents whose status, in theory, would give them an 'organic' stake in the performance of government agencies and officials. On the contrary, they are very much outside the public revenue streams upon which claims for accountability and entitlement are commonly based (Johnson, 2005).

Donors have been trying to square this circle through the introduction of results-based management (RBM). This means focusing on results and a systematic approach to monitoring the actions of all parties. RBM has the apparently positive effect of donors requiring that (as a *quid pro quo* for receiving aid) recipient governments introduce a similar system in their own country. The performance information thus acquired serves the needs of both governments in responding to citizens' demands that the public sector delivers value for money against stated objectives. Thus, donors and recipients can learn together about what works and what doesn't work in terms of effective aid. Chapter 2 critiques this approach, and from a complexity perspective explores why RBM may, in fact, be counter-productive to helping both donors and recipients achieve their goals because it constrains learning through relationships.

At first glance, '*mutual* accountability' appears to assume an already existing equality of relationship without any apparent need to reverse or diminish previously established hierarchical relations of power. Thus, the principle of mutual accountability is cited as the foundation for the New Partnership for Africa's Development (NEPAD), recognizing that policies and actions of both developed and developing countries have an impact on the effectiveness of aid and on the outcomes of development efforts (Makonnen, 2003).

In the preparations for the 2005 G8 Summit at Gleneagles, citing the *Commission for Africa Report*, President Obasanjo of Nigeria 'emphasized that partnership is based on mutual accountability and clearly defined obligations. In this regard, he expressed concern about the unfulfilled pledges made to Africa by its development partners in the past' (Africa Partnership Forum, 2005). Since then African governments have been asking why donor commitments made at the 2005 summit appear not to have been met. They can complain there; but there are no sanctions on donors should they default on their commitments. Furthermore, neither the donors nor their recipient partners are prepared to use the language of *downward* accountability because that would reveal the covert but shared knowledge that the relationship is, indeed, an unequal one.[8]

In contrast to ActionAid, DFID in Peru emphasized (along with responsiveness and transparency) mutual, rather than downward, accountability between donors and partners. Staff saw this as one of the elements of a rights-based approach with partners encouraged to practise similar rules of engagement with their fellow citizens/members (see Chapter 6). Using only small pockets of money in a context where their ideas and convening power were appreciated as much as their financial support, DFID staff did not perceive themselves as being in a hierarchical power relationship. However, through DFID's relational network approach, Wilson and Eyben suggest that it may have been running the risk of reinforcing existing social patterns of patronage, putting in jeopardy the good governance principles of transparent horizontal and vertical lines of accountability. If the DFID office had not closed, it might have been in the position of exploring more fully the implications of practising an aid relationship based more on the informal rather than the formal networks identified by Sida's learning group (see Chapter 4).

Nevertheless, a relationships approach to aid, despite its potential perils of falling into patronage traps (the shadow side of friendship), may go further than the mutual accountability principle. It can explore how a shared construction of knowledge, with an explicit recognition of the operations of power, may lay the foundations for trust and transparency that Pasteur and Scott-Villiers (Chapter 5) state to be the critical precursors for collaboration. Yet, the challenge becomes greater when we consider its implications for money management, where the details of accountancy practice fundamentally shape the aid relationship.

While programme/policy staff may be committed to downward accountability, innovation and empowerment, financial management staff are bound by systems of regulating financial matters that have evolved over the last 200 years as a means of combating discretion and flexibility. In Chapter 8, Shutt explores what happens to medium-size recipient development organizations as a result of these bureaucratic financial procedures that are applied with increasing rigour as the money passes down what she describes as the aid chain. She notes the damage that this causes in circumstances of highly unequal power relations.

In considering the impact of these procedures on learning, Shutt picks up the theme discussed in Chapter 2 of regressive and transformative learning. She argues that a necessary condition for achieving the latter is that the organization which holds the money in relation to the next one down the chain integrates managing the money within its wider moral relationship with the recipient. Thus, money needs to be procured and managed in such a way as to reinforce rather than to hinder relationships working for aid to reduce poverty and secure social justice. As described in relation to ActionAid's ALPS (Chapter 7), Shutt argues that this can be achieved through a better integration of the financial and programme planning cycles in order to avoid the financial tail from wagging the programmatic dog.

Such integration is not easy. ActionAid tried to do this by diversifying its sources of funding away from child sponsorship in order to release itself from the powerful grip of its own marketing team and the pressure of one-way accountability back to the donor. However, it found that it had jumped from the frying pan into the fire. Government donors, such as DFID, proved to be equally insistent on reporting procedures that focused on their needs, rather than being accountable for performance to the citizens in the South for whom ActionAid exists. A lofty organizational intention of 'reduced reporting' upwards is only feasible if the organization operates in a kind of vacuum vis-à-vis other funders – which is unlikely these days given the efforts to reduce transaction costs for recipients through joined-up or harmonized procedures.

Shutt argues that overstretched organizations would benefit from a reduction in their transaction costs if all their donors were to harmonize their financial reporting requirements. This case has already been successfully made, although often not yet practised, in relation to government-to-government aid. However, whether harmonization – for example, by donors putting their money in the recipient government's budget instead of funding their own discrete projects – supports or hinders more egalitarian power relations between donor and recipient governments is a highly debatable point. On the one hand, it can empower recipients by enabling them to take a systemic rather than a project-based approach to budgetary planning. On the other hand, it can disempower them through donors ganging up together.[9] Unless the operations of power are named and tackled, the harmonization solution to problems of aid fragmentation may create even bigger difficulties for the recipient. Accountability arrangements cannot be successfully reformed unless they are understood as a political as well as a technical issue, a point that still largely escapes the attention of official donors.

Conclusion

This book makes the case for a relationships approach to international aid as the necessary foundation for donors and recipients taking collective responsibility for shared transformative learning – that is, learning that results in action leading to irrevocable changes for the better. On the other hand, such mutual learning will fail without a constant awareness of, and response to, power that permeates the web of aid relationships, shapes actions and produces knowledge.

The current context is not an easy one. Since the IDS workshop in May 2001, a time of global doubt and anxiety has replaced the heady optimism of aid agencies during the new millennium and its MDGs. There is a fear that the commitment to rights and justice for all signalled at the great United Nations conferences of the 1990s is being rapidly eroded and that the new instruments of international aid, rather than supporting diversity and empowerment, are constructing hegemonic visions of the world.

Yet, international aid is full of contradictions. The fact that this book has seen the light of day is due to the financing that the IDS and many of the individual contributors have received from those very aid organizations which we suspect of hegemonic pretensions. Where we see the unbridled play of power and arrogant amnesia, we also note serious and innovative efforts to create a more democratic world, to support transformative learning and to strengthen accountability. When things appear at their darkest, there are often the greatest opportunities for radical change. Finally, some of the ideas put forward in this book may only take effect over the long term 'through gradually shifting the policy debate and opening up for a distant future some possibilities now inconsistent with the conventional volitions that guide society' (Lindblom, 1990, p262).

Notes

1   'Reflective' and 'reflexive' are both commonly used terms to describe this process. For some speakers, they are synonymous, while for others reflexivity implies a greater degree of discursive self-consciousness. This Introduction has opted for 'reflective'; but some of the other contributors to this book prefer to use 'reflexive'.
2   Pers comm with Sarah Ladbury, 15 October 2005.
3   De Landa prefers the term 'meshworks'.
4   Haugaard (2002, p1) provides a very helpful schematic diagram showing the historical evolution of different concepts of power in the Western intellectual tradition. Power as it relates to development practice is discussed in a number of chapters in Alsop (2005).
5   See the discussion on the issue of apparent compliance in order to minimize actual funding influence over core activities in Ebrahim (2005).
6   See Taussig (1999) on the theme of power and secrecy.
7   See, for example, www.keystonereporting.org. The website states: 'accountability is about performance. In development terms, this means holding organizations to account for their different contributions to real social change' (accessed 15 November 2005).
8   Of course, there are donors who have many lines of accountability, upwards, downwards and sideways, in terms of power and of varying significance in terms of the strength of the relationship (see Eyben and Ferguson, 2004).
9   Edgren (2003) notes the conflict in interpretation on this point in two different Sida-commissioned studies on donorship and ownership (see also Eyben, 2005).

References

Africa Partnership Forum (2005) Communiqué issued at the end of the Fourth Meeting of Africa Partnership Forum, 9–10 April, www.g8.gov.uk/, accessed 2 October 2005

Alsop, R. (ed) (2005) *Power, Rights and Poverty Reduction*, World Bank, Washington, DC

Commission for Africa (2005) *Our Common Interest: Report of the Commission for Africa*, July 2005, www.commissionforafrica.org/

Cooper, F. and Packard, R. (1997) 'Introduction', in *International Development and the Social Sciences*, University of California Press, Berkeley and Los Angeles

Crush, J. (ed) (1995) *Power of Development*, London, Routledge

De Landa, M. (2000) *A Thousand Years of Non-Linear History*, Swerve Editions, New York

Ebrahim, A. (2005) *NGOs and Organizational Change: Discourse, Reporting and Learning*, Cambridge University Press, Cambridge

Edgren, G. (2003) 'Donorship, ownership and partnership', in *Sida Studies in Evaluation*, Sida, Stockholm

Eyben, R. (2005) 'Donors' learning difficulties', in *Increased Aid: Minimising Problems, Maximising Gains*, IDS Bulletin vol 36, no 3, September, pp98–107

Eyben, R. and Ferguson, C. (2004) 'Can donors be more accountable to poor people?', in Groves, L. and Hinton, R. (eds) *Inclusive Aid*, Earthscan, London

Ferguson, J. (1990) *The Anti-Politics Machine*, University of Minnesota Press, Minnesota

Fowler, A. (2000) *NGOs, Civil Society and Social Development: Changing the Rules of the Game*, Geneva 2000 Occasional Paper no 1, United Nations Research Institute for Social Development, Geneva

Goleman, D. (2001) 'Emotional intelligence: Issues in paradigm building', in Cherniss, C. and Goleman, D. (eds) *The Emotionally Intelligent Workplace: How To Select For, Measure and Improve Emotional Intelligence In Individuals, Groups and Organizations*, JosseyBass, San Francisco

Groves, L. and Hinton, R. (eds) (2004) *Inclusive Aid: Changing Power and Relationships in International Development*, Earthscan, London

Harris, T. (1969) *I'm OK, You're OK*, Harper and Row, New York

Haugaard, M. (2002) *Power: A Reader*, Manchester University Press, Manchester

IMF (International Monetary Fund) (2002) *Financing for Development: Implementing the Monterrey Consensus Paper Prepared by the Staff of the World Bank and the IMF for the Spring 2002 Development Committee Meeting*, 11 April, IMF, www.imf.org

Johnson, C. (2005) *Social Accountability*, Unpublished report of a workshop organized for the Swiss Agency for Development Cooperation, Berne, October 2004

Lindblom, C. (1990) *Inquiry and Change: The Troubled Attempt to Understand and Shape Society*, Yale University Press, New Haven

Makonnen, E. (2003) 'Mutual accountability and policy coherence', Presentation to the Committee of Experts, Economic Commission for Africa, 29 May, Addis Ababa, www.uneca.org/eca_resources/Speeches/2003_speeches/052903speech_by_Elene_Makonnen.htm, accessed 2 October 2005

Mawdsley, E., Townsend, J. and Porter, G. (2005) 'Trust, accountability and face-to-face interaction in North–South NGO relations', *Development in Practice*, vol 15, no 1, pp77–81

Pomerantz, P. (2004) *Aid Effectiveness in Africa: Developing Trust between Donors and Governments*, Lexington Books, Lanham

Schön, E. (1983) *The Reflective Practitioner*, Temple Smith, London

Taussig, M. (1999) *Public Secrecy and the Labor of the Negative*, Stanford University Press, Stanford

Part 1

FRAMING THE ISSUES

1

Learning for Development

Katherine Pasteur

Introduction

Learning our way into a mysterious future calls for continuously revisiting what might be going on, what we are doing and achieving, and the way we are doing it. (Flood, 1999, p90)

The environment in which development agencies are working is characterized by complexity and uncertainty. The development process itself is non-linear, unpredictable and poorly understood: a complex range of social, economic and political factors are at play over which donor organizations, and even partners, have very little control. Furthermore, decisions are shaped by personal behaviours and organizational norms and constraints. Organizational learning is considered a key discipline for dealing with the 'white water'; of dynamic, unfamiliar and uncertain contexts. When individuals are in the position of doing things they have little experience with or have never done before, effective learning is a clearly a critical skill (Vaill, 1996).

How can development professionals gain a more nuanced understanding of the highly contextual and often ambiguous environments and relationships in which they are involved to make appropriate choices and decisions? More consistent and collaborative processes for holistic and profound reflection and learning are seen as fundamental to improving practice in this respect. This requires new theories, methods and tools for learning, as well as shifts in attitudes and relationships to permit greater openness and honesty. The implications for personal behaviour and institutional norms and procedures must also be taken into account (Chambers et al, 2001).

This chapter briefly scans the breadth of literature on organizational learning before focusing in on a closer interrogation of learning as reflection and reflexivity, leading to the reframing of knowledge and understanding, and improved actions and outcomes. Organizational learning is more than the transfer of knowledge around an organization: it implies additional analysis and judgement to translate knowledge into new insights and action. Improved strategies for personal and collaborative reflection that seek to build a more holistic understanding of an issue or problem are necessary to achieve the kinds of insight that result in profound learning and change.

The implications of this type of learning for an organization are thus less to do with knowledge management systems and processes, and more concerned with developing new tools for dialogue and holistic analysis, and attitudes and skills for working collaboratively. There are also implications for the guiding ideas (or paradigms) upon which organizational practice is founded, and the types of organizational culture, structures, incentives and procedures that dominate.

What do we mean by learning and the learning organization?

The literature on organizational learning is vast. This body of work, coming principally from the private sector, covers a range of disciplinary perspectives, with many different but often overlapping understandings of the goals, dynamics and problems associated with learning. A summary of these different perspectives on organizational learning is outlined in Box 1.1. As a result, Easterby-Smith (1997, p1085) argues that 'the creation of a comprehensive theory is an unrealistic aspiration'.

BOX 1.1 DIVERSE PERSPECTIVES ON ORGANIZATIONAL LEARNING

- *Management science*: concerned with gathering and processing information in and about the organization.
- *Sociology and organization theory*: focuses on the broader social systems and organizational structure where learning becomes embedded and which affect organizational learning.
- *Strategic perspective*: focuses on competition and the ways in which learning gives one organization an advantage over another.
- *Production management*: looks at the relationship between learning and organizational productivity and efficiency.
- *Cultural perspective*: describes how organizational and national cultures are a significant cause and effect of organizational learning.
- *The learning organization*: concerned with implementation and the characteristics of organizations which are able to effectively share and use knowledge to achieve organizational goals.

Source: Easterby-Smith (1997)

Interest in organizational learning in the context of development has tended to concern itself principally with issues of either monitoring and evaluation, or knowledge management (e.g. Korten, 1984; Marsden et al, 1994; Davies, 1998; King and McGrath, 2002; for a full review, see Hovland, 2003). Both are important ways of understanding and practising organizational learning. They do not, however, fully respond to the deeper concerns and contextual challenges described in the introduction. More recent literature, including a recent issue of *Development in Practice* (2002) and a volume edited by Groves and Hinton (2004) describe and analyse experiences of innovative learning and reflection methods and practice that greatly advance the thinking and understanding in this field. These will be referred to in more detail later in this chapter.

This section will briefly explore some of the different understandings of knowledge and learning. Given the wide array of meanings, the purpose of this section is to try to articulate and contextualize an understanding of learning as reflection and reflexivity in practice.

The nature of knowledge

How does organizational learning differ from other similar concepts such as information management and knowledge-sharing? Ackoff (1989) identifies a hierarchy stretching from data, through information and knowledge, to the pinnacle of wisdom. The distinction between each of these stages is the degree of cognitive processing of raw data or experience, from mere assimilation through memorizing, to transformation into new insight and action.

Data and information principally provide answers to 'who', 'what', 'where' and 'when' questions. Application of data and information leads to the building of knowledge, or 'know-how'. This distinction is similar to Nonaka et al's (1996) distinction between explicit and tacit knowledge and their differing means of transmission. Explicit knowledge – like Ackoff's information – is unequivocal and readily observable. As such, it is clearly transmittable in formal systematic language, and therefore can be documented or articulated with relative ease. Tacit knowledge, on the other hand, is often based on experience and skills. Such first-hand experiential knowing is naturally personal and often context-specific. It is much less easy to express and can only really be transferred through socialization processes, such as jointly performed tasks, face-to-face discussions, informal meetings, communities of practice, etc. (Nonaka and Takeuchi, 1995). There has been considerable increase in interest and investment in these forms of information management and knowledge-sharing amongst development non-governmental organizations (NGOs) and some bilaterals and multilaterals during recent years (King and McGrath, 2002; Hovland, 2003).

Ackoff takes his hierarchy two stages further. First, while knowledge results in learning, which improves efficiency, *systematic* ongoing learning and adaptation require a further level of understanding: knowing 'why'. Understanding is achieved through enquiry, analysis and diagnosis. Finally, wisdom is the pinnacle of the hierarchy. It involves a greater element of evaluation and judgement, and is more greatly influenced by values, ethics, aesthetics and morality – that is, it takes into account long-range as well as short-range consequences of any act (Ackoff, 1989; King and McGrath, 2002).

Machine-based systems can help to share data, information and even knowledge. However, understanding and wisdom require higher-order mental faculties to be able to analyse, diagnose and make judgements. These can only be achieved through human psychological and social systems, whether at individual or interactive level (Ackoff, 1989; King and McGrath, 2002).

Data/information 'who', 'what', 'where' and 'when'	Knowledge 'how'	Understanding/wisdom 'why'

Source: based on Ackoff (1989)

Figure 1.1 *An information, knowledge and learning continuum*

People who have understanding and wisdom can use it to improve effectiveness, rather than merely to increase efficiency of actions and outcomes (Ackoff, 1989). They can reinterpret and adapt knowledge and thus are able to improvise in different or unforeseen situations and environments. Knowledge is transformed into something that generates more generic insights, and so performance can be improved in a wider range of contexts. Learning is therefore less concerned with capturing and storing knowledge than with transforming knowledge and experience into improved action:

> *Taking in information is only distantly related to real learning. It would be nonsensical to say: 'I just read a great book about bicycle riding – I've learned that.' Through learning we become able to do something we were never able to do. Through learning we re-perceive the world and our relationship to it.* (Senge, 1990, p13)

Thus, several authors view learning as something distinct from the mere assimilation of information and knowledge. It implies the creation of deeper understanding and insight, which expands the range of action options. Learning in this sense principally requires processes of human interaction and socialization, rather than technological systems. Snowden (2002, p3) notes that learning is both a thing (something absolute, awaiting discovery) and a flow – that is, an 'ephemeral, active process of relating'. He suggests that learning is more than the acquisition of information and knowledge: it implies the creation of new understanding and insight through more holistic reflection, dialogue and analysis. It is not merely the content of learning that is important, but also the context within which it happens, and the quality of the narrative or relationship through which it flows. In terms of learning context, it is 'more about providing space and time for new meaning to emerge' than it is about moving bits of information to accessible places (Snowden, 2002, p10).

Learning, as outlined above, should not necessarily be considered superior to information systems or knowledge-sharing – only distinct. Different types of information systems, knowledge-sharing and learning processes are appropriate to different types of work settings; thus, the strategies or mechanisms employed will differ accordingly.

Appropriate learning within different work settings

Pickering (2002) notes that the characteristics of particular work settings and, thus, of the particular learning needs of each will depend upon:

- the level of interdependence of actors – that is, the level of cross-functional or cross-organizational collaboration required by the job;
- the complexity of work tasks – that is, the degree of judgement or improvization that is required.

This highlights four distinct types of work setting as illustrated in Figure 1.2.

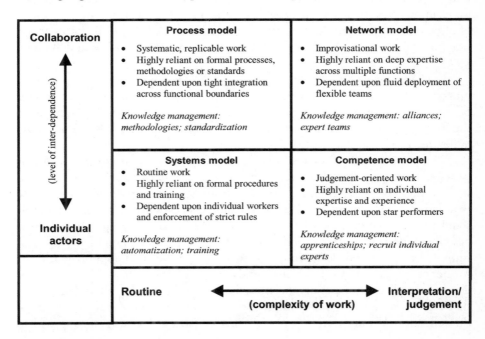

Source: adapted from Pickering (2002)

Figure 1.2 *Work styles matrix*

The systems and process models are appropriate for work settings that are highly routine and do not require elements of judgement or interpretation. In other words, what is needed to perform tasks is principally 'know-how'. Learning in the context of systems and process work settings takes place through more standardized mechanisms, such as generalized training or 'how to' guidance materials and sharing evaluations and other reports.

Network- and competence-model work settings involve far greater levels of judgement to carry out tasks and are dependent upon deeper understanding and insight, and an ability to improvise amongst staff. In these types of work environment, standardized instructions, or even generalized lessons from other contexts, are not always directly applicable. Work tasks in the development context – whether project based, negotiation or policy influencing – clearly fit within these two domains and, principally, within the network model. Thus, the context of learning will differ from that of routine tasks, being more associated with interactive formats, as well as individual expertise based on reflection on experience.

Learning leading to action

Much literature on learning in the context of knowledge management focuses on ways of improving access to knowledge based on the assumption that more knowledge leads to better outcomes. This assumption has been questioned (see, for example, Ackoff, 1989; Senge, 1990). The purpose of learning in the context of organizations is to improve practice – that is, there should ideally be an action outcome (Binney and Williams, 1995; Pedler et al, 1991; Pedler and Boutall, 1992).

Learning is viewed by many authors as a cyclical process whereby people reflect on actions, knowledge and experience, and, as a result, reframe their perceptions of their original experience or strategy, leading to new actions or strategies in the future (Kolb, 1984; Pedler and Boutall, 1992; Boud et al, 1985; Binney and Williams, 1995) (see Figure 1.3).

The stage of reflection and questioning is critical to an effective learning cycle, while the quality of the reflection process is crucial to achieving the next stage in the cycle: the reframing of the initial understanding or beliefs relating to that action. This outcome makes the learning process different from the simple acquisition and application of new knowledge (Pedler and Boutall, 1992). Dewey describes reflection as 'active, persistent and careful consideration of any belief or supposed form of knowledge in the light of the grounds that support it and the further conclusions towards which it tends' (Dewey, 1933, p118). The greater the depth, breadth and honesty of reflection, the greater the insight and understanding that can be gained. The following section explores in more detail the nature of the reflection or questioning processes that constitute learning, as opposed to knowledge assimilation.

Source: based on Pedler and Boutall (1992)

Figure 1.3 *A cycle of action and reflection*

Individual and organizational learning

The preceding sections described characteristics of knowledge and learning that often refer to individual rather than organizational processes. What is the meaning, then, of *organizational* learning? Prange (1999, p27) notes that 'one of the greatest myths about organizational learning is probably the who question – that is, the way in which learning might be considered *organizational*'.

Some authors view organizational learning as both individual and team learning in the organizational context, while others propose that organizational learning is somehow an aggregate or cross-fertilization of individual learning or a process (distinct, though perhaps similar to individual learning) by which an organization as an entity learns and adapts (Prange, 1999). Even within the latter interpretations, what constitutes an organization as an entity is open to dispute (Morgan, 1986). Taylor et al (1997), for example, note three sets of learning relationships within organizations: between individuals acting together; between individuals and the organization; and between the organization and others outside it.

This review does not aim to reconcile these different perspectives, but has merely drawn attention to them for the sake of clarity. In each of the interpretations the content, context and quality of individual and team learning are considered important to producing relevant insights, actions and outcomes at an individual, team or organizational level.

Organizational learning and the learning organization

This section is principally concerned with furthering an understanding of what is meant by learning and reflection processes. However, it is also pertinent to briefly touch on the significance of the literature on the learning organization. This gives insight into an effective *environment* for learning and reflection, which will be returned to in the section on 'Challenges to reflective learning'. Definitions of learning organizations highlight characteristics such as adaptability, responsiveness, vision and transformation (see Box 1.2).

BOX 1.2 SOME DEFINITIONS OF THE LEARNING ORGANIZATION

... [an] organization with an ingrained philosophy for anticipating, reacting and responding to change, complexity and uncertainty. (Malhotra, 1996)

A learning company is an organization that facilitates the learning of all its members and continuously transforms itself. (Pedler et al, 1991, p1)

Learning organizations [are] organizations where new and expansive patterns of thinking are nurtured, where collective aspiration is set free, and where people are continually learning to see the whole together. (Senge, 1990, p3)

Much of the learning organization literature is aspirational – that is, it seeks to describe the organizational ideal where learning is maximized. It tends to be focused on practical implementation, as well as generating action and change to create an environment that is conducive to learning. There is an emphasis on creating the kinds of conditions in which individual and collective creativity and performance flourish, thus contributing to the organization's ability to achieve results. Some of the key organizational challenges to reflective and reflexive learning in the development sector are returned to in more detail in 'Challenges to reflective learning'.

Characteristics of learning and reflection processes

As noted in the Introduction, implementing the shift towards influencing and supporting policy processes, and working in closer relationships to ensure ownership by partner countries, pose new challenges to development professionals. Hinton and Groves (2004) identify a number of key dimensions of learning and change that are central to achieving more effective impact:

- Shift from linear, outcome-oriented perspectives on development towards a more complex systemic understanding of the aid system, its actors and the relationships among them.
- Understand power and politics, and the ways in which they influence actions and relationships at many levels, from interpersonal to international.
- Question the ways in which procedures might be reinforcing pernicious cultural and political dynamics.
- Recognize and reflect on the role of the individual, as well as the organization, in transforming and implementing the poverty reduction agenda.

What does a learning process based on reflection and reflexivity that can fulfil these aims look like? This section will explore some key theories and concepts that help to inform an improved understanding of reflection and learning processes. Principally, they are methods that encourage a broader and more inclusive analysis of issues and problems, putting emphasis on individual, personal reflection on one's own attitudes, beliefs and how these influence learning, decisions or actions. Four broad areas of theory and practice are reviewed: systems thinking, exploring assumptions, reflection through enquiry and dialogue, and reflexivity or self-reflection.

Systems thinking

Systems thinking highlights the need to see, or think, in 'wholes' rather than in parts, drawing attention to the importance of recognizing relationships and feedback loops in the complex and dynamic environments in which people work, interact and learn (Checkland and Scholes, 1990; Senge, 1990; Flood, 1999, 2001):

> Systems thinking is a framework for seeing interrelationships rather than things, for seeing patterns of change rather than static 'snapshots'... Systems thinking is a discipline for seeing the 'structures' that underlie complex situations, and for discerning high from low leverage change.
> (Senge, 1990, pp68–69)

Western education teaches from an early age to break things into parts in order to make them more manageable and to enable us to study the isolated elements. But reality is complex, and it is important to recognize and appreciate the interdependency of the different elements of any system (detail complexity), as well as changes over time (dynamic complexity), in order to fully analyse and understand our environment (Senge, 1990, p92).

Flood (1999) likens systems thinking to opening contrasting 'windows' on a particular bounded-action area to generate a more holistic appreciation of issues and dilemmas (see Figure 1.4): 'Each window opens up your vision to one aspect of a complex activity... A holistic perspective of the interrelationships ... is formed in this way' (Flood, 1999, p96).

∾ **Systems of** *processes*	∾ **Systems of** *structure*
Processes are flows of events undertaken for a particular activity, including operational processes and management processes. Reflecting in this context involves analysing efficiency and reliability.	*Structure refers to organizational functions, rules and procedures, including forms of coordination, communication and control.* Are rules and procedures appropriate and efficient, given the particular action or the organization as a whole?
∾ **Systems of** *meaning*	∾ **Systems of** *knowledge power*
Meaning refers to ways in which people define their relationships with others and the world, shaped by their norms, values, ideology, thought and emotion. Is there coherence or contradiction, consensus or conflict between actors involved?	*What is considered valid knowledge and, hence, valid action, and who has the power to determine this?* This involves being sensitive to issues and dilemmas of knowledge and power in relation to particular actions.

Source: based on Flood (1999)

Figure 1.4 *Four 'windows' on learning*

Human thought is not capable of knowing the 'whole'; but it is capable of seeing greater connectedness between the known elements, and of recognizing and appreciating better what is unknown. Viewing an action or situation through all these windows and recognizing the interrelatedness of the issues and dilemmas revealed by each will suggest more creative courses of action and transformation from which improvements can be made. Taking a systemic approach to an issue in a social organizational context (as would be the case for many development issues) will reveal a number of interpretations of any particular action context. The aim of systems thinking is not to achieve a new and improved model of 'reality', but that interpretations or models should be used to explore and discover, in this way generating a more meaningful understanding of the context in question:

> *It might be reasonable to conclude that more learning has occurred when more and more varied interpretations have been developed because such development changes the range of the organization's potential behaviours.* (Huber, 1991, p102)

Senge (1990) highlights the importance of systems thinking in the context of organizational learning. It helps people to recognize their connectedness to the world and the consequences of their actions; it constitutes a shift from linear thinking, helps people to reflect on their current mental models and, thus, exposes prevailing assumptions (this concept will be expanded upon in the following section on 'Exploring assumptions'); it provides a shared language for improved team discussion and dialogue; and it allows a shared vision to emerge through collaborative feedback processes.

The learning methodology (the 'tensionometer') applied by Guimarães and Larbi-Jones (2005) to learning about partnerships in Brazil followed a systemic approach. Alongside tracing flows of events, they tried to gain insight into the broader structural, procedural and political context within which those events were taking place, the ways in which those involved interpreted their relationships, and their emotional responses to events and outcomes. This was achieved through facilitating self-reflection with individual partners. Triangulation of that information gave useful insight into the UK Department for International Development's (DFID's) role and approach to partnership.

Exploring assumptions

While systems thinking, at its simplest, calls for an expansion of the *range* of factors that are taken into account in developing understanding and insight within a particular learning context, Argyris and Schön's (1978) theory of learning similarly calls for a *deepening* of the level of questioning. They note a tendency in organizations towards 'single-loop learning' in which the emphasis is on more immediately observable processes and structures, while taking organizational goals, values, frameworks and strategies for granted. This type of learning leads to adaptation, but only within the existing organizational framework for action. Double-loop learning, in contrast, involves questioning the role of the framing and learning systems that underlie actual goals and strategies:

> *Single-loop learning is like a thermostat that learns when it is too hot or too cold and turns the heat on or off. The thermostat can perform this task because it can receive information (the temperature of the room) and take corrective action. Double-loop learning occurs when error is detected and corrected in ways that involve the modification of an organization's underlying norms, policies and objectives.* (Argyris and Schön, 1978, pp2–3)

Thus, double-loop learning emphasizes closer examination and questioning of organizational values, beliefs and assumptions upon which actions and strategies are based. Exploring these governing variables and their implications can help the learner to see the problem in a new light, to develop new concepts, policies and strategies, and to change existing standards of judgement. Double-loop learning leads to fundamentally new ways of looking at the issue in question or a reframing of the problem (see Figure 1.5).

At a practical level, Senge (1990) proposes the five 'whys' as a useful tool for steering away from blaming first-order causes or individuals, and reaching a deeper level of understanding of the factors underlying the issue. When the question 'why

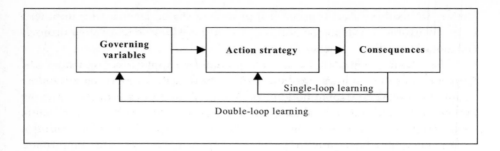

Source: based on Argyris and Schön (1978)

Figure 1.5 *Single-loop and double-loop learning*

is this happening' is asked in relation to a particular problem, rather than taking the first answer(s) as the cause(s) of the problem, one should ask the question 'why' again in relation to each response. As the levels of probing become deeper, the tendency is to move from specific technical aspects towards broader questioning of values, incentives or policies.

Chapter 5 documents experiences with learning processes that also aimed to question assumptions in a more fundamental way. A reflective learning process carried out in a DFID programme in Uganda questioned a range of stakeholders on their perspectives on events that had taken place and asked them to question why they believed others had behaved in the ways they did. This helped to avoid a culture of blaming and to seek deeper causes of particular actions and consequences.

Reflection through enquiry and dialogue

Enquiry is a means by which further information is obtained that can help to build a better understanding of the bigger picture and to interrogate and challenge assumptions. Enquiry can take a range of forms, whether as an individual or group process, or through activities of observation, investigation or dialogue.

Some authors view the reflective process as essentially an individual mental activity in which others are not involved (Dewey, 1933; Boud et al, 1985; Schön, 1983). In contrast, others, especially proponents of systems thinking, maintain that learning requires dialogue with, and even the participation of, others (Flood, 2001). A range of tools or methodologies for enquiry and dialogue exist that facilitate communication and exploration of values and understandings, and the emergence of shared meaning (Preskill and Torres, 1999).

Some strategies that have been used to improve the quality of dialogue and enquiry include those from the discipline of action research, such as action learning, cooperative enquiry and participatory enquiry (see Chapter 4). These approaches involve the establishment of small groups or 'sets' of participants who meet on a regular basis. In action learning, each brings to the group a situation or problem that they are engaged in – for example, a policy that they are working on or an issue relating to work relationships. They share their experiences relating to the issue with the group and through reflecting together gain a deeper understanding of the issue, its dynamics and dilemmas. On the basis of new insights, ideas for action are developed. Between group meetings, participants consciously reflect on their current methods of working, and explore new and better ways of operating to address the particular issue under enquiry. They then return to the group with an account of the consequences of their actions for further reflection and exploration (Pedler and Boutall, 1992; Reason and Heron, 1999).

Forms of enquiry can differ in the number of participants involved, whether they have individual or shared questions around which to enquire, and the nature of the actions taken between meetings (active research or simple reflection on practice in the light of discussions) (Reason and Heron, 1999).

Workshops, meetings, retreats and even email discussion or online communities of practice can also be used as spaces and opportunities for improved learning through dialogue and enquiry. This can require developing particular skills and disciplines to be attentive to what others say and to be tolerant of multiple interpretations of events. Such events require attention in their planning and execution to ensure an environment that supports and facilitates honest reflection and sharing (see Chapter 5). People need to become practised in reflecting, talking more openly and making their assumptions explicit so that conversations can become more incisive (Senge et al, 1994). Alternatively, skilled facilitators can help to elicit learning by encouraging different directions for reflection and drawing attention to assumptions.

Reflexivity: Self-reflection

Argyris and Schön (1978) note the tendency not to question organizational or other broader underlying assumptions; in later work, they also highlight the tendency of learners not to question personal values and assumptions (Argyris and Schön, 1996). Marshall (2001), similarly, contrasts two simultaneous streams of enquiry, which she calls her inner (personal) and outer (external) arcs of attention. Mental models, cognitive maps, paradigms and other schema shape how individuals interpret information and experience. Unless individuals explore what underlies their *own* typical thinking and action, they are likely to make superficial changes to existing strategies, which will limit the potential for more fundamental learning and change (Preskill and Torres, 1999).

Chambers, in much of his work, including *Challenging the Professions* (1993) and *Whose Reality Counts* (1997), has pointed out the importance of the role of the individual development practitioner in achieving development goals, in particular their attitude and behaviour in relation to those with whom they are working. He defines reflexivity as:

> *... self-critical epistemological awareness. It means critical straining for honest reflection on how one's own ego, mindset, institutional context, and social and political interests combine to select and shape personal knowledge.* (Chambers, 2002, p153)

Hence, a reflexive approach requires individuals to be aware of who they are and what they are bringing to the table: the position and power they hold, the biases they have and the assumptions that they as individuals are making (Marshall, 2001; Reason and Bradbury, 2001; Chambers, 2002; McGee, 2002; Eyben, 2004).

How does personal reflection take place in practice? Marshall (2001) notes that each person's enquiry approach will be distinctive and disciplines cannot be cloned or copied. She has made a conscious commitment to self-reflective practice; as such, she dedicates time to this purpose, making notes to capture and track her sense-making processes. Chambers (2002) also notes that the act of writing a diary helps reflection and gives one something to return to when later experiences may have caused unconscious manipulation of memory.

Another stimulus for reflection is challenging oneself through exposure. Immersion programmes involve development agency staff who are principally based in cities or developed countries undertaking extended visits to the field to spend time with poor people. These are key opportunities for learning more about poverty through enquiry and dialogue, but also for reflecting on one's personal assumptions and testing them against the realities observed. Accounts of such reflective processes are often quite powerful and reveal radical shifts in thinking. As Ravi Kanbur[1] reflected on his ten-day exposure trip: 'this programme ... has been one of the most educational and moving experiences of my life' (cited in McGee, 2002, p28).

Chambers (2002) and Eyben (2003) both note the challenges of reflexivity in practice. Chambers identifies three constraints to self-reflection:

1   fear of exposing oneself;
2   loyalty to colleagues and friends;
3   space and time.

Eyben, after leaving her post as head of country office for DFID in Bolivia, did find the time to deeply reflect upon and analyse her experiences there. She admits that while in the post, she was so engaged in action she often forgot to observe herself. Only having left the post could she legitimately take the opportunity to reflect, and was released from the relations of power and position that might have made such reflection uncomfortable:

> *Reflexivity is particularly challenging for a person of relatively high status and power. It is not comfortable for anyone committed to social and political justice to enquire into one's own behaviour as a member of an elite cosmopolitan group, the donor community.* (Eyben, 2003)

Challenges to reflective learning

The preceding section explored some key concepts and methods that facilitate improved learning and reflection. However, translating these ideas into organizational practice is likely to pose a number of challenges. What is required is an organizational environment that facilitates such practice: the environment of a 'learning organization'. Senge et al (1994) capture some key dimensions of change required to build a learning organization in a useful framework (see Figure 1.6). These dimensions are adopted as the structure for this section.

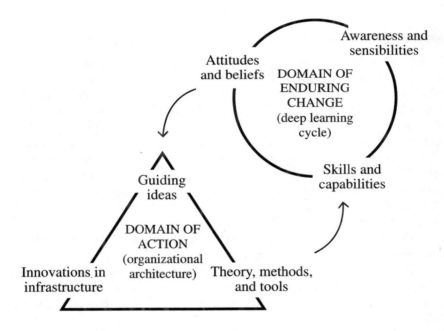

Source: Senge et al (1994), p45

Figure 1.6 *Key dimensions of change to build a learning organization*

Guiding ideas

According to Eyben (2003), there is a dominance of positivism in development practice, and dominant professionals have been economists. Bureaucratic organizations, based on a positivist paradigm, tend to find reflection difficult due to their centralized control, mechanistic thinking, high levels of specialization, and over-specification of plans (Morgan, 1986; Olson and Eoyang, 2001).

Despite the high levels of uncertainty within the development environment, there is a pressure to be able to predict and to appear infallible. Ellerman (2002) notes a tendency amongst donors to seek a 'one best way' to achieve poverty reduction outcomes and to become wedded to these 'official views'. This attachment to single solutions seriously limits learning within the organization and the ability of partners to share ideas and learn together.

It is argued, therefore, that a shift in fundamental assumptions – a new paradigm – is needed for development agencies to become learning organizations (Ellerman, 2002; Eyben, 2003; Hinton and Groves, 2004). The alternatives proposed include an 'open learning model' (Ellerman, 2002), a complex systems approach (Hinton and Groves, 2004) or critical theory (Eyben, 2003) – the key characteristics of all being a more open and experimentalist holistic and pragmatic perspective, as well as the encouragement of greater collaboration.

Theory, method and tools

Achieving a paradigm shift might seem a daunting proposal. Change begins to happen through the introduction of new theory, tools and methods, and the elimination of old ones (Senge et al, 1994; Hobley and Shields, 2000; Chambers and Pettit, 2004). In Chapter 7, David, Mancini and Guijt observe that, while the philosophy of ActionAid promoted the participation and rights of a range of stakeholders, their internal procedures did not reflect this. They recount how ActionAid reinforced their guiding ideas by developing more consistent accountability and reporting methods. This meant a shift from a traditional upward reporting system to a more participatory 360-degree learning approach called ALPS (the Accountability, Learning and Planning System). Other alternative theories, tools and methods that facilitate reflective and reflexive learning have been outlined earlier in this chapter, including action learning, systems thinking, double-loop learning, participative enquiry and immersions.

In Chapter 5, Pasteur and Scott-Villiers recount examples of adapting and improving existing methods and tools (such as workshops and meetings) to better the quality of learning that takes place within them, rather than introducing wholesale change.

Some tools, such as the logframe, embody the linear logic and elimination of unpredictability associated with a positivist paradigm; these need to be modified or alternatives must be sought if they are to reinforce a new development philosophy (Chambers et al, 2002; Eyben, 2003).

Innovations in infrastructure

Infrastructure refers to the means through which an organization makes resources available to support people in their work – in other words, time, management structures, incentives, money, information and contact with other colleagues (Senge et al, 1994). This raises a whole range of issues and areas for change to facilitate learning.

In terms of management, decentralized structures allowing for participation, flattened hierarchies that reduce power differentials, and small units that communicate and interact well with one another all facilitate better learning relationships (Finger and Brand, 1999). In development agencies, 'silo' mentalities often associated with disciplinary training and departmental membership, and strong hierarchies associated with more bureaucratic agencies, are counter to learning (Hobley and Shields, 2000). They tend to result in relationships of competition or fear, and do not foster openness and sharing.

Recruitment, job descriptions, training, performance assessment, incentives systems and promotion criteria can all be adapted to ensure capacity and incentives for reflection and learning (Chambers et al, 2001; Hobley and Shields, 2000). Chapter 5 highlights the importance of creating space for learning – ensuring that time is available for learning and that this activity is valued by managers – and that existing procedures could be better adapted to help facilitate learning. Pasteur and Scott-Villiers note tendencies within DFID, which may be typical of other development bureaucracies, to reward competition and independence over team working, honest reflection and sharing. The drive to spend budgets also tends to devalue the investment of time in other aspects of the aid delivery process, such as understanding the working context and investing in relationships. On a more positive note, Eyben (2004) recognizes that a shift in DFID towards the recruitment of national staff is helping to improve staff investment in institutional relationships that aid learning.

Skills and capabilities

Relevant skills and capabilities are also essential if individual organizational members are to be able to apply new theories, tools and methods. Skills such as reflection, effective dialogue and systemic conceptualization may not come naturally to people and are not typical components of academic training (Senge et al, 1994). Organizations may need to invest in awareness-raising, training and skills development in this area to ensure that organizational policy is effectively transformed into practice (see Chapters 5 and 7).

ActionAid used channels such as an impact assessment network in country workshops and a set of guidance notes to help develop understanding of ALPS and skills when applying the new approach (see Chapter 7). Bloch and Borges (2002) describe in some detail how they developed new skills for more effective listening, dialogue and communication, linking these to the monitoring and evaluation system so that they could monitor qualitative improvements over time. This required considerable investment of time and effort in order to achieve profound change in team behaviour. However, they note: 'there are no miracles – changes take time' (Bloch and Borges, 2002, p468).

Awareness and sensibilities

Senge et al (1994) suggest that as new skills and capabilities are learned and practised, new awareness will emerge: an ability to 'see' the underlying structures driving behaviour, and assumptions and practices that may previously have gone unquestioned. This type of sensitivity is viewed by some authors as emotional intelligence (Goleman, 2001) or interpersonal and intrapersonal intelligences (Gardner cited in Smith, 2002). The authors of Chapter 5 use the term 'relational intelligence'. It is concerned with a person's ability to be sensitive to others, to recognize their own emotional response and to use this awareness effectively in interaction. This sensibility is important to learning because, as noted earlier, the context and narrative within and through which learning happens are crucial (Snowden, 2002). Both reflection and enquiry processes often centre on issues of tension, and power dynamics are often at play (see Chapter 5 and Guimarães and Larbi-Jones, 2005).

Power dynamics can have an incredibly powerful impact on learning through generating fear or silencing the voice of weaker parties, while blocking the ears of the powerful who don't believe that they need to listen or learn. Different forms of power are not always easy to observe. Gaventa (2003) describes three types of power that operate to inhibit or enhance people's ability to speak their minds: visible, invisible and hidden. Visible power might be manifest in a meeting between a president in a large office and a representative of a poor people's movement unused to opulent surroundings. Hidden power involves the unseen context in which a relationship is taking place – for example, the history of relations between one organization and another will affect present relations. Invisible power is where the participants have internalized who has power to do what, whether or not that is true – so younger people may feel that they have less valuable opinions than older individuals in a given culture. Chapter 5 cites real examples of how power dynamics can impact on opportunities for learning and exchange.

Awareness and sensibility towards interpersonal (including power) dynamics is hard to learn; however, as individuals or groups consciously attend to these factors in their practice of reflection, dialogue and reflexivity, it will begin to become apparent. Nevertheless, in cases where there is a significant power difference, the use of a third-party facilitator can be an effective means of keeping an eye on the balance of power, addressing inequities, helping to maintain focus and resolving conflicts that might arise.

Attitudes and beliefs

Changes in attitudes and beliefs represent a shift at the deepest level of an organization's culture. This signals that learning has really become embedded in the organization, rather than being merely an espoused value (Schein, 1992). Characteristics such as an ability to surrender control and to admit uncertainty or fallibility; a broadening of one's analytical perspective; increased levels of risk-taking; and improved communication, transparency and trust all start to become internalized (Finger and Brand, 1999).

As attitudes and behaviours start to become internalized within the organization, this should not imply the achievement of a new steady state. The principle of questioning assumptions holds for notions about learning, as well as about other areas of organizational practice. This process of reflecting on the learning process itself is termed by Argyris and Schön (1978) as 'triple-loop learning', or as 'deutero-learning' by Bateson (1972), and involves enquiring into the context as well as the content of learning.

Learning in development organizations: An achievable goal?

It is increasingly recognized that an organization's ability to evolve and improve its impact depends greatly upon the capacity of its staff to reflect collaboratively and to envision change. Recent literature illustrates a growing interest in questioning the meaning and practice of reflection and learning in the development sector (*Development in Practice*, 2002; King and McGrath, 2002; Hovland, 2003; Groves and Hinton, 2004).

As experience and analysis in this field increase, personal behaviour and working relationships emerge as fundamental issues to be addressed. The implications for this are not just operational, but also depend upon shifting guiding ideas, power, culture and values (Roper and Pettit, 2002). As Chambers and Pettit (2004) note, becoming a learning organization:

> ... *is about instilling new norms and behaviours that value critical reflection and enable fundamental changes in an organization's direction and strategy. The goal is not simply to improve effectiveness, but to create conditions for rethinking basic organizational principles and values.*

These are long-term processes of change requiring strong organizational backing and commitment.

The following chapters illustrate important and encouraging examples of changes in learning practice in development agencies. Such experimentation and documentation are critical to stimulating and facilitating more sustainable long-term change. It is hoped that this work will stimulate further adaptation of existing concept theories and methods to ensure their relevance to the development sector, as well as encourage the analysis, documentation and sharing of such experiences to ensure that learning and change in this field continues.

Notes

1 Leader of the World Bank team commissioned to write the *World Development Report 2000/2001: Attacking Poverty* (World Bank, 2001).

References

Ackoff, R. L. (1989) 'From data to wisdom', *Journal of Applied Systems Analysis*, vol 16, pp3–9

Argyris, C. and Schön, D. (1978) *Organisational Learning: A Theory of Action Perspective*, Addison-Wesley, Reading, UK

Argyris, C. and Schön, D. (1996) *Organisational Learning II: Theory, Method and Practice*, Addison-Wesley, Reading, UK

Bateson, G. (1972) *Steps to an Ecology of Mind*, Chandler, San Francisco

Binney, G. and Williams, C. (1995) *Leaning into the Future: Changing the way People Change Organisations*, Nicholas Brealey, London

Bloch, D. and Borges, N. (2002) 'Organisational learning in NGOs: An example of an intervention based on the work of Chris Argyris', *Development in Practice*, vol 12, nos 3 and 4, pp461–472

Boud, D., Keogh, R. and Walker, D. (1985) *Reflection: Turning Experience into Learning*, Kogan Page, London

Chambers, R. (1993) *Challenging the Professions: Frontiers for Rural Development*, Intermediate Technology Publications, London

Chambers, R. (1997) *Whose Reality Counts: Putting the First Last*, Intermediate Technology Publications, London

Chambers, R. (2002) 'Power, knowledge and policy influence: Reflections on an experience', in Brock, K. and McGee, R. (eds) *Knowing Poverty: Critical Reflections on Participatory Research and Policy*, Earthscan, London

Chambers, R. and Pettit, J. (2004) 'Shifting power: To make a difference', in Groves, L. and Hinton, R. (eds) *Inclusive Aid: Changing Power and Relationships in International Development*, Earthscan, London

Chambers, R., Pettit, J. and Scott-Villiers, P. (2001) 'The new dynamics of aid: Power, procedures and relationships', *IDS Policy Briefing*, vol 15, August

Checkland, P. and Scholes, J. (1990) *Soft Systems Methodology in Action*, John Wiley and Sons, Chichester, UK

Cornwall, A., Pratt, G. and Scott-Villiers, P. (2004) 'Participatory learning groups in an aid bureaucracy', *Lessons for Change in Policy and Organisations*, no 11, IDS, Brighton, UK

Davies, R. (1998) 'An evolutionary approach to organisational learning: An experiment by an NGO in Bangladesh', in Mosse, D., Farrington, J. and Rew, A. (eds) *Development as Process: Concepts and Methods for Working with Complexity*, Routledge and ODI, London

Development in Practice (2002) Issue on 'Development and the learning organisation', *Development in Practice*, vol 12, nos 3 and 4

Dewey, J. (1933) *How We Think: A Restatement of the Relation of Reflective Thinking to the Educative Process*, DC Heath, Chicago

Easterby-Smith, M. (1997) 'Disciplines of organisational learning, contributions and critiques', *Human Relations*, vol 50, no 9, p1085

Ellerman, D. (2002) 'Should development agencies have official views?', *Development in Practice*, vol 12, nos 3 and 4, pp285–297

Eyben, R. (2003) *Donors as Political Actors: Fighting the Thirty Years War in Bolivia*, IDS Working Paper 183, IDS, Brighton, UK

Eyben, R. (2004) 'Relationships matter for supporting change in favour of poor people', *Lessons for Change in Policy and Organisations*, no 8, IDS, Brighton, UK

Finger, M. and Brand, S. B. (1999) 'The concept of the "learning organization" applied to the transformation of the public sector', in Easterby-Smith, M., Araujo, L. and Burgoyne, J. (eds) *Organizational Learning and the Learning Organization*, Sage, London

Flood, R. L. (1999) *Rethinking the Fifth Discipline: Learning within the Unknowable*, Routledge, London

Flood, R. L. (2001) 'The relationship of "systems thinking" to action research', in Reason, P. and Bradbury, H. (eds) *The Handbook of Action Research: Participative Enquiry and Practice*, Sage, London

Gaventa, J. (2003) 'Towards participatory local governance: Assessing the transformative possibilities', Paper prepared for the Conference on Participation: From Tyranny to Transformation, Manchester, 27–28 February

Goleman, D. (2001) 'Emotional intelligence, issues in paradigm building', in Cherniss, C. and Goleman, D. (eds) *The Emotionally Intelligent Workplace: How To Select For, Measure and Improve Emotional Intelligence In Individuals, Groups, and Organizations*, Jossey-Bass, San Francisco

Groves, L. and Hinton, R. (eds) (2004) *Inclusive Aid: Changing Power and Relationships in International Development*, Earthscan, London

Guimarães, A. C. and Larbi-Jones, E. (2005) 'Working for pro-poor change in Brazil: Influencing partnerships?', *Lessons for Change in Policy and Organisations*, no 10, IDS, Brighton

Hinton, R. and Groves, L. (2004) 'The complexity of inclusive aid', in Groves, L. and Hinton, R. (eds) *Inclusive Aid: Changing Power and Relationships in International Development*, Earthscan, London

Hobley, M. and Shields, D. (2000) *The Reality of Trying to Transform Structures and Processes: Forestry in Rural Livelihoods*, ODI Working Paper 132, ODI, London

Hovland, I. (2003) *Literature Review, Knowledge Management and Organisational Learning*, ODI, London

Huber, G. (1991) 'Organizational learning: The contributing processes and literature', *Organization Science*, vol 2, pp88–115

King, K. and McGrath, S. (2002) 'Knowledge sharing in development agencies: Lessons from four cases', Draft paper, October

Kolb, D. (1984) *Experiential Learning: Experience as the Source of Learning and Development*, Prentice-Hall, Englewood Cliffs, NJ

Korten, D. (1984) 'Rural development programming: The learning process approach', in Korten, D. C. and Klauss, R. (eds) *People-Centred Development: Contributions Toward Theory and Planning Frameworks*, Kumarian Press, West Hartford

Malhotra, Y. (1996) *Organizational Learning and Learning Organizations: An Overview*, www.brint.com/papers/orglrng.htm

Marsden, D., Oakley, P. and Pratt, B. (1994) *Measuring the Process: Guidelines for Evaluation of Social Development*, Intrac Publications, Oxford

Marshall, J. (2001) 'Self-reflective inquiry process', in Reason, P. and Bradbury, H. (eds) *Handbook of Action Research: Participative Enquiry and Practice*, Sage, London

McGee, R. (2002) 'The self in participatory research', in Brock, K. and McGee, R. (eds) *Knowing Poverty: Critical Reflections on Participatory Research and Policy*, Earthscan, London

Morgan, G. (1986) *Images of Organisation*, Sage Publications, Beverly Hills, California

Nonaka, I. and Takeuchi, H. (1995) *The Knowledge Creating Company*, Oxford University Press, New York

Nonaka, I., Takeuchi, H. and Umemoto, K. (1996) 'A theory of organizational knowledge creation', *International Journal of Information Management*, vol 11, nos 7–8, pp833–845

Olson, E. and Eoyang, G. (2001) *Facilitating Organisational Change: Lessons from Complexity Science*, Practicing Organisational Development Series, Jossey-Bass/Pfeiffer, San Francisco

Pasteur, K. and Scott-Villiers, P. (2004) 'If relationships matter, how can they be improved? Learning about relationships in development', *Lessons for Change in Policy and Organisations*, no 9, IDS, Brighton

Pedler, M. and Boutall, J. (1992) *Action Learning for Change: A Resource Book for Managers and Other Professionals*, National Health Service Training Directorate, Bristol

Pedler, M., Boutall, J. and Boydell, T. (1991) *The Learning Company: A Strategy for Sustainable Development*, McGraw-Hill, London

Pickering, A. (2002) *Knowledge Management: New Research from the Institute for Strategic Change*, PowerPoint Presentation given at ODI, Accenture Institute for Strategic Change, London

Prange, C. (1999) 'Organisational learning – desperately seeking theory', in Easterby-Smith, M., Araujo, L. and Burgoyne, J. (eds) *Organizational Learning and the Learning Organization*, Sage, London

Preskill, H. and Torres, R. (1999) 'The role of evaluative enquiry in creating learning organisations', in Easterby-Smith, M., Araujo, L. and Burgoyne, J. (eds) *Organizational Learning and the Learning Organization*, Sage, London

Reason, P. and Bradbury, H. (eds) (2001) *Handbook of Action Research: Participative Enquiry and Practice*, Sage, London

Reason, P. and Heron, J. (1999) *A Layperson's Guide to Co-operative Enquiry*, www.bath.ac.uk/carpp/layguide.htm

Roper, L. and Pettit, J. (2002) 'Development and the learning organisation: An introduction', *Development in Practice*, vol 12, nos 3 and 4, pp258–271

Schein, E. (1992) *Organisational Culture and Leadership*, Jossey-Bass, San Francisco

Schön, D. (1983) *The Reflective Practitioner*, Basic Books, New York

Senge, P. (1990) *The Fifth Discipline: The Art and Practice of the Learning Organisation*, Doubleday, New York.

Senge, P., Kleiner, A., Roberts, C., Ross, R. and Smith, B. (1994) *The Fifth Discipline Fieldbook: Strategies and Tools for Building A Learning Organization*, Nicholas Brealey, London

Smith, M. K. (2002) 'Howard Gardner and multiple intelligences', *The Encyclopedia of Informal Education*, www.infed.org/thinkers/gardner.htm

Snowden, D. J. (2002) 'Complex acts of knowing: Paradox and descriptive self-awareness', *Journal of Knowledge Management*, special edition, vol, 6, no 2, pp100–111

Taylor, J., Marais, D. and Kaplan, A. (1997) *Action Learning for Development: Use Your Experience to Improve Your Effectiveness*, Juta and Co Ltd, South Africa

Vaill, P. (1996) *Learning as a Way of Being: Strategies for Survival in a World of Permanent White Water*, Jossey-Bass, San Francisco

World Bank (2001) *World Development Report 2000/2001: Attacking Poverty*, Oxford University Press for the World Bank, New York

2

Making Relationships Matter for Aid Bureaucracies

Rosalind Eyben

Large aid agencies of the kind discussed in this volume face similar challenges. They are bureaucratic organizations whose edifice of rules, procedures and systems is predicated on cause-and-effect thinking, in which process is seen as a transaction cost undermining efficiency. Second, they have a common goal of progressive social change. Finally, they find learning difficult. Drawing on complexity theory, this chapter explores how these characteristics provide both opportunities and challenges for a relationships approach to aid, in which donors learn to become more accountable to citizens at both ends of the aid chain.

Bureaucratic characteristics that shape views on relationships

That aid is a matter of relationships would seem self-evident. Yet, despite the recent popularity of such terms as 'partnership', those responsible for aid policies and management take little interest in their staff being equipped with the skills, values and attitudes for positive relationship management, including self-knowledge through reflective practice. To explore why this should be requires enquiring into bureaucratic modes of organization; considering the traditional split between policy and implementation; the emphasis on treating all citizens or clients in an equally impartial manner; the centrality of rational, 'objective' thinking rather than feeling as the basis for decision-making; and the lack of direct external feedback mechanisms for modifying practice.

In government organizations, staff are primarily viewed as implementers of policy that has been decided by politicians.[1] The presumed technical role of officials is reinforced by the bureaucratic ideal that requires perceiving the people they serve as *objects* of attention, not as living and breathing people with emotions to whom the official as an individual might feel attracted or repelled. Orders of superiors must be implemented without personal preferences. Bureaucrats cannot have friends or, indeed, passions (Jassey, 2004).

Compared with modes of public administration based on partiality, where an official may treat people very differently depending upon personal or familial ties, or upon common religious, gender, class or ethnic identity, this ethic of disinterestedness is admirable (du Gay, 2000; Courpasson and Reed, 2004). A more critical view, however, would note that a bureaucratic mode of organization also reflects, enacts and contributes to maintaining the values and power relations of the society of which it is part, and is perfectly capable, for example, of practising institutionalized racism or gender discrimination, albeit in a non-emotional and objective fashion (Bauman, 1989).

Relationships involve emotions and, therefore, are out of place at work (Mawdsley et al, 2005). When emotions burst out there is a general sense of embarrassment and discomfort, as at the workshop for UK Department for International Development (DFID) staff in Brazil described in Chapter 5.

The ideal bureaucratic form of organization is rational, basing decisions on objective evidence scrutinized by experts working in a hierarchical system where all obey the established procedures. The power of knowledge based on rational scientific method, rather than the power of relationships, is the essence of a modern public bureaucracy (Courpasson and Reed, 2004).

This attitude to knowledge shapes what is considered as evidence and, therefore, influences from whom and how bureaucracies learn. In parliamentary democracies the feedback mechanism for public-sector performance has been indirect, via the politician. For voluntary organizations, feedback is provided by their private donors. The implications of these traditions for systems of accountability of international aid are discussed later.

Public-sector bureaucracy shares the same philosophical roots as liberal economic theory (Hare, 1981). Societal processes and outcomes are seen as the sum of discrete, intentional acts by autonomous actors, pre-constituted rather than defined through their relations with others. The theory of rational choice connects to the idea of utilitarian contract. The least time I need to spend with someone in coming to a contractual agreement, the more efficient is my performance in terms of maximizing my utility. Thus, from the rational choice perspective, a relationship is a transaction cost rather than what underpins society. This theory has become naturalized in the world of aid. People do not realize that they are using it.

Thus, proposing that a bureaucratic organization equip its staff with relationship skills is contrary to the ethos of an organization that looks for controlling, emotion-less, objective patterns of behaviour in which time spent with other people can only be justified by a cost–benefit analysis. This is the challenge facing those wanting relationships to work in aid. The fact that a relational approach can now even be mentioned is due to wider social changes, including changing gender relations at work and development of 'the network society', resulting in post-bureaucratic tendencies where relationships, influence and emotions are beginning to be seen as essential attributes of current working practices. This is the subject of the next section.

Networks as an alternative approach to making relationships matter

The last two decades have seen a body of theory develop to explain societal change in the so-called 'developed world'. The old organizational hierarchies are dissolving, replaced by global capitalistic networks of power and information, which in turn, are resisted by other emerging networks of civil society (Castells, 1997).

Organizational theorists have used networks to explore how bureaucracies are changing in response to the 'information age'. Information, typified by the internet, is more democratically available rather than controlled by hierarchical authorities. Working in DFID during the transition from the pre-internet era, I noted how the new technology stimulated the horizontal spread of ideas and gossip. This was followed by changes in office layout. Previously, clerical staff would share a large room together, while those higher up the hierarchy sat isolated, each in their own room behind closed doors. Rank or grade was determined by the size of the room, the type of furniture and the presence of carpeting. Those visiting DFID today will find an open-plan arrangement, making it difficult to discern status from the appearance of the workplace.

Unlike fixed status in a bureaucracy, a network is more dynamic and action-oriented: in a network, one *works* (Mazlish, 2000). Nowadays, many large organizations are adopting the network as an organizational principle, sometimes with effects considered undesirable by many of their staff. Non-hierarchical teams are established for short periods to produce a product or idea; they then dissolve and others form. Because these are not long-lasting networks, it has been suggested that institutional learning is at risk, and new networks may start all over again on an enterprise perhaps already undertaken and forgotten (Wittel, 2001).

A recent review of policy coherence in DFID, following the reorganization of its policy division into a large number of network-based teams, noted the challenge in sustaining a common narrative. Many staff expressed a desire to return to a more structured arrangement in which clear directions were sent down from the top (Ladbury, 2005).

Organizations have increasingly fuzzy boundaries, with greater mutual interdependence than previously (Hajer and Wagenaar, 2003). Even long-serving employees may have stronger loyalties to persons in their trans-organizational network than to the formal organization that provides their salary (Hewitt, 2000). Networking also implies a breakdown in the bureaucratic ideal of strict separation between the private citizen at home and the public official at work. Not only are many increasingly working from home, but networking means inviting work colleagues into your house or meeting them for social events (Wittel, 2001).

Networks and relationships have probably always been significant for aid staff when posted in recipient countries. The split between home and office is much harder to maintain where most of the life of staff members centres round the job. Field staff may come across other modes of organization, such as (in Weberian terms) 'patrimonial' in government offices or 'charismatic' in NGOs. They may find the ideal of a strict separation between private life and official function alien to many of their interlocutors. Although they may be part of a satellite office following the same procedures as the head office, much of their job may be outside that familiar space of order and control. They often find that they cannot make a difference by giving orders down the hierarchy, but only by influencing change through networking.

The 'network' has also reshaped theories of policy-making. Policy-making, traditionally regarded as a hierarchical process where those at the top of the pyramid make decisions and transmit them down for implementation, is viewed today as a contested activity of interest groups and networks in which nothing is ever permanent but always open to renegotiation:

> *Terms such as ... 'networks', 'complexity', 'trust', 'deliberation' and 'interdependence' dominate the debate, while terms such as 'the state', 'government', 'power', 'loyalty', 'sovereignty' ... have lost their grip on the imagination.* (Hajer and Wagennar, 2003, p1)

On the other hand, *informal* networks always existed within and between organizations, potentially subverting formal hierarchies of authority and decision-making (Peters, 1995). When an organization abandons some of its more hierarchical manifestations of bureaucracy, the outcome may simply be confusion or may even make it more vulnerable to favouritism. A relational approach can bring its own problems if not developed in association with reflective practice and greater accountability.

Networks possess their negative side. While they may be more democratic than patron–client relations – the precursor of impartial bureaucracies – they present some of the same problems regarding exclusion of the powerless from the web of personal connections that shape policy and allocate resources (Mazlish, 2000). Making relationships work for aid brings its own risks due to the highly unequal power relations in the aid web. In discussing DFID's approach in Peru, Chapter 6 notes the need to critically explore what lies beneath the surface: how networks as an organizational form are structured not only by good intentions, but also by power relations, hierarchy and exclusivity.

Thus, the key question becomes whether adopting a strong relational and networking approach to promote rights might contradict some of the basic principles that DFID advocates, such as accountability. To avoid this trap, should donors be more transparent about the kind of relationships that they want and the values underpinning them?

The quality of relationships depends upon the values that support them. Shifts away from project-based work and direct engagement in the field to managing large disbursements and policy work have led some to alienation from the values with which they came into development and a loss of a sense of purpose.

Today, the design and monitoring of autonomous projects have become less important than negotiating deals with colleagues from other aid agencies and with staff in recipient ministries of finance. Successful aid, defined in terms of securing a grant agreement and disbursing money, is dependent upon networking skills and is reflected by staff demanding training on negotiation and methods of influencing.[2]

Networking for influencing, even when terms such as 'partnership' are used, may imply a wish for one-way influence – the power to make other people do what *you* want, rather than working with them to do things that *you both* want or supporting them in doing things that *they* want. The pressure to disburse funds against the agency's policy objectives can make a relationship appear manipulative. This is likely to be the case where networking is guided by a desire to control, rather than to support, an agenda identified by local persons who are working for societal change that can improve life in that country. Although aid may be less visible in the countryside because of fewer projects, 'by insinuating themselves firmly within the transnational policy community that oversees governmental expenditures, one could argue that aid has never had a greater impact on the management of public affairs', as Gould (2004, p3) suggests for Tanzania.

A relational approach would expect a country office to regularly test the quality of relationships through iterative feedback, reflection and change. Such analysis is still very unusual in aid agencies. Its rarity may be due to the strong goal orientation of aid: it views and acts in the world according to the way it would like the world to be. Learning about local context and history may lead to limited objectives governed by pragmatic feasibility and continuous adaptation to changing circumstances; such modesty does not fit well with international aid's vision of saving the world.

Another issue is the extent to which senior management at head office is prepared to recognize that relationship-building is inevitably a political exercise. When working with state institutions, aid agency officials have tended to see the reform of public administration as a technical issue divorced from politics. Donors may introduce systems for greater accountability and transparency without reference to the perspectives of those in power and the citizens whom they presumably represent. Donors may prefer to do this, rather than become embroiled in the issues of power and politics that necessarily occur when they assume a brokerage or facilitation role. In discussing DFID's involvement in the health sector, Chapter 6 comments on the risks of political discord and breakdown when engaging in complex and controversial policy arenas.

To sum up, networks possess many of the required characteristics for making relationships matter in achieving the goals of international aid. However, unless aid agencies are prepared to recognize that they operate in a messy political environment shaped by power and privilege, the switch from a bureaucratic to a network mode of organization offers few advantages. The following section explores how complexity theory can provide some pointers to supporting networks that do promote progressive social change.

Complexity: An explanatory framework for a relationships approach in aid

Although there is a growing literature on the application of complexity theory to the policy domain, it has so far had little effect on the strategic thinking of bilateral aid agencies (Morgan, 2005).[3] However, I suspect that many international aid staff, while unaware of the theory, may be applying complexity thinking in their day-to-day practice. My own experience as an aid practitioner has led me to the conviction that relationships management is as important for effective aid as money management; only subsequently did I discover the theory that explained what I had learned through practice.

As discussed in the Introduction to this book, complexity theory postulates that change is unceasing. Organized efforts to fully direct it confront the impossibility of completely understanding a system in constant flux. The system, composed of innumerable elements that are continuously shaped and reformed through their interaction, is constantly creating new elements that, in turn, may affect (loop back) and change existing ones. Thus, we cannot predict all the effects that our actions may have on the wider system or, indeed, on ourselves. Small 'butterfly' actions may have a major impact and major ones very little.

A complexity approach does not see aid as a catalyst. As Edgren (2004) argues, a catalyst exerts an impact or change on another component within a system without itself changing. Seeing aid as a catalyst implies that the donor can intervene without being affected by the relationships of which its staff are part. A donor agency that is ready to be influenced by local actors would examine more closely with whom it relates and which relationship networks it supports.

The 'default' meta-theory of donor governments is one of order, rather than complexity. It is based on certainty, rationality, predictability and cause-and-effect linkages, in contrast to complexity theory, which suggests that these may be partially but never completely achievable (Geyer, 2003). Complexity theory provides a way of thinking about social change and aid's role in promoting change in it that embraces rather than ignores paradoxes, of which there are many in the aid relationship. Staying 'open to paradox' suggests *improvisation* as the most effective action. As in jazz, the players have a shared idea of what they might play; but the interaction of the instruments as they perform is different each time, so the score becomes a living reality rather than something determined in advance (Clegg et al, 2004). The audience judges the performance by what they actually hear. Trust between members of the band is a fundamental ingredient of good jazz: whom you play with shapes your product.

Four key elements of complexity theory are most relevant for a 'relationships matter' approach to aid:

1   Change commonly occurs by self-organization of elements in the system through interaction with each other: this understanding privileges relationships, processes and networks rather than structures.

2   There are multiple causes, multiple effects and multiple solutions (for example, to poverty reduction).
3   Anyone's diagnosis of the problem and its solution(s) is necessarily partial because the information they possess about the complex system will be limited and their understanding will be influenced by prior conceptions of how change happens.
4   In unbounded problems (where there is no clear agreement about exactly what the problem is), there may be non-proportionality of cause and effect, there is ambiguity as to how improvements might be made, and there are no limits on the time and resources the problem could absorb (Chapman, 2002).

The next section asks what donors can do differently to respond to a 'complexity' understanding of the world of international aid. I suggest that their first priority is to tackle their learning difficulties.

Donors' learning difficulties

Arguably, by their very nature, all bureaucratic organizations find it difficult to learn through reflection (Morgan, 1997). However, the more uncertain their environment, the more difficult they may find it and, thus, the less they can achieve their objectives. In the last decade, the international aid community has scaled up its vision from fairly limited projects to taking on the burden of Atlas. Donors have adopted an enormously ambitious goal, no less than the eradication of world poverty, with all the risks, conflicts and ambiguities associated with such an agenda. Donor bureaucracies work in a highly uncertain environment. Operating in a volatile and contradictory world, the pressure grows to pass themselves off as infallible, thus depriving themselves of the ability to learn (Beck, 1992). Para-doxically, whereas reflective practice could help in such messiness, it may be very difficult to admit ignorance to systematically dismantle the pretence of being in control.

As discussed in Chapter 1, organizational and systems learning has developed within the for-profit sector. Corporations have learned the danger of top-down approaches that reject information which challenges their understanding of the world (Weick and Sutcliffe, 2001). Businesses that ignore the contradictions and paradoxes of their environment 'plot their own demise' (Clegg et al, 2004, p487). In theory, the same risk would apply to the public sector, where the equivalent of business's bottom line is the satisfaction of citizens, which governments must maintain in order to stay in power. Nevertheless, Whitehall (for example) is not very good at learning. The political environment that shapes public-sector cultures is averse to experimentation. It maintains traditions of control and secrecy that stifle feedback (Chapman, 2002; Common, 2004).[4] However, at the same time, in a functioning democracy politicians are helped to learn through the power of the ballot box. In the aid arena this feedback mechanism does not exist. I suggest that this is why aid agencies particularly suffer from learning difficulties.

When I worked for DFID in Bolivia, I tried to undertake some kind of 'reality check' every two months. However, usually I only truly listened to what I wanted to hear. When villagers complained about the disappearance of aid projects, I saw this as evidence of clientelist dependency. I impressed upon them the radical significance of the Poverty Reduction Strategy, whereby they would be empowered as citizens to hold their government to account for the expenditure of its whole budget, not just the aid money. Enthused by my vision of a radically changed world, I did not reflect upon *their* view based on long experience – that whereas before they got a little bit out of aid, now they would get nothing because the corrupt elitist government would take it all. I failed to ask them and myself what we could do together to change things in small feasible steps from the desperate mess in which Bolivians found themselves. I had avoided that difficulty by constructing an imaginary world of great sweeping changes where aid could solve Bolivia's problems. I was surprised that people in the villages did not share my enthusiasm; but I did not change my mind. To do so, I would have had to admit the relative insignificance of aid. I would have had to unlearn my expertise in order to start learning, and I was not ready to do so.

In his discussion of 'the troubled attempt to understand and shape society', Lindblom (1990, p219) comments that 'the impossibility of anyone's ever achieving a full grasp of the relevant complexities of society compels action in ignorance'. Relations of mutual respect between citizens, experts, officials and others allow them to learn together the results of such ignorant actions and to deliberate upon what they want to do next.

In Chapter 1, Pasteur explores the kind of learning that would help aid organizations to work more effectively in an uncertain and complex socio-political environment. She argues that organizations need to adopt attitudes that allow them to use deliberative and dialogic tools for democratic horizontal relations with their partners in the development enterprise. This requires learning through relationships of mutual respect, where good enough solutions are identified through processes of discussion and information-sharing, in which one party does not use its greater resources to dominate the process. This means radically reforming the way in which international aid organizations currently conceive their task to be results-based management. The following section discusses how results-based management constrains transformative learning and damages aid relationships.

The effects of results-based management

If stakeholders do not have a common view regarding solutions to the unbounded problems that are typical of international aid, such as reducing global poverty, then to whom should aid agencies be accountable for solving them? I mentioned earlier the idea of *improvisation* – shared learning through action. This recognizes that there are different perspectives on the problem and on what counts as success, unlike results-based management (RBM), which determines in advance both the expected result and the kind of evidence acceptable to determine whether that result was achieved. RBM is a product of a bureaucratic mode of understanding the world. I now turn to the challenges that aid agencies face in shifting to a relational view that would allow them to respond more effectively to the challenges of complexity.

RBM is usually attributed to taxpayers and voluntary gift givers growing increasingly suspicious, wanting to know in advance how their money will be spent and checking afterwards that it has been spent that way (Pentland, 2000; Meier, 2003). It may also be a response to the 'risk society'. The public sector, operating in a volatile and contradictory world, feels a growing pressure to demonstrate its infallibility through logic, control and the use of 'objective' evidence for decision-making (Beck, 1992). The resulting 'audit cultures' (Strathern, 2000) require an agreement between those in the accountability relationship about what is acceptable as evidence. To deliver that evidence, organizations may have to change their values and ways of working (Power, 1996; Pentland, 2000). RBM can give aid organizations more control. However, it can also create unintended consequences of resistance.

A donor may often have the upper hand in defining what is acceptable knowledge. It not only reshapes the recipient's organization so that it is capable of delivering the required information, but influences how the recipient describes itself (Strathern, 2000). One effect of this process may be 'decoupling'. This is when an organization goes through the ritual of imposed procedures but has not internalized their logic or the values underlying them. In this case, the more emphasis on measuring performance, the greater the likelihood for the organization to become deviant and secretive (Pentland, 2000, citing Power, 1996).

Another effect may be what has been termed 'colonization' – a rather sensitive word when used in the context of the aid relationship. Here the donor effectively shapes the recipient organization in its own image (Power, 1996; Pentland, 2000). For recipients, 'colonization' may offer a real possibility of *transformative learning* – seeing the world in a new way that helps them to act differently in order to achieve their goals more easily, or perhaps even to change their goals. On the other hand, it can encourage what has been termed *'regressive learning'*, one of compliance (Vince, 2001), or conversely what could be termed *'resistance learning'* or the 'weapons of the weak', where the donors' power generates its own resistance. I return to this later.

Most organizations in the aid web are, of course, both recipients and donors of funds. These different kinds of learning – transformative, regressive and resistance – can occur at the individual, organizational and trans-organizational level in all parts of the aid chain where money flows from the ministry of finance in a donor country down to local government or community-based organizations (CBOs) in the recipient country.

Regressive learning by recipients reinforces donors' claims that they know what the problem is and have the solution to it. Thus, the process has a negative impact on the donors, who have no incentive or challenge to revisit the way in which they understand the problem. They are discouraged from transformative or 'double-loop' learning and make only single-loop adjustments to their practice, otherwise known as 'managing for results'.[5] They only learn in connection to how they have previously defined the problem, rather than being open to learning through acting in a state of admitted ignorance (Lindblom, 1990).

A further negative effect is that RBM – with its imperative for upward reporting to donors who have used their power to define the problem and the solution – may reduce recipient governments' accountability to their own citizens. The same effect may manifest itself in projects. At a workshop that I facilitated recently in Switzerland, I introduced an exercise on mapping lines of accountability in a donor-funded project. Participants discovered that although the project's aim had been to strengthen accountability between local actors, the strongest accountability link was to the donor government. In such circumstances, staff time that could have been devoted to strengthening responsible horizontal relationships is diverted to reporting to the donor, the only actor in the project's network of relationships who can apply sanctions if the accountability obligation is not met.[6]

My argument so far is that RBM may have three perverse effects. First, it may distort or weaken recipients' accountability to their own citizens or intended end-users. Second, it may constrain transformative learning by both donors and recipients, the very kind of learning required for managing the non-bounded problems that aid agencies are tackling. Third, RBM may encourage resistance learning.

The French sociologist De Certeau has suggested that while the modern world appears to be dominated by an ideology of rational bureaucratic processes, ordinary people are resisting in a multitude of ways. He describes these as 'popular tactics' where order can be tricked by 'artifice, networks of connivances and sleights of hand' (De Certeau, 1988, Chapter 2).

James Scott (1985) has developed similar ideas, referring to 'weapons of the weak' and even going so far to suggest that the bureaucracy itself may turn a blind eye and connive in these popular tactics to ensure its own survival (Scott, 1998). He cites the example of agricultural production in the former Soviet Union, where food supply to the cities substantially depended upon members of collective farms diverting their labour, seeds and fertilizers to their minute private plots, which were vastly more productive than the bureaucratic, rule-bound collective farms. Thus, in pursuit of their own ends, the peasants unintentionally allowed the bureaucracy to continue pretending that it was in control.

It would be interesting to explore the extent to which resistance learning throughout the aid web has allowed aid to have some positive impact, providing 'evidence' that aid works and thus allowing the justification of its continued existence. Such learning may be in connivance with those inside the bureaucracy who 'bend the rules'. These examples of aid working might multiply if bureaucracy could shed the pretence of control. Thus, resistance learning by the recipient and single-loop learning by the donor could both be changed to mutual transformative learning.

This vision seems particularly challenging where power relations are highly unequal. However, even the vision, let alone efforts at practice, are almost absent in the world of aid. The next section considers whether this is because of the weakness of aid agencies' accountability to citizens in giving and receiving countries.

Responding to accountability failures

Aid organizations face a particular accountability dilemma. They are not account-able to those receiving their services, but only to those providing the funds. Paradoxically, in practice aid organizations are not even very accountable to those who fund them. This is because of the spatial and conceptual distance between the source of money and the scene of action. As a local government council taxpayer, I know that if the dustmen do not take away my rubbish on the scheduled day, I can easily complain. When I give money to an aid agency, either through taxes or as a donation, it is difficult for me to know whether the commitment has been fulfilled. At the other end of the aid chain, villagers in Bolivia are unaware of what promises were made back in the donor country, how much money was committed and who is accountable. One of the most significant achievements of ActionAid's Accountability, Learning and Planning System (ALPS) is that the new financial openness towards communities and partners (NGOs, CBOs and networks) has acted as a powerful symbol of intent to be transparent, which triggered an improved quality of relations (see Chapter 7).

On the other hand, even ActionAid finds it a challenge to communicate complexity to its funders. Its UK website claims that certain amounts of money can deliver specific outcomes – a literacy class, a duck-breeding programme or a school roof. However, these outcomes result from ActionAid staff members building relationships and learning to work with the communities receiving the aid. ActionAid's staff also strengthen civil society's political capacity and mobilize citizens to demand government delivery of public services and infrastructure. Yet the website does not emphasize that point. Like all other aid agencies, ActionAid stresses money over relationships, fearing that givers would view staff as a 'transaction cost' or 'administrative overhead', rather than as the people who make the difference. Aid agencies thus find themselves trapped into making complexity simple: give us the money and we will do the job. How can they move into a process of mutual learning with their donors so that they gain support not by claiming that they know what to do, but that they are acting in ignorance?

The complex nature of social change and the impossibility of predicting that a particular action will lead to a certain outcome suggest a possible approach: donors could work to develop long-term, consistent *relations* with selected recipient organizations who are pursuing a social change agenda that is compatible with the donor's own values and mission. Rather than aiming to achieve a predetermined concrete change in which the recipient organization is treated as an *instrument* of that change, the focus of donor effort would be to support that organization's own efforts in what may be a rapidly changing policy environment.

Given the donor consensus during the mid 2000s on the 'right way' to do aid – spend money to achieve pre-fixed targets (Manor, 2005) – an effort to make a general movement back towards a more relational approach would need to be supported by asking citizens in donor countries to consider the world in a new light. This means that those campaigning for more money to aid or more debt relief should switch their slogans to better and more equal relationships. At the global level, such a change is already observable – for example, in the World Social Forum – but it has yet scarcely penetrated the organization and practice of aid. Staff in aid agencies would be able to encourage wider citizen interest when they can demonstrate that learning through relationships helps aid to work more effectively for their fellow global citizens at the receiving end. This requires individuals and organizations to develop relationship skills – something, as I pointed out at the start of this chapter, that is intrinsically difficult for bureaucratic organizations. It is even harder given current commitments to spend more money. However, as I shall now discuss, there are changes under way.

Accountability by learning through relationships

A condition of transformative learning is to admit a state of ignorance. In 2002, Nick Stern, chief economist of the World Bank, made a speech about the Millennium Development Goals. He said that lack of knowledge was not an issue in achieving the goals. We knew the solution. We knew what do. All we needed were the resources.[7] Similar speeches were made that same year at the Monterrey Conference on financing development. The *UN Millennium Development Project Report* notes that a perception that aid quality is low discourages citizens from supporting increases in the aid budget (UN, 2005). The RBM response to such perceptions is to demonstrate what money can deliver in terms of tangible results: so many bed nets or other 'quick wins'. Aid has set itself a giddily ambitious agenda – the elimination of world poverty; yet its leaders claim they know what they are doing and the task is easy, provided the resources are available.

It would appear difficult to say, 'Please give us the money, although we are not sure what the answer is and we have to invest in relationships, rather than focus uniquely on outcome, if we are to make progress.' Here lies the challenge of learning and accountability. Can we find ways of encouraging everyone to learn, given that learning is essential for accountability?

The germs of such accountability may lie in efforts to find out what others, particularly aid recipients, think about a donor's values and actions. ActionAid introduced this idea in ALPS through a process of annual participatory reviews and reflections. A *social audit* is a method for securing regular and systematic feedback from partners and other stakeholders on the performance of the agency. Although DFID senior management did not accept social audit as a standard procedure, DFID has begun to take seriously some of its underlying principles, particularly in those countries where it feels itself less powerful. For example, the Asia director's annual plan for 2003 stated that DFID needed to be 'much more open to being influenced by others, to building genuine partnerships and to demonstrating its transparency and accountability to local communities' (cited in Eyben, 2004). Terms of reference produced in early 2005 for evaluating DFID's country programmes stress the importance of seeking stakeholder views.

Nevertheless, learning through relationships will not succeed if power relations are not addressed. Unlike DFID, the Agency for Personal Service Overseas (APSO) (the Irish international volunteer service, funded by an allocation from the Irish aid budget) decided to adopt social auditing. However, when an evaluation was undertaken of the exercise:

> *It was repeatedly highlighted by interviewees that as most APSO key stakeholders were totally dependent on APSO for assistance and resources, they were unlikely to engage in a process where they might criticize and potentially alienate the only hand that feeds.* (O'Dwyer, 2005, p285)

Not only did issues of asymmetrical power relations make the social audit flawed, some stakeholders objected to restricting their involvement to commenting on performance against APSO's mission, rather than having the chance to discuss whether this mission was the appropriate one (O'Dwyer, 2005) In other words, the social audit did not provide an opportunity for double-loop learning. Even worse, despite the flaws in the process itself, some interesting findings did emerge; but a powerful board watered them down before they were published.

O'Dwyer (2005) points out that a tool such as a social audit cannot by itself contribute to organizational learning and change without the leadership subscribing to stakeholder empowerment and democratic dialogue. ActionAid could not have introduced ALPS and used it relatively successfully to reduce the asymmetrical power relations in the aid web without very strong commitment from its senior management. Even so, as Chapter 7 describes, there was considerable resistance within the organization.

The fact that honest feedback *can* be elicited from stakeholders when they have the option of ending the relationship again indicates the significance of power to the quality of relationships. Eyben, Keeley and Li Shi carried out semi-structured interviews and small workshops in China with staff from government departments that were receiving DFID project funding. There was as much negative as positive feedback, including comments on the validity and relevance of DFID's mission in the country and the lack of financial transparency. Our report was sent to all of those we had interviewed, and the DFID country office drew up an action plan to implement the recommendations that it found acceptable (the criterion for acceptability being largely what would be satisfactory to senior management in London). The relative success of this exercise can be attributed to the roughly equal power relations between DFID and its partner organizations in China (Eyben, 2004).

To sum up, the argument for what Lindblom (1990) calls a 'self-guided' solution is based on an idea of mutual responsibility derived from shared learning through trial and error. This privileges relationships as a means of problem-solving in a world where it is uncertain how to make improvements. Because any one of us has only very limited information, a 'complexity approach' favours an investment in relationships. Differently positioned actors can be encouraged to work with each other so that they can get a better grasp of the whole through mutual communication of their knowledge of the system. Such an approach also helps to build domestic accountability for aid within both recipient and donor countries because government invites the participation of many stakeholders. However, unequal power relations mean that partner governments and donors must see this as an aspiration to aim for, rather than something that is easily achievable.

Conclusion

When an organization uses its power to avoid accountability to its end users, it has no interest in double-loop learning. Such an organization, interested in history only insofar as it confirms its own preferences, will be both ignorant and forgetful. Its power to practise 'historical amnesia' (Foucault, 1980) will deafen it to the voices and views of others. Instead of inviting their assistance, it ignores their understanding of the world, and through its exercise of control, it may incite resistance, not cooperation. I have proposed an alternative that values differences, where donors are better able to respond to the complex environment in which aid operates.

Recognizing complexity does *not* justify complicated aid interventions. Rather, what may be required is 'planned opportunism'.[8] It requires the capacity to judge when an intervention might trigger major social change, with active communications between all those involved concerning what they are learning from the effects of the initial intervention. It emphasizes modest step-by-step actions: this means a change of mindset. While, in some circumstances, a focus on concrete results can enhance performance through strengthened accountability to the end-users, an indiscriminate use of RBM will distort relationships, hide much that should be understood, reduce responsibility and block the capacity to learn in an unpredictable world. The current enthusiasm for RBM, with its central role for causality, ignores other ways of understanding the world and weakens the effectiveness of aid.

It would be increasingly possible to make a difference if the single-minded concern for results gave way to a greater emphasis on choice and the quality of the relationships, upon which donors depend to create real-world effects. Donors should negotiate accountability in terms of mutual responsibility.

Donors are already learning some of this. The DFID's recent policy paper on fragile states (DFID, 2005) demonstrates an awareness of the futility of rushing straight up the hill. It emphasizes modest and incremental actions that acknowledge the uncertain and contingent environment of international aid. Its paper recognizes that aid has caused problems in the past and that donors themselves are political actors. This is good progress.

We are also witnessing greater responsiveness. The Monterrey Agreement to monitor donors, as well as recipients, is being implemented in Tanzania through the Independent Monitoring Group (Killick, 2004). Donor governments that have most embraced rights-based approaches, such as in Sweden, are asking recipient governments to evaluate their aid programmes. Compared with a decade ago, donors are more transparent about their budgets, including the costs of their own staff. This signals a real concern to promote recipient ownership (Eyben and Ferguson, 2004).

In this chapter, I have argued that aid can be more effective through developing relationship-building skills and practising planned opportunism, combined with initially modest objectives. In order to achieve this, donor agencies must understand the specific context by investing in relationships with diverse local individuals, organizations and networks involved in change. Donor agencies must also deploy sufficient staff to create, support and strengthen alliances, bringing ideas, as well as money, to these alliances. This means rejecting the proposition that more money can be spent more effectively with fewer staff. It also means accepting that there is no necessary correlation between the magnitude of the resources and the impact. Finally, it means recognizing and responding to the historical landscapes of power within which aid relationships are located.

Notes

1   When, in 1999, I made an early presentation in DFID on my 'relationships matter' thinking (Eyben, 2004), the then Secretary of State warned me that such an approach risked treading on the terrain of the politicians. This reflected a viewpoint that has long been held in theories of government that public administration lies outside the sphere of politics (Peters, 1995).

2   See also the House of Commons Committee on International Development's report no 8, where the Permanent Secretary says that DFID staff needed skills to influence governments (House of Commons Committee on International Development, 2004, para 61).

3   Morgan cites only two other publications relating complexity theory to aid: Rihani (2002) and Groves and Hinton (2004).

4   Recently I was at a meeting of a small number of civil servants from two different departments discussing why Whitehall was not interested in learning. They unconsciously emphasized the point through their nervous comments that whatever they said should not go beyond 'these four walls'.

5   'Managing for results is an iterative management approach... Based on constant feedback of performance information from audits, management reviews, performance measurement ... and evaluations, the inputs and activities can be modified' (Meier, 2003, p24). This is a classic description of 'single-loop learning' by the head of the RBM unit in the Canadian International Development Agency (CIDA).

6   See also Carlsson and Wohlgemuth (2000).

7   I heard this speech at the Annual Bank Conference on Development and Economics in Oslo in June 2002. As I am reporting from memory, this is the gist of what I remember and may not be verbatim.

8   I am grateful to Andy Batkin for this phrase.

References

Bauman, Z. (1989) *Modernity and the Holocaust*, Polity Press,London

Beck, U. (1992) *The Risk Society*, Sage, London

Carlsson, J. and Wohlgemuth, L. (2000) 'Introduction', in Carlsson, J. and Wohlgemuth, L. (eds) *Learning in Development Co-operation*, EGDI Study 2000, vol 2, Ministry of Foreign Affairs, Stockholm

Castells, M. (1997) *The Power of Identity*, Blackwell, Oxford

Chapman, J. (2002) *System Failure: Why Governments Must Learn to Think Differently*, Demos, London

Clegg, S., Vierra da Cunha, J. and Pinha e Cunha, M. (2004) 'Management paradoxes: A Relational View', *Human Relations*, vol 55, no 5, pp483–503

Common, R. (2004) 'Organisational learning in a political environment: Improving policy-making in UK government', *Policy Studies*, vol 25, no 1, pp36–49

Cooper, F. and Packard, R. (eds) (1997) *International Development and the Social Sciences*, University of California Press, Berkeley and Los Angeles

Courpasson, D. and Reed, M. (2004) 'Introduction: Bureaucracy in the age of enterprise', *Organisation*, vol 11, no 1, pp5–12

De Certeau, M. (1988) *The Practice of Everyday Life*, University of California Press, Berkeley

Department for International Development (DFID) (2005) *Why We Need to Work More Effectively in Fragile States*, DFID, London

du Gay, P. (2000) *In Praise of Bureaucracy*, Sage, London

Edgren, G. (2004) 'Aid is an unreliable joystick', in Pronk, J. et al (eds) *Catalysing Development? A Debate on Aid*, Blackwell, Oxford

Eyben, R. (2004) 'Relationships matter in supporting change in favour of poor people', *Lessons for Change*, no 8, Institute of Development Studies, Brighton

Eyben, R. and Ferguson, C. (2004) 'How can donors become more accountable to poor people?', in Groves, L. and Hinton, R. (eds) *Inclusive Aid*, Earthscan, London

Foucault, M. (1980) *Knowledge/Power: Selected interviews and other writings* (C. Gordon, ed) Pantheon Books, New York

Geyer, R. (2003) 'Beyond the Third Way: The science of complexity and the politics of choice', *British Journal of Politics and International Relations*, vol 5, no 2, pp237–257

Gould, J. (2004) 'Introducing aidnography', in Gould, J. and Marcussen, H. S. (eds) *Ethnographies of Aid – Exploring Development Texts and Encounters*, Occasional Paper no 24, International Development Studies, Roskilde

Groves, L. and Hinton, R. (2004) 'The complexity of inclusive aid', in Groves, L. and Hinton, R. (eds) *Inclusive Aid*, Earthscan, London

Hajer, M. and Wagenaar, H. (2003) 'Introduction', in Hajer, M. and Wagenaar, H. (eds) *Deliberative Policy Analysis, Understanding Governance in the Network Society*, Cambridge University Press, Cambridge

Hare, L. (1981) *Bentham and Bureaucracy*, Cambridge University Press, Cambridge

Hewitt, T. (2000) 'A hybrid or a third way? Contemporary thinking on inter-organizational relationships', in Robinson, D., Hewitt, T. and Harriss, J. (eds) *Managing Development: Understanding Inter-Organizational Relationships*, Sage Publications in association with the Open University, London

House of Commons Committee on International Development (2004) Report no 8, www.publications.parliament.uk, accessed 15 October 2005

Jassey, K. (2004) 'The bureaucrat', in Groves, L. and Hinton, R. (eds) *Inclusive Aid*, Earthscan, London

Killick, T. (2004) 'Monitoring partnerships. Aid-based relationships. A note', *Development Policy Review*, vol 22, no 2, pp229–234

Ladbury, S. (2005) *DFID Policy Coherence Review*, Final report, 3 January, unpublished, DFID, London

Lindblom, C. (1990) *Inquiry and Change: The Troubled Attempt to Understand and Shape Society*, Yale University Press, New Haven

Manor, J. (2005) 'Introduction', *Increased Aid: Minimising Problems, Maximising Gains*, IDS Bulletin no 36, p3

Mawdsley, E., Townsend, J. and Porter, G. (2005) 'Trust, accountability, and face-to-face interaction in North–South NGO relations', *Development in Practice*, vol 15, no 1, pp77–81

Mazlish, B. (2000) 'Invisible ties: From patronage to networks', *Theory, Culture and Society*, vol 17, no 2, pp1–19

Meier, W. (2003) 'Results-based management: Towards a common understanding among development cooperation agencies', Discussion paper prepared for the Canadian International Development Agency, Performance Review Branch, for consideration by the DAC Working Party on Aid Effectiveness and Harmonisation, www.managingfordevelopmentresults.org/, accessed 7 February 2005

Morgan, G. (1997) *Images of Organisations*, Sage, London

Morgan, P. (2005) *The Idea and Practice of Systems Thinking and Their Relevance for Capacity Development*, Report from the European Centre for Development Policy Management, March

O'Dwyer, B. (2005) 'The construction of social account: Case study in an overseas aid agency', *Accounting, Organizations and Society*, vol 30, pp279–296

Pentland, B. (2000) 'Will auditors take over the world? Program, technique and the verification of everything', *Accounting, Organizations and Society*, vol 25, pp307–312

Peters, B. G. (1995) *The Politics of Bureaucracy*, Longman, Whiteplains

Power, M. (1996) 'Making things auditable', *Accounting, Organizations and Society*, vol 22, no 123, p146

Rihani, S. (2002) *Complex Systems Theory and Development Practice: Understanding Non-Linear Realities*, Zed Books, London

Scott, J. C. (1985) *Weapons of the Weak: Everyday Forms of Peasant Resistance*, Yale University Press, New Haven

Scott, J. C. (1998) *Seeing Like a State*, Yale University Press, New Haven

Strathern, M. (2000) 'Accountability and ethnography', in Strathern, M. (ed) *Audit Cultures*, Routledge, London, pp279–304

UN (United Nations) (2005) *Investing in Development: UN Millennium Development Project Report*, www.unmillenniumproject.org/

Vince, R. (2001) 'Power and emotion in organizational learning', *Human Relations*, vol 54, no 10, pp1325–1351

Weick, K. E. and Sutcliffe, K. R. (2001) *Managing the Unexpected. Assuring High Performance in an Age of Complexity*, Jossey-Bass, San Francisco

Wittel, A. (2001) 'Toward a network sociality', *Theory, Culture and Society*, vol 18, no 6, pp51–76

Part 2

REFLECTIVE PRACTICE

3

Relations with People Living in Poverty: Learning from Immersions

Renwick Irvine, Robert Chambers and Rosalind Eyben

Introduction

This chapter is about the practice and the potential of immersions.[1] Immersions are occasions when professionals learn directly from encounters with people living in poverty by staying with them and reflecting on the experience. Those taking part may be the staff of bilateral and multilateral agencies, diplomats, parliamentarians, government officials, NGO staff, academics or other development professionals.

We set out to:

- describe types and purposes of immersions;
- review practical experience with immersion design, logistical organization and the host community;
- assess the rationale and impact of immersions, including better awareness of the realities of poor and marginalized people, personal and institutional learning and change, reinvigorated commitment, and influence on decision-making and policy;
- identify enabling conditions for making immersion experiences a normal, regular and expected activity for development professionals, together with good practices.

Why immersions?

I have asked myself what would have happened if I had spent one week per year in a village somewhere over the last decade. I am quite sure it would have made a difference to me. Ten different contexts, and a

number of faces and names, to have in mind when reading, thinking,
writing, taking decisions and arguing in our bureaucracy.[2]

Most development professionals are directly or indirectly committed to the reduction of poverty and injustice. At the same time, most of us are isolated and insulated from poor and marginalized people and lack opportunities for direct experiential learning about their lives and conditions. Today, aid agency staff spend much of their time on policy dialogue, in workshops and meetings, and on the donor coordination and aid instruments that support this dialogue. The pressures of upward reporting and managing programmes make it only too easy for staff to become distant from the day-to-day realities of living that confront those whom their work is meant to serve. Reports, useful though they can be for understanding some aspects of those realities, are no substitute for personal insights gained from living and learning *in situ.* These have proven to be particularly helpful in triggering the 'double-loop learning', which reframes a problem or issue (see Chapter 1).

One of the crucial factors helping an organization achieve its goals is knowledge of its staff. Direct, lived experience of the environment that the organization is seeking to change is an important source of such knowledge. Direct experience generates energy, confidence and commitment, and gives staff the authority to make a policy case derived from face-to-face encounters. Reading or participating in seminars on poverty can and should also be undertaken in the same reflective learning approach; but *direct* experience can engage the learner more deeply and, as Senge (1990) says, provide more opportunity for looking at the world and the way in which we relate to it in new ways. It provides the kind of learning that helps agencies to respond intelligently in different or unforeseen circumstances. As realities on the ground are rapidly changing, it also means constantly refreshing that direct experience; otherwise erroneous decisions may be made on the basis of out-of-date information.

If they do not make the effort to engage directly with poor people, aid agency staff may be unintentionally signalling that their agency's publicly stated concerns for participation and accountability need not be taken seriously, and that poor people's own experience and ideas about their condition are considered irrelevant for poverty reduction policies.

Two of the international development organizations that have most engaged with immersions, the World Bank and ActionAid International, appear to be at different ends of the aid spectrum; yet their rationales for immersions are similar. The introduction to the World Bank's Village Immersion Programme says that they are 'an opportunity for the Bank staff to shed their Bank hats, live the lives of the poor and understand poverty in all its dimensions' (World Bank, 2003). Similarly, ActionAid India states that the purpose is 'to gain social empathy and experiential learning, through living with people in poverty, about dynamics and processes of their impoverishment, oppression, discrimination and marginalization, and to apply these learnings professionally and personally' (Chachra, 2003).

Immersions are a means of achieving such understandings. They are distinct from normal brief field visits that are often highly structured and 'red carpet' in style, vulnerable to a rigid pre-planned schedule, formality, shortage of time, a constraining political environment and encouraging behaviour designed to please or gain benefits from the visitor as donor. As one expatriate informant put it: 'The whole process is highly ritualized and fraught with political significance around what foreigners can and cannot see.' Such visits also have other biases (Chambers, 1983, pp10–25) and carry the risk that one short encounter or constrained conversation with one specially briefed local inhabitant may disproportionately influence perceptions and subsequent recommendations or decisions. Immersions, in contrast, are designed for visitors to stay for several days with their hosts, practising reflective observation and participating in the day-to-day lives of their hosts, in this way gaining fuller, more grounded and more realistic insights.

Of course, development professionals such as aid agency staff can meet poor people in their everyday lives, from riding in buses rather than private cars, to shopping in downtown markets. Nevertheless, setting aside a few days at regular intervals for the experiential learning offered through immersions can provide a different quality and depth of exposure, as much for government officials and national professional staff in aid agencies as for expatriates. Immersions can be as relevant for ground-truthing of macro-policy as for the micro-management of services.

Types and purposes of immersions

In development practice, there has been a long history of organized immersions; but during the past ten years, a new movement of organized immersions has been quietly gathering momentum, with the lead taken by the Exposure and Dialogue Programme (EDP) of the German Association for the Promotion of North–South Dialogue (APNSD, 2000, 2002a).[3] Founded in 1985, the association has since carried out over 50 EDPs in different parts of the world. Development agencies that have participated include the Gesellschaft für Technische Zusammenarbeit (GTZ), the Bundesministerium für wirtschaftliche Zusammenarbeit und Entwicklung (BMZ) and the World Bank. The methodology and its continuing evolution owe much to its initiator Karl Osner. The major aim of EDPs has been to 'give poverty a face' and to motivate key persons in politics, governmental institutions, civil society and the churches. EDPs have been organized in collaboration with many organizations, including the Grameen Bank in Bangladesh, the Self-Employed Women's Association (SEWA) in India and the Centre for the Development of Human Resources in Rural Areas (CENDHRRA) in the Philippines.

The World Bank's Grass Roots Immersion Programme (GRIP) was developed during the mid 1990s as part of the Executive Development Programme for its senior staff. The aim of the immersions was to complement the academic part of the programme at Harvard with a reality check, to reinforce 'fighting poverty with *passion* [emphasis in the original]' (World Bank, circa 1998) and to bring about value-based change. The Village Immersion Programme (VIP) in the South Asia region is a parallel programme of experiential learning involving a wider range of staff. The first VIP immersion was in Pakistan in 1996; since then, over 200 staff have taken part. The purpose is for staff to understand and appreciate the reality of the poor people who are the World Bank's clients, and to rekindle their commitment to eliminating poverty (World Bank, 2003).

Following on from a number of immersions organized for their own staff and for the UK Department for International Development (DFID) in India, Viet Nam and China, in 2005 ActionAid International undertook two pilot programmes in Bangladesh and Ghana that sought to draw on the lessons from good practice of these earlier initiatives. From these pilots, ActionAid is now developing the concept of immersions as a facilitated workshop with learning outcomes.

Immersions have also been undertaken by *individuals* on their own initiative. During the 1960s and 1970s, Shri Mathur, a senior Indian Administrative Service (IAS) officer responsible for agricultural extension in India, made a personal reality check by spending one week each year living in a village in Bihar. Social anthropologists have long practised self-organized immersion visits as part of a research programme or consultancy assignment, as have a few others in development agencies and governments. Self-organized immersions have, though, been exceptional. They have faced institutional constraints of time and approval and have sometimes only been done by taking leave.

Immersions can have *different specific purposes*. In 2000, SEWA in India initiated EDP immersions for its organizer staff as part of their induction and orientation, and so that they would understand SEWA members, what keeps them poor, and their strengths and strategies (Bali, 2002). SEWA management perceives immersions as important for creating or maintaining a pro-poor organizational culture and enabling new staff members to have a wider base of knowledge and understanding. ActionAid India has also used immersions to sensitize staff and to develop their capacity in rights-based approaches by becoming familiar with the dynamics and processes of the impoverishment, oppression, discrimination and marginalization of people in poverty.[4]

Immersions have also had more thematic purposes. They have been used for participatory rural appraisal (PRA) training, for developing a new strategy or policy, as an integral part of a workshop or conference process, as part of research, or for combinations of these. From 1989 onwards, for example, village immersions were part of PRA development and training in India. The Swiss Agency for Development and Cooperation (SDC) has used brief immersions twice in Tanzania. In the first, during 2001, donor and NGO staff spent a day and night in poor communities as an integral part of a 'learn shop' on poverty and change held at Ifakara. In the second, during 2002, SDC staff were trained as researchers and spent days living with and helping very poor families (Jupp, 2004). In January 2004, Cornell University, SEWA and Women in Informal Employment Globalizing and Organizing (WIEGO) broke new ground with a joint EDP in Gujarat. They preceded a dialogue on labour market, trade and poverty issues with 'exposure to the lives of six remarkable women' in whose homes they stayed for two nights and a day (Chen et al, 2004, pp9–11).

Designing and organizing immersions: The challenge of power relations

An immersion can run the risk of reinforcing unequal power relations as well as stereotypical views that may be held by hosts and visitors alike. Hence, the design of immersions requires considerable thought and sensitivity. Practical details are discussed in an earlier version of this chapter (Irvine et al, 2004).

Most organized immersions appear to take place in rural areas. There are fewer urban accounts, although some SEWA/EDP immersions have had an equal rural–urban split. Remote villages that are difficult to reach differ from those that are easily accessible and are often more deprived. Yet, immersions in inaccessible areas entail the trade-offs between travelling time and immersion time, and may cost more, though travel itself can be a significant experience. They may also be harder to set up: the facilitating organization for a two-person immersion by Eyben and a Bolivian colleague had to make special arrangements to contact the leader of a Guarani community so that they could be met at an agreed time at the road head and be guided through the forest to their hosts' community.

The most commonly documented immersions have lasted from three days to two weeks. For convenience, a common length has been five to six days, taking a week together with travel time, and involving between 8 to 16 people. It may be worth keeping the overall programme down to a week to encourage greater participation.

The relative seniority of the members of the group matters. Power dynamics and institutional hierarchy have been observed in some World Bank immersions. Achieving a balanced and diverse composition of the group in terms of gender, range of experience, subject area and seniority is emphasized in one set of guidelines (APNSD, 2002b).

Immersions range from the highly structured or closed to the unplanned or open. Closed immersions have a sequence of prearranged activities, such as meeting local officials, visiting schools, co-operatives and other local institutions, and participating in 'cultural' events. In these there is little scope for deviance from the set plan. Somewhat more open-ended have been immersions where PRA activities have been used to gain insights into aspects of a community, such as its resources, institutions, problems and ways of working. Also more open-ended is the common practice of time spent with the family hosts, being taught by them and helping them in their everyday activities, such as collecting water or firewood, cooking, washing, going to market and working in the fields. Other immersions have a theme or topic to be explored but no prearranged programme. In the most open of all, as in the pilot immersion organized by ActionAid in Ghana in 2005, there is full freedom to wander around, to go with the flow, to see what hosts wish to show or share, and to follow up on whatever is significant, surprising and unexpected. The best combination is often a mix, depending upon context, purpose and the interests of both visitors and hosts.

An immersion usually requires the services of a *facilitating organization* (FO) that is already well known in the region to be visited and has the trust and confidence of local communities. This could be, for example, an NGO, a local government body, a research institute, a consultancy company, a faith-based group, a network of local community organizations or, as with SEWA, a trades union. Mutual expectations and objectives of the contracting and facilitating organizations need to be understood in advance, with agreement that the major purpose is experiential learning for the visitors, not public relations for the FO. Ideally, the presence of the FO should be low-key and not hamper free communication between host and visitor.

Good facilitators and translators can make the difference between a fruitful and a difficult immersion. Their role is to enable the guests to have a real meeting with their hosts, to understand each other and to achieve a close personal exchange (APNSD, 2002b). Care is needed for additional translation where some in a host community, often disproportionately women, do not speak the *lingua franca* of a country, such as Mandarin in China or Spanish in much of Latin America.

For participants, the most challenging aspect of an immersion is often lack of or minimal basic amenities and possibly no privacy for bathing and toilet needs. The issue may be more sensitive for women, a problem that may be partially offset by pairing female participants together. Failing to provide reassurance on these matters may be one reason why some people are reluctant to participate in immersions. Thus, the level of support given to participants may entail a trade-off between encouraging them to undertake the immersion and making it unrealistically comfortable. However, the less the support provided, the more the sense of isolation and insecurity which some have found significant experiential learning:

> *I battled with the urban squalor, the urban foraging by cows, the ani-mal excreta everywhere, the lack of access to water once we left the home. I battled with the noise of the city, and the air pollution was an assault; Leelaben saw me battling with it and said it was a factor in her own depression.* (Frances Lund in Chen et al, 2004, p72)

On the other hand, one respondent commented:

> *Asking bureaucrats to immerse themselves in contexts in which their practical arrangements are very stressful can be counterproductive – if all the time is spent wondering how to cope with everyday needs, it detracts from the building of relations with others.*

Psychologically preparing the participants for living in villages with very basic amenities can help to optimize benefits from the experience.

Health can be a major concern and appropriate measures should be taken to ensure the well-being of the participant. Mosquito nets are provided where necessary in organized immersions. While these can be seen as sending negative messages to the communities, creating barriers between visitors and hosts, they can also make suitable and natural presents to leave behind in the community.

Personal safety issues are another common concern, including how safe it is for staff to go into remote areas because of political disturbance or risks of natural disasters. ActionAid in Ghana arranged for two plainclothes policemen to be stationed in the community during the immersion, raising questions for the participants as to why they should receive protection while their hosts normally had no access to the police.

Host communities or groups within them can take responsibility for much of the organization of an immersion, as with Win–Win trainings (Joseph, 1995). The potential for organized and empowered groups such as Reflect[5] circles to host immersions is yet to be explored. So far, it has been more common for the facilitating organization to make the arrangements, including selection of host families, although in the case of the immersion organized by ActionAid Ghana, that choice was left to the community's male elders. This particular immersion threw into relief some issues of power and relations between women and men that appear to have been rarely discussed in previous reports on immersions.

Participants may sometimes consider the host community to be too closely associated with a particular facilitating organization with an 'agenda', risking the distortion of perceptions and experiences. In some cases, the Village Immersion Programme has been in 'World Bank affected' villages so that the immersees can get closer to the real 'clients'. However, one immersee commented that having clients as hosts 'brought the baggage associated with being a donor, of offering money, being attached to service delivery or benefits which distort what people tell you' – precisely what the immersion aimed to avoid.

Payment for an immersion is usually through the facilitating organization, distancing participants from having to negotiate costs. However, in some cases, direct payment has been made to the family involved (as by ActionAid Viet Nam), making transparent the payment for a service received. In other cases, payment has gone into community funds to support local development. Options for one-off individual immersions include bringing as gifts items that are not easily obtainable for communities living far away from a town or a market.

Views differ on gifts. SEWA strongly discourages them: immersions are a regular practice for SEWA staff, and gifts would change relationships and raise others' expectations in the future. In other immersions, giving small gifts for hosts or children is a common gesture of friendly appreciation. Insensitive or large gifts can, however, draw undue attention to social and power differences and undermine the spirit of an immersion.

Ethical issues are often raised, most notably regarding the impact that outsiders have on the community, on the host family and on how the power dimensions play out between visitors, facilitators/interpreters and the host community. A helpful approach is to draw up a code of conduct at the outset (Narayanasamy and Boraian, 1997). Responding to personal questions may be challenging. When a World Bank staff member was asked in Indonesia how much he earned, he answered honestly. He then found himself forced to justify his salary by explaining purchasing power parity; but, as he recognized, this fell somewhat short of a satisfactory explanation.

An immersion can raise expectations of direct benefits to a community. Normally there will be none, and consistent clarity is needed on this. If there are to be benefits – for example, payment to a community fund – that also needs to be completely clear. Despite best efforts, expectations may still be raised. In Ghana, the village chief in his goodbyes to the immersion participants remarked: 'A mother waits to see if she has a true daughter or not', meaning that even though a grownup daughter leaves the village, she should send gifts thereafter.

Some who have participated in immersions have commented upon the trouble and inconvenience that the hosts were put to by 'looking after' them. This feeling of unease can be reduced by full involvement in daily activities and chores, and being sensitive as to when it is best to step back and observe.

Koy Thomson of ActionAid International wrote in his back-to-office report:

> One of my expectations of the immersion was to 'unlearn'. But I realized that you cannot really report what you 'unlearned'. Unlearning is not a happening but an attitude of mind. For me, at least, the immersion was a safe and secure place to be allowed to let go, open out and be vulnerable. For if you can't do that, how can you listen, value what you hear, and notice what the hell is going on? But what did Funsi get from the immersion? Well, according to some of the village elders: 'The rains came, no one died, and there was no bad news. This was a blessing from God for welcoming strangers.'

The benefits of immersions: Personal, institutional and policy learning and change

Potential and actual impacts of immersions are personal, institutional and policy related, affecting commitment, insights, practices and policy. A successful immersion can lead to personal change through experiential learning; to institutional change through what participants do later in their organizations; and (with decision-makers) to changes in policy grounded in the realism of the experience.

Personal impact, learning and change are central to immersions. For McGee (2002, p36) 'policy-makers' disposition for personal involvement with poor people in learning about poverty affects the soundness of the knowledge claims they can make'. Since experiential learning, both emotional (in how things are felt) and intellectual (in how they are framed) is at the core of immersions, impact varies according to personal predispositions and motivation. The quality and depth of the learning depends upon the preparation and upon what happens during the immersion; but most of all, and critically, it depends upon adequate time and space for reflection and questioning.

Some people welcome and eagerly anticipate the challenge and learning of an immersion, while others are nervous and hesitant. Positive predispositions and motivation may centre on a desire to better understand the realities of poor and marginalized people, coming from combinations of:

- social empathy: concern for those who are less fortunate;
- reflective awareness of personal isolation from and ignorance of the lives of poor people;
- professional interest in topic-related learning and doing a reality check;
- wanting to deepen and strengthen personal and professional commitment;
- a desire to be more professional – for example, in policy dialogue to be able to speak and argue with the authority of direct personal experience.

Views vary on how important personal predispositions are to a good immersion. One view is that a successful immersion requires an 'inner readiness' of participants. On the other hand, some who started as sceptics later reflected that they have 'got a lot out' of the experience. For example, one participant in the 1997 World Bank village immersion in Tamil Nadu commented: 'I am convinced that it is necessary for all economists in the World Bank to have spent such time in close and informal interaction with such members of society' (Narayanasamy and Boraian, 1997, pvi).

The experiential nature of an immersion means that there are no benchmarks for how people have changed. Participants' different starting points in emotional intelligence, life experiences, local knowledge and so on make it difficult to compare or measure change across individuals. The main evidence is personal testimony. For Ravi Kanbur (1999), his immersion was 'one of the most educational and moving experiences of my life'.

An immersion can also change a professional view. After staying with a SEWA member and watching a minimum-wage negotiation, Gary Fields, a macro-economist, wrote:

> Because of what I saw on the ground, my professional judgement about minimum wages and supplementary benefits changed. With the standard labour economics model in mind, I had worried that the minimum wage might hurt the very women it was meant to help because of a loss of jobs. In this context, though the minimum wage does not act as a wage floor, it acts as an aspirational target... The very fact that a minimum wage is set at so (relatively) high a level strengthens SEWA's negotiating position... This kind of 'wage' increase is something that I favour. Without this experience on the ground, that is not something I would have said two days earlier. (Chen et al, 2004, p36)

Emotional engagement frequently comes out in immersion reports. There are stories, precious moments, anecdotes, surprises, relationships built up, new insights, and shifts of perception and attitude, some of which may only emerge later with recollection and reflection. After a World Bank EDP with SEWA, Judith Edstrom wrote:

> ... and my feeling that I have learned so much from this courageous woman, that my own sense of adversity pales next to what Kamlaben [the hostess from SEWA] has confronted and overcome. I feel humbled by this woman and believe that when a challenge confronts me in the future, I can honestly ask myself one of two questions: first, 'Would Kamlaben have this option?', to put the query in perspective, or, second, 'What would Kamlaben do in this situation?' Not in the sense of being confronted with the same challenges, but of seeking to find the straight-forward answer that keeps close to the truth – family, health, spirituality and, most of all, a sense of personal dignity.

How motivating an immersion can be was expressed by a GRIP participant:

> On the surface, I saw nothing new during my trip. However, experien-cing poverty at first hand, witnessing the life of a family [who] has no assurance that it can survive until the next harvest, going to bed at 8 pm because there is no light and nothing else to do, and talking with parents and children who have no expectation that government will improve their lives had a remarkable effect on me. It leaves me even more committed to our mission.

Institutional

Institutional change through organizational learning can take many forms through changes in perception, behaviour and practice. Such changes may be difficult to document. If it is often difficult for participants to realize the changes that they have undergone; it may be even harder to assess the long-term impact of their immersions on their organizations.

The human resources and finance departments of any organization play a big part in forming and sustaining organizational cultures. Their staff may also be among those whose learning could have most impact. Dorothee Fiedler of the BMZ wrote that one important outcome of her EDP immersion with SEWA was seeing 'that we have to be much better able to listen to the poor, instead of telling them what should be done to improve their situation'. Since then, when recruiting new staff she puts more emphasis on listening skills as a core competence (D. Fiedler, pers comm, November 2002). Changes like this may seem small and almost imperceptible; but their effects may be deep, wide and enduring.

Impact on policy and practice

A combination of empirical evidence and experiential understanding of poverty is powerful for influencing and guiding development actors. As an ActionAid staff member commented on an immersion in Viet Nam, the objective was 'to have that feeling of poverty myself, so that the experience would guide my thoughts and actions'. The immersion directly influenced his approach to policy and guided the thinking, planning and design of programmes to take much more account of the felt needs of the poor.

Immersions can give policy-makers grounded empirical evidence and a clear picture to inform decision-making. As pointed out in the EDP guidelines, 'it is considerably easier for a person to defend opinions which are the result of vivid personal experiences' (APNSD, 2000). As one participant in an immersion in Sri Lanka in 1999 commented: 'As for the relevance of the experience, I can emphatically say that it was of great value to the work I do on rural development... This has given me some comparative framework to my current work on rural development strategy.' One clear instance of policy impact comes from Ravi Kanbur's (1999) immersion, which gave him confidence, confirming the importance of risk and vulnerability that were to be prominent in the very influential *World Development Report 2000/2001: Attacking Poverty* (World Bank, 2000).

The impact of an immersion depends upon many factors, not least the quality of the preparation, facilitation and arrangements, and the orientation, commitment and influence of the participant. Beyond these, three ways of enhancing the impact of immersions stand out: reflection, feedback, and follow-through and reinforcement.

A repeated weakness of immersions is inadequate time and process for reflection. Where time is short, the normal reflex is to protect the immersion itself. The trade-offs here are hard to judge. Suffice it to say that it is a common complaint that there was too little time for personal reflection. Taking notes, recollecting details and thinking through what has been felt and learned should occur close to the time of the experience, and always before returning to business as usual.

The forms of feedback and dissemination after an immersion affect the depth and breadth of impact. The acts of writing and speaking about the experience help to develop, clarify and embed the learning. The World Bank required each immersee to file a memo to the president of the Bank, in no more than two pages, regarding:

1 location and experience;
2 how this affected you;
3 can you use this work to strengthen your work in the Bank? (World Bank, circa 1998)

Distortions were possible when 'people write what they think Jim [Wolfensohn] expects to hear' (respondent). Written reports do have their value, not least relative permanence, and some of them can be very moving.

Praful Patel, vice president of the World Bank for South Asia, produced and distributed on email a striking visual diary of photographs and commentary illustrating his experience. Verbal feedback has its own power. Informal conversations and stories that are told and repeated have a capacity to affect not just individuals, but organizations (Denning, 2000). Personal presentations have the added strength that we say things we would not write, say them more vividly than we would write them, and convey feelings directly. In the SDC Tanzania *Views of the Poor* study, researchers did not write reports, but were debriefed in pairs (Jupp, 2004, p10). After a SEWA immersion in Gujarat in November 2003, Dorothee Fiedler gave five presentations with slides in response to demand from her colleagues in BMZ, and Judith Edstrom of the World Bank had this to say:

> *What has surprised me as I recounted my experience to colleagues at a departmental meeting is that for every person who might be sceptical about the realism of this experience, there are more who have been touched by it – the Ugandan staff assistant who came up to me after the meeting and said, simply, thank you for doing that; the Ghanaian consultant who came and showed me a picture of his poor mother sitting on the floor of her home; the Romanian staff member who immediately wrote me an email saying how my talk evoked the times when he lived behind the Iron Curtain and Westerners would come for home stays, and how they would talk about human rights and other issues he dared not speak about with fellow citizens. Have you had such experiences?* (J. Edstrom, pers comm, 2003)

Nevertheless, memory fades and commitment wanes unless reinforced. The value of follow-through on the implications of what has been experienced and learned is obvious. In addition to the feedback of written accounts, stories and presentations, other forms of follow-through include:

- Keep a reflective diary throughout and refer back to it.
- Maintain contact with hosts, the FO and with co-participants.
- Encourage colleagues to undertake immersions and help them to do so.
- Make an immersion an annual event.
- Work with human resources departments and others to institutionalize immersions as part of good professional practice.
- Have a feedback reflection or reunion some months after the immersion in order to review the extent to which changes initially identified have taken deeper root (APNSD, 2002a).
- Enhance the enabling conditions as discussed in the following section.

Enabling conditions

A significant institutional change is for organizations to adopt immersions as policy for their staff, as SEWA has done. While this occurred in the World Bank, at the time of writing we do not know of any other multilateral or bilateral aid agency that has followed, although individual managers in the Swedish International Development Agency (Sida), DFID and SDC have encouraged their staff. The way in which a participant reports on his or her experience may influence the perceptions of senior management regarding the wider benefits of immersions. Those who seek to promote immersions need to be sensitive to their organizations' culture and priorities and what might or might not make a difference. These cultural differences might imply alternative ways of deciding who and how to influence within the organization selected to promote immersions. Where there is a strong value placed on solidarity with people living in poverty, immersions might be seen as a means of reinforcing that value. In an organization where there is an emphasis on evidence-based policy, the advantages of immersions might be stressed rather differently.

Immersions are useful for agencies who want staff to be reflective practitioners, imaginative and purposeful in working to the agency's poverty reduction objectives. The following factors can enable immersions to become a routine activity in a development agency:

- Senior management should set an example and take the lead in participating in immersion visits. Regional and country directors have an important role, as well as those at the top of the agency.
- Build immersions into existing management development and staff training and induction programmes, including language learning.
- Make immersions an integral part of country strategy planning and evaluation processes.
- Have someone in the organization responsible for maintaining up-to-date information about design, budgets, terms of reference and contact details of facilitating organizations, names of former participants, etc.
- Provide concise objectives and clear and sensitive feedback mechanisms, co-established between the facilitating organization, the participant(s) and the sending institution. This gives a good basis for immersions.
- Develop a structure that is sufficiently flexible to be adapted to a particular context, followed and agreed to by all. However, some 'non-negotiables' may help (such as the need for a thorough briefing, joint objective setting, sufficient time in the communities, a long enough reflection period and a personalized write-up). These depend upon the nature of the institution.
- Provide momentum through a critical body of immersion alumni to help spread the message and encourage colleagues to engage in the process. This requires a dissemination strategy that includes different members of staff, goes beyond a written Back to Office Report (BTOR) or memo, and creates alternative forums where experiences can be shared.

- Facilitating organizations and experienced immersion facilitators need to be supported by the donor organizations, both financially and with a long-term commitment to immersions. This may not be an expensive undertaking, but part of pre-existing alliances and partnerships (such as initially between Nijera Kori and DFID in Bangladesh). Equally, a careful assessment is required of how much the 'voice' of the FO comes through in the immersion to ensure that the exposure is not overly determined by the FO perspective.
- Newly arrived agency staff in-country would benefit by spending some time in the villages/poor urban areas. This could be easily included as part of the induction process, and would have the added benefit of establishing rapport with a more established member of the particular mission (who should be able to do an immersion periodically). It could also be tied to language learning.
- The trade-off between scaling up immersions and their quality is tricky. However, as and when the opportunity arises to go to scale with institutionalizing immersions, it may be too good to miss. This may be true for both champions within institutions and FOs. Maintaining quality could be sought through strategic dissemination of good practice, a sharing of experience and inter-organizational training.

Conclusion: Good practice for immersions

Immersions are a useful means of experiential learning that can lead to a more profound understanding of the reality of the lives of people living in poverty – and to a process of rethinking policy and practice in order to be more effective in supporting their efforts to achieve better lives. Immersions are likely to be most effective if integrated within a wider systemic process of personal and organizational learning – a process that values reflection and relationship-building as emphasized elsewhere in this book.

As we have seen, key good practices for immersions include preparation through reflection on the purpose of the immersion and the group and individual learning outcomes, as well as adequate and appropriate space and time for reflection afterwards, and for sharing and providing feedback to others. Ethics are basic and participants need to be fully briefed and sensitive to behaving well and in a culturally appropriate manner in their encounter and relationship with their hosts. Models in which hosts join in the reflection process are particularly to be welcomed, and innovation in terms of 'reverse' immersions could be explored. Practical preparations are also important. The choice of a facilitating organization is crucial, and issues of when, where and how matter very much if participants are to reap optimum benefit from the experience.

Immersions have shown their potential for experiential learning, for generating commitment and for grounding in realism. If widely valued, adopted and expected in development organizations, immersions could help to transform power, insights and relationships, and make pro-poor policy and practices more focused, relevant and effective. Those who have experienced them often have a sense of achievement, confidence and re-energized commitment. Yet, in 2006, immersions are still exceptional. When asked, development professionals rarely question their value and often say that they would welcome the experience. But then nothing happens. There are obstacles to confront: personal (anxiety, hesitation and reluctance), practical (being uncertain of who to approach in order to make arrangements) and institutional (the demands of routine, negotiations, meetings, reporting and workshops; dealing with visitors and the like; and lack of incentives and the absence of immersions in human resources practices and appraisals). Some obstacles can also be interpersonal, such as having managers with other priorities or who do not see the point. But none of these is insuperable. Perhaps it is best to take the bull by the horns and get on with it, to experience and learn from immersions, and then to promote them, encouraging and giving space to others to do likewise:

> *Lying on a mud floor, in the middle of the night, looking up to the skies through big holes of a palm roof and not being able to sleep really makes you think 'There has to be a better way for these people'.* (Ridwan Ali, VIP participant, World Bank, Colombo, 1999)

Notes

1   This chapter started life as a report by Renwick Irvine. In the autumn of 2003, he undertook an extensive literature review and conducted telephone and email enquiries into the design and practice of immersions. We are grateful for responses to Renwick from Alana Albee, Tamsin Ayliffe, Dyuti Baral, Stephanie Barrientos, Marilyn Carr, Martha Chen, Ian Curtis, Teresa Durand, Rosamund Ebdon, Judith Edstrom, Phil Evans, Alistair Fernie, Eric Hanley, Goran Holmqvist, Ramesh Khadka, Jennifer Leith, Harsh Mander, Richard Montgomery, Andy Norton, Fred Nunes, Praful Patel, Jillian Popkins, Albert Silvo, Caroline Skinner, Melanie Speight, Sheelagh Stewart, Imraan Valodia and Sharon White.

The authors discussed the report at a small workshop at the Institute of Development Studies (IDS) during 15–16 December 2003 with Richard Ackermann, Qazi Azmat Isa, Sandeep Chachra, Sam Joseph, Sammy Musyoki, Karl Osner and Mallika Samaranayake. Those at the workshop have been trailblazers in designing and organizing immersions, and we are most grateful to them for their support and encouragement in helping to bring immersions to a wider audience. Finally, the authors are grateful to Kath Pasteur for her helpful comments on an earlier version of this draft.

2   Respondent to Irvine's email survey.

3   The legal name is now Exposure and Dialogue Programmes. Since the papers cited were produced under the old name, we are retaining that for the purposes of this chapter.

4   Communication from Sandeep Chachra, 2003.

5   Reflect combines Freirean and PRA approaches for empowerment and literacy, and is now used by over 350 organizations in 60 countries.

References

In writing this chapter, we have drawn on unpublished reports and guidelines. Most of these are available for consultation in the Participation Resource Centre at the Institute of Development Studies (IDS).

APNSD (Association for the Promotion of North–South Dialogue) (2000) *Guidelines for Reflection and Dialogue in Exposure and Dialogue Programmes*, APNSD, www.exposure-nsd.de/Publications.htm

APNSD (2002a) *Development has Got a Face: The EDP of the Association for the Promotion of North–South Dialogue – A Brief Profile*, APNSD, www.exposure-nsd.de/engl.html

APNSD (2002b) *Guidelines for Facilitators of Exposure and Dialogue Programmes*, APNSD, www.exposure-nsd.de/engl.html

Bali, N. (2002) 'Introduction', in SEWA (ed) *Tana Vana*, SEWA, Ahmedabad

Brock, K. and McGee, R. (eds) (2002) *Knowing Poverty: Critical Reflections on Participatory Research and Policy*, Earthscan, London

Chachra, S. (2003) *Experience with Immersions*, ActionAid India, available from sandeep@actionaidasia.org or sandeep@actionaidchina.org

Chambers, R. (1983) *Rural Development: Putting the Last First*, Longman, Harlow, UK

Chen, M., Jhabvala, R., Kanbur, R., Mirani, N. and Osner, K. (eds) (2004) *Reality and Analysis: Personal and Technical Reflections on the Working Lives of Six Women*, Working Paper 2004-06, Department of Applied Economic and Management, Cornell University, Ithaca, New York, April, www.aem.cornell.edu/research/researchpdf/wp0406.pdf

Denning, S. (2000) *The Springboard: How Storytelling Ignites Action in Knowledge-Era Organizations*, Butterworth and Heinemann, Boston

Irvine, R., Chambers, R. and Eyben, R. (2004) 'Learning from poor people's experience: Immersions', *Lessons for Change in Policy and Organisations* no 13, Institute of Development Studies, Brighton

Joseph, S. (1995) 'Win–Win trainings', *Participation in Action*, vol 5, August, available from participation@ids.ac.uk

Jupp, D. (2004) *Views of the Poor: Some Thoughts on How to Involve Your Own Staff to Conduct Quick, Low Cost but Insightful Research into Poor People's Perspectives*, available from djupp@tiscali.co.uk

Kanbur, R. (1999) *EDP Report/Memo in World Bank for WDR 2000/01*, www.worldbank.org/poverty/newsl/oct99b.htm

McGee, R. (2002) 'The self in participatory poverty research', in Brock, K. and McGee, R. (eds) *Knowing Poverty: Critical Reflections on Participatory Research and Policy*, Earthscan, London, pp14–43

Narayanasamy, N. and Boraian, M. P. (eds) (1997) *Towards Rural Immersion: A World Bank Journey*, PRA Unit, Gandhigram Rural Institute, Deemed University, Tamil Nadu

Osner, K. (2004) 'Using exposure methodology for dialogue on key issues', in Chen, M., Jhabvala, R., Kanbur, R., Mirani, N. and Osner, K. (eds) *Reality and Analysis: Personal and Technical Reflections on the Working Lives of Six Women*, Working Paper 2004-06, Department of Applied Economic and Management, Cornell University, Ithaca, New York, April, www.aem.cornell.edu/research/researchpdf/wp0406.pdf, pp85–94

Participatory Rural Appraisal Unit (PRAU) (1998) *Village Immersion Programme 1998: Report and Reflections*, PRA Unit, Gandhigram Rural Institute, Deemed University, Tamil Nadu

Patel, P. (2003) *GRIP Program at SEWA in India, 9–14 November: Notes and Photographic Record of the Salt Workers Team*, Collaborative Programme of SEWA and the World Bank, Ahmedabad

SDC (Swiss Agency for Development and Cooperation) (2003) *Views of the Poor: The Perspective or Rural and Urban Poor in Tanzania as Recounted through Their Stories and Pictures*, SDC, Berne

Senge, P. M. (1990) *The Fifth Discipline: The Art and Practice of the Learning Organization*, Doubleday, New York

SEWA (Self-Employed Women's Association) (2002) *'Tana Vana': Warp and Weft of Life*, SEWA and APNSD, Ahmedabad, January

WIEGO (Women in Informal Employment Globalizing and Organizing) (2002) *WIEGO General Meeting 2002*, www.wiego.org/meeting/index/shtml

World Bank (circa 1998) *Grass Roots Immersion Programme (GRIP) Guidelines Memo*, World Bank, Washington, DC

World Bank (2000) *World Development Report 2000/2001: Attacking Poverty*, Oxford University Press, New York

World Bank (2003) *The VIP Report*, World Bank, South Asia

World Bank, Colombo (1998) *Summary Report of the Village Immersion Program, Sri Lanka*, World Bank, Colombo, Sri Lanka

World Bank, Colombo (1999) *Report of Village Immersion Programme, 25 February–8 March*, World Bank, Colombo, Sri Lanka

4

Making Connections: Learning about Participation in a Large Aid Bureaucracy

Seema Arora-Jonsson and Andrea Cornwall

Today's development talk is full of relationship words such as participation, ownership and partnership. Yet, most development organizations offer little opportunity for staff to reflect upon what these words mean for their everyday work. This chapter describes an experiment in using a participatory methodology in the headquarters of an aid bureaucracy, the Swedish International Development Agency (Sida), to engage a cross-departmental learning group of desk officers in reflecting and acting upon Sida's stated commitment to enhancing the participation of the poor in development processes and the everyday constraints to putting these fine-sounding ideals into practice. Our work sought to address two kinds of learning challenges for development organizations. One is developing the reflective and reflexive capabilities of those who work for them – that is, the capacity for self-critical awareness and being able to step back from a situation and look at it from different perspectives (Schön, 1983). The other is to find ways for the increasingly busy and beleaguered bureaucrat to gain opportunities of connecting with others in their organization who think differently and who work with different aspects of development, and to deal competently with the different realities, forms of knowledge and challenges that are part of development work and for which bureaucratic processes and procedures are often so inadequate.

Learning about participation

Amidst the debates circulating amongst participatory development practitioners during the mid to late 1990s, the dilemmas of 'institutionalizing' participation loomed large (see Blackburn and Holland, 1998). Large aid bureaucracies had long been the target of advocates of popular participation in development. By the late

1990s, debates on 'mainstreaming' participation had come to focus on the dangers of a preoccupation with techniques and technicalities, and the 'routinization' of participatory processes. Donors were widely regarded by practitioners as the source of the problem (Cornwall et al, 2001). The verdict was that donors were both subject to bureaucratic procedures which made it difficult for them to become flexible enough to actually work effectively with participation, and that those who worked for donor agencies did not really understand well enough what participation was all about.

Donor agencies were often regarded in these debates as monoliths. People talked of 'DFID said ... ' or 'Sida thinks ... '; practitioners moaned about the stupidity of donors and talked about the need to 'educate' them; activists got fired up about misdirected funding, mismanaged projects and mismatched solutions; and development academics would often be quietly dismissive about the intellectual capabilities of those who worked for donor agencies, seeing bureaucrats as second-rate thinkers who need to hire in consultants to tell them what they should do. Policy documents – necessarily – give none of the game away of the differences in position or perspective within such agencies, or the politics of the processes of arriving at agreed-upon statements: they present in cool, unequivocal terms a position that those outside donor agencies might come to assume is 'the position'. And yet, as anyone who has worked for one of these agencies can tell you, different positions co-exist – not always easily – within and among departments and divisions. What an idea like 'participation' comes to mean in such a setting is by no means as straightforward as the policies would have it, nor is it as cleanly put, nor as uncontested, as the apparent orthodoxy – tyranny, even, for some observers (Cooke and Kothari, 2001) – of participation in development would imply.

What would happen, then, if a process were to be created that engaged some of those who worked for donor agencies in thinking through what participation really meant in their work settings *and* sought to engage them in considering how existing procedures limited their responsiveness and what they might do about it? What if this process harnessed the wisdom of participants, who often know their situations and the solutions that might be required better than outsiders to whom the problem might be more apparent, but who rarely have solutions that take account of local complexities? What if, in engaging bureaucrats in such a learning process, it was possible to develop an approach that could be used to initiate change that might bridge stated policies and everyday practice through the small acts that those bureaucrats could carry out as part of their current jobs, as well as the influence that they may come to have on internal policies and procedures? An ambitious idea was slowly germinated by Andrea Cornwall and Patta Scott-Villiers at the Institute of Development Studies (IDS), together with Katja Jassey, who held the brief for participation in Sida and for whom the gap between Sida's excellent policies and what actually happened to them in the context of the organization's work had become both a frustration and a challenge. This chapter describes this experiment and what it taught us about participation and about learning in a large donor bureaucracy.

Laying the ground

The project came into being through a confluence of interests representing a range of objectives that were considered together over the course of the programme. Each of those involved – seven desk officers from across Sida's departments and divisions, two IDS resource people and two Swedish researchers – had different preoccupations and reasons for engagement. These differences oscillated within the group, creating excitement, boredom, frustration and anxiety. A sense of progress might be coupled at any time with an awareness that we were really going nowhere: what delighted one person would dismay another. This was an unusual process of which no one involved really had any experience.

Influenced by Peter Reason and John Heron's (Heron, 1996; Heron and Reason, 2001) work on cooperative enquiry, we sought to take their main methodological principles and adapt them to the exigencies of bureaucratic life in Sida. By engaging in loops of action and reflection over a succession of meetings, we attempted to develop our capacities for reflection and reflexivity, in the process generating different kinds of knowledge about how the organization worked and about everyday meanings and practices of participation. The group would bring their changing understandings of participation and of Sida to our six-weekly meetings and work with it as their 'data' in an ongoing process of collective analysis. This analysis would then feed into changes in everyday working lives, with potential knock-on effects on projects, meetings and policy processes. It would also radiate out from individuals' own practice to influence their colleagues.

To the ingredients of cooperative enquiry, we added a pinch of action learning.[1] Each member of the group was encouraged to have a particular project or activity in which they would intervene and regularly report back on. These 'action situations' would be foci for developing a richer and deeper understanding of the dilemmas of participation in practice: they would also be grist to the collective mill, illustrating the range of possible situations that donor bureaucrats might find themselves dealing with. This also seemed a useful way of building peer support for tackling the challenges that people were facing in their work, and of gaining broader insights from other people's experiences.

Our idea was that meetings would begin and end with collective reflection, and weave in sharing and analysis of desk officers' individual projects. Group members would be encouraged to write up these projects as case studies, which we would then produce as a collection of donor-authored pieces that illustrated the complexities and conundrums of participation in practice. Recognizing time constraints, we adapted the process to include research support from two Swedish researchers, Seema and Lotta. This chimed with the desire of Sida managers to strengthen Swedish capacity, rather than having to rely upon external expertise. The Swedish researchers would work with the group between meetings and help to facilitate the group's research activities.

The project began with a training course at IDS, geared both at recruiting our learning group and seeding interest in participation in a wider constituency in the organization. A lively and diverse group of people from all over Sida came together for three days to explore the intersection between participation and organizational learning, in the process opening up some of the issues that we were to continue to learn about during the coming months.

Early days

At the end of the course, seven staff from different departments and divisions in the Stockholm headquarters sat together in the dingy lounge of a downtown Brighton hotel for their first meeting. Amidst a host of water metaphors and talk of swimming, floating and drowning, differences in the group's expectations began to emerge, while differences in the motives that had brought people to the group were voiced. Some spoke of their anger about the inconsistencies and contradictions in the way that policies worked in Sida; some talked of a desire to learn about participation and to solve some of the riddles that their daily work presented them with (was participation an end or a means, and was all the energy spent in participating a good investment of resources or a waste of time?); others saw in this process a chance to find the time to think and reflect and share ideas, something that they felt they absolutely lacked in their everyday work; and some saw the learning group as presenting an opportunity for a new network, one that spanned 'the house' (as Sida's headquarters was known by those who worked there) and offered connections that they hadn't made before.

Patta Scott-Villiers and Andrea Cornwall facilitated a very organized and to-the-point second meeting in Stockholm, coupling a visual expectations exercise – in which the group were able to emphasize the need for us to be as efficient as possible with the time they had made available for this work, a key issue for dutiful civil servants – with some getting-to-know-you identification of key themes, dilemmas and questions with which the group wanted to engage. The group was provided with a briefing note on methodologies that it might want to use in finding out about participation in Sida. These methodologies ranged from the conventional (ethnography) to the experimental (photo voice). We thought of the note, at the time, as short, informative and informal; but it was pages long, written in the kind of language that only an academic can call accessible, and it remained unclear as to whether anyone actually read any of it. We didn't linger as long as we ought to have done on methodological questions, fearing that people would get bored or bogged down. Rather, we began talking about people's everyday work – what they *did* – as an entry point for collective reflection.

Round the group we went, with everyone introducing an 'action situation' that they wanted to work on. Then we opened up a general discussion about participation, drawing together key themes, questions and dilemmas. As people told us later, the image of IDS as a place that exudes competence inspired a kind of confidence in what we were doing that placed us almost beyond question. And there was, as in any process, a need for people to place themselves in our hands and to allow us to guide them. Kalle, one of the group members, would joke that he and his colleagues were our 'guinea pigs'. We would all laugh; and yet we knew perhaps more than anyone just how much we were experimenting with something that none of us had ever actually done before.

Since there were now several resource people, a division of labour was mooted. Seema would work with group members, interviewing them between meetings to capture their reflections. Lotta would support the documentation needs of the group, putting together materials that they might need at any particular time. They would take it in turns to write up the minutes of learning group meetings. Patta and Andrea would attend alternate meetings. Katja set up an internet-based project room to house documents and engage in conversations, using it also for the learning group's work. We resolved to complement formal meetings with an informal 'clinic' with the resource team in the afternoon, which any group member could attend and to which people could bring individual learning projects.

So far, so good. By the time the third meeting came, however, there was a distinct lack of energy in the group. Round the room we went, each person reporting on their own experiences during the last six weeks and ruminating about what that had taught them about participation. These were rich experiences. Yet, no one in the group seemed particularly energized by the discussion. And when it came to moving from analysing these experiences to thinking a bit more about what exactly the group would like to produce, there was an even more perceptible drop in energy. As in any group, some members have more of an impact on the group's mood than others: during this meeting, one of these people spent most of their time gazing out of the window at the busy Stockholm street below. The afternoon's discussions were unremarkable. Things were not going quite as well as we'd hoped. The idea of individual learning projects had come out of the interest people had in exploring aspects of their work. But it had also caused anxiety about what would be expected in terms of products. And while some of the group had done their 'homework' – having preliminary discussions with colleagues or finding out a bit more about what participation meant to those involved in projects outside the office – it wasn't altogether clear where this would take us.

Formal meetings were complemented by other, more informal, spaces. Visits to the pub on the evening of the meeting became one such space and gained a certain subversive character. While formal meetings were attended by all, it was usually only just over half of the group who came to the pub, creating a different dynamic. We had labelled our process the Participation Action Learning Group, which didn't exactly roll off the tongue or produce a nice-sounding acronym either. In the pub after one of the early meetings, we played with alternatives. One of member the group came up with the Swedish term *lagom*, which means 'just enough, not too much and not too little', but also connotes a distinctively Swedish spirit, one which speaks to ideals of flattened hierarchies and of moderation in all things. Amidst our amusement, we'd found ourselves a name. As we came to reflect later, it spoke volumes that the name was never debated or even formally adopted; it simply got taken up in the pub and became who we were.

It was in the pub, on a wickedly cold Stockholm night following the second meeting, that the idea was hatched to 'hijack' an ailing project, one that had been around for some years and that no one really cared much about, and breathe new life into it via an injection of participation. This would be something concrete, something real; it would also be something that the group could work on together. Once back in the formal space of Sida, ambitions for what might be done were trimmed back. But an idea was proposed that terms of reference for a study that was being commissioned might be used as an opportunity to learn more about how to put ideas about participation into practice. There was enthusiastic agreement.

At that point, the process took a decisive shift. The model we'd been working with in the first two meetings consisted of group members sharing what they'd experienced that had taught them something about participation since the previous meeting. A discussion then followed that analysed these reflections, guided heavily by Andrea and Patta. It focused on using individual experience to generate collective understanding. The opportunity to do something *together* created a very different learning dynamic. The group began to convene its own meetings and to have its own internal email communications in Swedish. Our next meeting was very different. Through a series of activities, structured by the resource team, the group picked apart the terms of reference and thought about what it was trying to achieve, and what this told each member about participation. The feeling at the end of the meeting was triumphant: this was the kind of practical activity that group members had wanted. The meeting was considered the best to date. But was this cooperative enquiry? What *was* cooperative enquiry, anyway? From what we'd read, it involved regular meetings, relatively systematic discussions, and individuals going off and doing their own enquiries and coming back together to systematize findings, generating different kinds of knowledge. Were we doing that? We'd more or less abandoned the action learning part of our process, when we ditched the focus on the individual and their 'action situation'; but was this a precipitous decision that we would come to regret? What exactly *were* we doing?

Going public

It was exactly at the point, when some of the resource team were becoming a little anxious about how the group was going to deliver what it had promised, whether in terms of learning or in terms of outputs, that other waves of anxiety began to ripple through the group. The cause of this anxiety was, however, rather different. At the second meeting in Stockholm, the group had decided that it wanted to do something to present itself to Sida: some kind of public occasion at which its purpose became evident to colleagues and managers, that legitimated what it was doing, that enlightened those around them *and* that encouraged colleagues and managers to ask questions about participation. This seemed an excellent idea. Like the training course, it would be a way of preparing the ground amongst a wider constituency for the lessons about participation that we were to produce and the changes that might be made as a result. As we sat in a most salubrious room in Sida, with our list of ten projects that we would do as a group and our idea of this public event that would inform and excite people about our work, we felt very pleased with ourselves.

Fast forward to the week before the planned public occasion, some five months later, and the group was feeling none too sure that this was, after all, such a good idea. It had, during the meantime, met several times to consider what it was going to do, and with the exception of one member of the group, Katja, whose enthusiasm for what would come to be called 'the event' knew no bounds, several were feeling increasingly uncertain. Spurning the familiar model of a verbal presentation followed by a question-and-answer session, the group – led by Katja – had opted for something closer to an art exhibition. No one quite knew how the idea had come about. Somehow fragments of different ideas had all merged. As 'the event' drew nearer, doubts built up until they reached a crescendo a couple of weeks before it was scheduled to take place. At a meeting held to review progress, things came to a head. The idea of showing Sida something of what the group was about, and inviting it to take a glimpse of our work and join in the 'quest for questions', had seemed an attractive one. But what had the group *done*? What did it have to show for the *time* it had spent (and, by implication, the use of taxpayers' money that it had incurred in the process)? And what would others in Sida make of this very unconventional way of communicating – would they regard the group as ridiculous? Doubts dissipated as debate picked up on the importance of opening a space for Sida staff members to think differently about what they were doing, and to begin asking themselves the kind of questions that the group was asking. But the anxieties about not being taken seriously didn't go away.

The event itself was magnificent. Conventional advertisements were cast aside and, instead, mysterious posters with photographs of Sida workers from the 1970s were put up in various parts of 'the house' with the heading 'In the mind of this Sidaite?' and a quote from one of Sida's policies. Unusually for Sida, the posters promised wine – paid for by the IDS team, rather than the Swedish taxpayer – and an unusual time of day for the event, an hour when the building is usually empty. It was also to be held in an unusual place: the basement sports hall rather than a seminar room. At lunchtime on the appointed day, a video screen was set up in the canteen in front of the lunch queue. A random selection of people in 'the house' had been asked what the word 'participation' meant to them; answers ranged from 'grassroots', 'something good' to 'impossible mission'. Those queuing for lunch were able to snack on sound bites as an aperitif to the evening's festivities.

The evening came. The sounds of Abba could be heard in the corridor leading up to the candle lit basement room, where the curious guests were first greeted by a huge timeline, which occupied an entire wall of the room. Filled with quotes representing policies, trends in development, landmark events and 'signs of the times' in the organization over the decades, the timeline had a graph superimposed on it of trends in development spending and numbers of employees posted in a sample foreign country (Tanzania, much beloved by many of Sida's older staff). People were encouraged to take brightly coloured Post-its and add their own memories and experiences. A fridge was covered with poetry made up of bureaucratic jargon, to which guests were encouraged to add their own 'Sida poetry'. There were glass bowls with marbles in different denominations and people were asked to guess how many policies Sida had. Colour photos of members of staff were plastered around the column, with guesses ranging from almost 200 to under 10 (the director-general himself did not win the competition). A washing line was strung with pictures of a senior bureaucrat who had been photographed at the same time every day over the course of a month. These pictures of him sitting by his computer, of his empty desk and of him on mission in an identical-looking room to those in 'the house', somewhere in Africa, were contrasted with posters advertising the evening tabloids, with blazing headlines of raids, deaths, hurricanes and war. Flipcharts invited people to add their own definitions of participation to those defined by Sida and international policy.

The timeline was perhaps the greatest attraction. For old-timers, it was a rare opportunity to discuss Sida's history and to look at what they were doing in perspective. It offered an opportunity to analyse changing policies by placing them alongside major international trends, as well as changes in Sweden's own policies and culture, and cultural changes in the organization itself. Many were amazed at the things that people wrote on the timeline: things that they themselves had not known or thought about. Bursts of discussions around various turns in Sida's history, policy and work took shape as Post-its continued to make their way to the wall. The spirit of the decade of 1965–1975 was reflected in comments such as 'liberation', 'sandals' and 'aid will do the trick'. The 1980s turned to 'Sida cheers for Mugabe' and 'from project to sector', while the 1990s were described by 'development pessimism' and 'neo-liberalism'. This was followed by 'more stress', 'masculinity' and 'beautiful words' – and the implied gap with which we began between those beautiful words and the realities of implementation.

Those who responded to the invitation to interact appeared to have found it beneficial. One of Sida's senior managers spoke fulsomely of the group's work at an event at the Ministry of Foreign Affairs some days later to host Deepa Narayan, one of the authors of the *Voices of the Poor* study (2000), describing what Sida's own enquiries into participation were showing. But others within Sida were bemused by it all, wondering what on earth it was all for. The group discussed follow-up, which resulted in an oblique one-liner on the intranet inviting people to click on the link to a series of questions about participation and impact. But energy quickly dissipated at the realization that many colleagues simply hadn't *got it*. It was hard to pin down what *it* was. It was a sort of understanding, but it seemed intangible. How do you describe arriving at a more in-depth understanding of your own workplace, rather than the more conventional task we'd embarked on of understanding 'participation' (which is always implicitly something that happens 'out there')? And how were we going to communicate all this to those in Sida who had been fired up by 'the event' and were now expecting something more?

A sense of collective unease grew in the group about the degree to which 'emergent design' had taken over from proper planning. As a result, the 'logframe' was born. Andrea and Patta were back in the driving seat again, and facilitated an exercise that resulted in neat columns and lists of objectives, outputs and activities that we jokingly came to call the 'logframe'. We didn't go quite as far as Objectively Verifiable Indicators (OVIs), but came close with a column on how we would know whether we'd made a difference. We had a plan. We had order. We now knew what we were doing. The logframe was more ephemeral than most ideas; it was forgotten soon after our meeting and never referred to again. But it had helped to structure our worries about showing what *Lagom* had done and planned to do by putting a plan onto paper. Once it was done, and the anxieties about spending time on something that was not generating concrete outputs and not conforming to the usual project style were assuaged, we could carry on as usual. The question after the event was: what now? The logframe answered it; a host of new activities and directions were charted out for *Lagom*. Group members who had missed the meeting remarked in interviews that it was with relief that they opened their emails with the logframe as an attachment. Many knew that the ambitious activities listed there might never be translated into practice. But it felt good all the same.

Reports and reporting

One of the major activities in the agenda was to produce a document that would inform others within Sida about what we had learned from this process about participation. It was to be a short piece, written in an accessible style so that busy bureaucrats would read it, and it was to be practical, something desk officers would actually use. It seemed easy enough in theory. However, putting the idea into practice brought up all the group's contradictory ideas about how to approach the rest of Sida, and made us realize how different our visions were of how to achieve organizational change.

The initial plan was to produce two documents: one paper on lessons learned about participation and the other on the methodology that we had used in the group. One of the group members began with a mini version of the methodology in her own department that was much appreciated by her colleagues. She argued that it was more effective for the group to create these kinds of spaces for *doing*, by small acts, than to have some kind of overarching document that no one would read. But others felt that they needed to address the whole of Sida, to make it take notice and start thinking and talking about participation. The greatest difference, however, turned out to be over the form that 'the product' (as it came to be called) was to take, rather than what it would say.

Katja arranged a retreat for the group in a conference centre outside Stockholm. We were to spend two days together, reflecting on what we had learned and then working in small groups to construct text for the product. After a rich and lively discussion, the groups were dispatched to write. Self-selection meant that some of the differences within the group came to be concentrated in writing groups whose style and focus varied substantially. Some individuals approached the task by writing a text that was as conventional as possible. Others felt that what was needed was an event-style document, something completely unusual – even shocking – that would get people talking and reacting and thinking. The retreat ended without us having a single document in our hands. Prudence Woodford-Berger, a seasoned Sida consultant who had by then joined us, was asked by the group to go off and make something out of a morass of incoherent pieces. She did what every good consultant does so well. She put together an excellent document: clear, to the point and full of useful information.

For some members of the group, this was exactly what was needed. For others, however, it was precisely this kind of document that was part of the malaise they suffered as desk officers. They were concerned that it would be binned along with the other papers landing up on people's desks every day. Ambivalence about the written word had been a long-standing feature of *Lagom*. Everyone knew that few of their colleagues had the time to read reports or books, except the executive summary. An alternative was mooted. Enlisting members in writing up the bits of their everyday experience that spoke to bureaucrats as *people*, Katja led a process of putting a second document together. It sought to reach out to people in Sida in ways that an official, objective, to-the-point document would not. It would speak to their frustrations of bureaucratic hurdles and fulfilling targets while seeking to work for goals that are often far removed from quantifiable results. It would also take a critical look at the work they were doing, and at the contradictions of wanting to change the world and remove poverty while living as rich expatriates in poor countries.

Called *The Voices of the Bureaucrats* (unpublished report), this second version of 'the product' was daring, cheeky and unique. It began with the image of a desk officer trudging to work in the snow to sit looking at a computer screen all day, thinking of how nice it would be to have a foreign posting in a sunny place. It featured the diary of a desk officer, replete with emails from the public, bargaining with colleagues to get decisions over spending through the system, and endless meetings. And it gave a pungent flavour of the everyday realities of the lives of those who work in Sida – too pungent, some of the group members felt, for it to be viable as a product. As with 'the event', anxieties began to rise about how such a document would be received. For example, if it were destined, in part, to justify the time the group had spent on the process and to advocate for processes such as these, would it have a disastrous effect? It was a document that got under the skin. It brought up discomforting reflections that some felt were best left alone.

The two documents represented polar opposites; they also spoke to the different visions that members of the group had about what could make change happen in their organization and how they could reach out to other Sidaites. The first, the 'official version', would justify creating spaces where the real work of change could begin – involving discussion, dialogue, questioning and reflection. The second, *The Voices of the Bureaucrats*, captured a more anarchic spirit by speaking to people as people; it would help to create another kind of space in which there could be some more honesty about what a development bureaucrat does. By recognizing bureaucrats as people, it would encourage them to use their discretion to make a difference. These were the main lines drawn in what was to become a protracted negotiation, with some refusing to sign off on one document, and others on the other. The result was that neither document ever saw the light of day.

It wasn't as if what was written in *The Voices of the Bureaucrats* had not been said or talked about animatedly by everyone in the group. It was just that it encoded these discussions in written form. In this context, it is important to note that official correspondence in Sweden is open to the public. As a result, informal discussions and ideas that are still provisional tend to be aired not on paper or emails, but in informal discussions, on the telephone and in smaller groups, away from the spectre of the ever-present public eye. Committing themselves to paper in something as bold and unusual as *The Voices of the Bureaucrats* was something the group feared not only because of the exposure it might entail of unconventional methods and unorthodox view – it was because it brought the informal into the formal domain, making the hidden and covert visible and official, fixing what would always remain provisional, and sealing unfinished dialogue with the stamp of consensus.

The red and the blue

It was at this point, when the group was still in limbo over which – if any – document might be officially adopted as *Lagom*'s product, that Seema had a flash of insight. At a workshop at IDS on organizational change, participants were asked to draw images of the organizations with which they were affiliated. Seema drew a picture of two networks, one red and one blue. The formal working forms in Sida were the red networks. People operating in the red networks did what was expected of them as bureaucrats in a manner demanded by the formal system. Documents produced during the course of such work were red documents. They represented official decisions and were circulated through official channels.

The group itself had begun as a red network. It attempted to understand how to incorporate participation, and what doing so really meant in the diverse contexts within which they acted. But the methodology opened up the space for the group to define the agenda. And this was a very diverse group that came from different Sida departments, each with varying agendas. The mix of the quiet, the steady, the hardworking, the creative and the adventurous in the group let loose a side of people that jarred with a red agenda. It created a space where some people felt frustrated that nothing concrete was being produced, and that there was no visible structure or plan so common in development work. For others, it was a place to be creative and to discuss issues that had been bothering them in their work. Above all, it was a space that offered an opportunity to discuss their organization and how they worked within it. At times, it was a mix between the red and the blue. Sometimes blue dominated – but when it did, there was always remorse about still wanting to make what we were doing red and acceptable in order to justify the luxury of taking time off from writing important documents and making decisions about money to be spent.

Heron and Reason's (2001) characterization of Apollonian and Dionysian styles of cooperative enquiry groups chimes with the tendencies we picked up in our group. The archetypical Apollonian process, they argue, is more structured, regular, predictable and ordered; Dionysian tendencies are more spontaneous, chaotic, creative and haphazard. So, too, with the competing tendencies and styles of doing things that had emerged as currents and occasionally simmered as tensions within the group, erupting in the build-up to the retreat and giving rise at different points to concessions, but never to a sufficiently consensual way of co-existing. The logframe was such a concession to red tendencies and expectations; but 'the event' was also one, to the 'blueness' within the group. Neither was fully accepted by all group members as necessary or even desirable; but they happened all the same.

The dilemma of how *Lagom* would present itself to Sida, which became so apparent in the discomfort with 'the event', resurfaced during the production of the document. The first document was bright red. The second document was bright blue, and the reason for this was precisely so that people wouldn't just disregard it as another red memo. It was about participation; but it was also about *them* as participants. It would be read and talked about; it might even create a bit of a stir. But it had the potential to make *Lagom* cause for ridicule. The red document reduced the burden of not having answers that were acceptable to the rest of Sida: it spoke authoritatively and spelled out in clear detail what desk officers may feel they need to know about participation. But it was rejected. Sida's routines had once again sneaked into the group. The red could not be accepted because the blue networks which ensured that it would work did not really support it.

Bringing in participation

The group often used the metaphor of swimming around, of trying to find out more about what it was doing. This was a luxury that Sida officers normally could not afford. The open-endedness of the group's process, however, created rich opportunities for learning, not necessarily the one definitive answer to what participation in Sida was about, but about the many ways in which it could manifest itself and the different ways in which desk officers could choose to work with it. As one of the group members put it, the group helped to make explicit what Sida was doing. The desk officers in the group used whatever opportunities they came across in their everyday work to bring in their new knowledge and ideas about participation, whether it involved asking questions where they would have once taken something for granted or detailed different terms of reference, or insisting that certain procedures be changed or certain processes applied. These are small acts that make a difference in an almost imperceptible way: a word here, a phrase there; saying yes when it was customary to say no; being able to overlook certain procedures and facilitate certain ways of doing things; the art of the bureaucrat put to the service of participation.

The group struggled throughout with the imperative to come up with results. As Pasteur notes in Chapter 1, there was a pressure to have the right answers and to be infallible. The learning within the group, on the other hand, had fostered deeper analysis of Sida's ethics and values and left it asking questions – about itself and the ways in which it worked – while it was expected to provide answers for others outside. So, while the process prompted reflexivity, new insights sat uncomfortably with familiar routines. Although each desk officer had considerable power to change things, they also had their limitations and realized that many insights challenged everyday routines and practices to which they had to conform in order to get things done. To be able to exercise that power, they were also expected to act in certain ways.

It is easy to overlook the importance of the incremental and personal changes that a process such as this was able to foster – after all, one could say, what is the point of working with such a small number of people and not coming up with anything concrete as a result? The results, however, are encoded in forms that would be difficult to name as 'impacts', but have significant institutional importance. *Lagom* members sat on committees that wrote major policies and revised procedures, to which they were able to apply what they had learned – things that could not be named because to do so would remove influence in small acts that may be hidden from view but that create ripples of change.

Fostering learning: What is a donor organization to do?

What, then, can be done to foster forms of learning such as those described in this chapter – forms that may be chaotic in their creativity and lack clear objectives or goals precisely because they seek to catalyse adaptive learning and create time to think? What should be done by senior managers to lend weight and give priority to the kind of adaptive learning that development workers need in order to respond to the changing realities of development? What incentives or procedures would support making time for learning? For busy bureaucrats, spending time on activities that might not be regarded as 'serious' or 'productive', rather than on meetings, memoranda or answering emails, may be difficult to square with their own perception of what learning is about – let alone the perceptions of their managers. Making learning fun calls for activities that mesh with everyday bureaucratic work, but also offer new perspectives on it – and gain legitimacy precisely because they build the competencies that today's bureaucrats are ever more in need of: competencies in making and managing relationships.

Creating space for reflection – space where people can test out and acquire new ideas, and gain new perspectives on routine activities – may be counter-cultural in many development organizations. But such reflective spaces can provide a way of fostering the kind of responsiveness that is ever more important in the world of contemporary aid. Our experience suggests that 'informalizing' interactions, building on shared values and interests, creating new networks for people to feel part of and learn from, and making space within them for experimentation might provide enough excitement as new and different 'communities of practice' (Wenger et al, 2002). These are the practices that might make a difference because by building relationships at the same time as building understanding, they help to create new networks, new understandings and new capabilities.

Notes

1 Liz Goold brought action learning methodology to our attention, and also gave us valuable advice at the outset about establishing and running groups like these.

References

Blackburn, J. and Holland, J. (1998) *Who Changes? Institutionalizing Participation*, IT Publications, London.

Cooke, B. and Kothari, U. (2001) *Participation: The New Tyranny*, Zed Books, London

Cornwall, A., Musyoki, S. and Pratt, G. (2001) 'In search of a new impetus: Practitioners', Reflections on PRA and Participation in Kenya, IDS Working Paper 131, IDS

Heron, J. (1996) *Co-Operative Enquiry: Research into the Human Condition*, Sage, London

Heron, J. and Reason, P. (2001) 'The practice of co-operative inquiry: Research with rather than on people', in Reason, P. and Bradbury, H. (eds) *Handbook of Action Research: Participative Inquiry and Practice*, Sage, London, pp179–188

Narayan, D., Chambers, R., Kaul Shah, M. and Petesch, P. (2000) *Voices of the Poor: Crying Out for Change*, World Bank/Oxford University Press, Washington/New York

Schön, D. (1983) *The Reflective Practitioner*, Basic Books, New York

Wenger, E., McDermott, R. and Snyder, W. M. (2002) *Cultivating Communities of Practice*, Harvard Business School, Boston

5

Learning about Relationships in Development

Katherine Pasteur and Patta Scott-Villiers

Relationships and interactions may be the stock in trade of aid; yet, development agencies have given relatively little attention to thinking about what limits or promotes learning within relationships, and to ensuring procedures and an organizational culture that foster capacities to select and engage with appropriate or necessary interlocutors and to end relationships well. International development cooperation is, at its foundation, based on human, organizational and political relationships. Why are we not learning about them? Whether a development agency is delivering projects, negotiating sector-wide approaches, influencing policy and opinion, or supporting national budgets, its resources are delivered through working with organizations and individuals in aid-recipient and aid-donor countries, in multilateral arenas and through a maze of interactions within the organization itself. A quick scan of daily activities in any of the big bilateral agencies would reveal thousands of meetings, in which the human relationships are the environment that creates new ideas, knowledge, agreements and action. It is within relationships that aid actors not only exert influence, but also learn much of what they know about development – about its context, processes, impact and possibilities. In the flow of relations between people within and beyond the boundaries of the organization, the development agency stores its greatest asset – its dynamic knowledge and its capacity to act well.

This chapter offers a perspective on how development agency staff and departments can engage in 'relational learning'. How can they make improvements to their understanding and performance by attending to learning within their inter-personal and inter-organizational relationships? We draw on case studies from work with the Department for International Development (DFID) in the UK, Brazil and Uganda, including our own experiences as a group of facilitators from inside and outside the organization. There are ideas in this chapter about how individuals can be reflexive and how they might facilitate team-based learning and sharing.

There are suggestions for management about the need for changes in organizational culture, incentives, skills and structures that can lead to the creation of better relationships and result in better aid. The chapter deals with how to investigate and improve people-to-people relationships and suggests that organization-to-organization relationships will also benefit. There is much, however, that is not covered here. For example, we do not discuss means of sustaining organizational relationships, such as all the possible organizational architectures and procedures. These important aspects of relational development need to be given serious consideration, and this chapter suggests that it is within a set of much improved person-to-person relationships that these means will be explored, implemented and adapted to circumstance.

The relevance of relational learning

The Organizational Learning Partnership was a small group that worked inside DFID between 2001 and 2003, looking for ways of promoting relational learning. Our team consisted of four people (one staff member of DFID, two researchers from the Institute of Development Studies, or IDS, and an external consultant) who set up, supported and appraised a number of reflection processes with DFID staff. Our first engagement was in Uganda.

In 2001 the DFID Uganda office contracted a group of consultants to carry out a study of a large public-sector reform process in the Uganda forest administration (Kazoora et al, 2002). DFID had been funding an expatriate company to work with the Ugandan government to provide a package of technical and facilitation inputs for the reform. It was hoped that the package would be comprehensive and appealing enough to overcome any local resistances from those who lost out in the substantial changes that were being pushed through. But a proposed new forest law, drawn up by the technical consultants with members of government, which included the formation of a new forest authority, was meeting mysterious blockages in parliament and in parts of the Ugandan bureaucratic system. The work of Kazoora and his colleagues explained the blockage, revealing a web of expectations and demands, good and poor lines of communication, strong power dynamics, competition for resources and contradictory accountabilities.

While DFID was accounting to British taxpayers, the Ugandan government was accounting to its own citizens, and the expatriate company was dually accountable to both the Ugandan and UK governments. As a result, communications between the parties were often at cross-purposes. There were strong internal political struggles within all the parties, particularly within the government of Uganda, where individuals and entire departments stood to lose and others stood to gain power, influence and control of resources. Some of Kazoora's interviewees wrote the tensions off as corruption and incompetence; others took a more nuanced view. The study described the intersection of a 'push culture' and a 'yes culture' – the donor drive to get things done (the push) and the Ugandan tendency to say 'yes' and then quietly, but effectively, resist.

In the process of one-on-one discussions with individuals and representatives of numerous affected offices, the expatriate company came in for criticism for 'exceeding its powers'. The role of the UK and Ugandan governments was also questioned: 'To have entrusted the restructuring of a government department to people not part of the government was to forget the political dimension of the reform', said one observer. 'We cannot question why DFID gave too many powers to [the expatriates] because when we asked about the content of negotiations between DFID and the government of Uganda, we were told by our fellow Ugandans that it was confidential', said another. The ambitions, policies and politics of individuals and departments, consultants and advisers emerged in a mosaic of counteracting interests. The message was clear: failure to deal explicitly with communication and power issues was threatening the progress of the reform. As we detail later, the study had a stimulating effect and, vindicating the instincts of those who commissioned it, helped to get the reform process back on track.

This example illustrates the convoluted nature and powerful influence of relationships in the development process and is not by any means unique to this one instance from Uganda. Relationships in aid delivery are nothing new; but expectations of them are changing and becoming more demanding. There should be *harmonization* with other donors and *partnerships* with government; investments should permit *participation* of a wide range of voices, build *ownership* of goals by various parties and be *transparent* and *accountable*. These words describe key elements of what is currently assumed to be good development practice; but these words are ambiguous and hard to translate into reality. In fact, recent enquiries by Robert Chambers reveal that these words have been perceived by DFID staff as highly hypocritical (Chambers et al, 2001). The Ugandans thought so, too. The words are open to interpretation and are politically laden. Lacking clarity, the concepts mostly fail to deliver on their multiple promises. The hubris of development officials' half-hearted attachment to these impossible concepts serves to undermine the efforts of development.

Our team made initial consultations with DFID staff in London and Uganda in the autumn of 2001 and with DFID Brazil in 2002. These consultations revealed concerns about new aid instruments, such as budget support, sector-wide approaches and poverty reduction strategy papers. People pointed out the difficulties and opportunities of operating at high levels of national policy, where political issues are heightened. They talked about how difficult it was to be sure that the interventions were pro-poor, noting their increasing isolation from poor people. For most people we talked to, important relations were with officials of governments, United Nations agencies and NGOs who, in turn, made relations with citizens and communities; yet, there was little appreciation of the difficulties that such a chain of dependent and political relationships might pose to development outcomes.

It emerged that many of the issues arising in the application of DFID's aid instruments were to do with the multiple and serial inter-personal and inter-organizational relationships needed to deliver them. Since the degree of donor technical control over the way in which funds were spent had decreased, so the importance of the *conversation* between donor and recipient had increased. However, the quality of donor–recipient or donor–donor relationships did not automatically improve with the increase in their importance. Learning about effective relationship-building was not emphasized in official procedures; therefore, the understanding that was being generated by DFID staff and their interlocutors across the world was not being recognized, formalized or shared. The extensive knowledge management systems of the organization (which include document databases, a sophisticated intranet, and numerous seminars, workshops, networks and research and documentation exercises) were not generating learning and debate on the subject of how to build and manage working relationships. It was as if the relationships business needed no attention because it was something innate. Anyway, said one, the prickly question of aid relationships is something people would prefer not to focus on.

Interactions are difficult to manage in the aid environment primarily due to the particularities of politics, culture clash, resource imbalance, gift-obligation dynamics and polar accountabilities that are peculiar to the sector. These forces imbue relationships with power and uncertainty. The reality of day-to-day development practice involves staff of bilateral agencies in a unique combination of moral, political, bureaucratic, economic and personal questions. As individuals, teams and departmental representatives deal with ambiguous concepts, so clarity is often an early casualty. They represent an influential moral and cultural perspective with funding attached. They also represent the current economic and political agenda of their governments – for example, promoting growth, stability and security. They operate within geographically extended, bureaucratic organizations and deal with other organizations with similarly complex profiles; yet their approaches have to be context and sector specific. They are continuously analysing and making choices about best approaches, and spending considerable time marketing those choices within the organization and beyond. They move from one country to another and from one sector or development 'idea' to another with regularity. Interpretations of all these expediencies are mostly up to the individual. Beliefs about each one of these, either explicit or hidden, play a strong role in the relations that development officials engage in every day.

In examining some of the internal cultural and bureaucratic reasons for difficulties in relationships, several staff members noted that the DFID suffers from, as one put it, 'innovation-itis', which means continuously moving the goalposts for partners, interlocutors and detractors, or moving to new partners altogether, sometimes losing both learning and goodwill in the process. How then, they asked, to develop the best capacities inside the organization for consolidating good practice and good relationships without hindering innovation and change?

The answer may lie in changing the view of what learning means within an organization: moving beyond the idea of knowledge as a fixed asset to be applied to problems, to seeing useful and dynamic knowledge as inseparable from the relationships in which it is formed and used. Relational learning would thus become a priority. Relationships and their concomitant knowledge are not 'owned' by or held within the organization, but exist between people and between one organization and another. Innovation and good ideas would thus be associated not with the imposition of imperious concepts, fashionable ideas and financial power by one organization over another, but generated as part of a set of effective and realistic relationships. If 'know-how' is seen in this way, then primary competencies in development would be a capability to understand the politics and impacts of influence, along with abilities to manage the human side of change.

Lessons from reality

In our two years of intermittent engagement with the DFID, we were involved in a number of cases of learning in action. Examples here from Brazil and Uganda, as well as the experience of our own partnership, point to ways in which approaches to relationship-learning can be developed. Here we introduce the three examples in brief.

In Uganda we briefly observed and worked alongside Kazoora's team of consultants carrying out the study in the forest sector. Ideas for new forms of learning to fit with new aid instruments were being encouraged within DFID at that time, and offices were seeking to experiment and develop good practice to share with the rest of the organization. The instigators of the Uganda study – the DFID adviser and the leader of the expatriate management team – were conservative in their choice of method, but brave in their choice of questions to ask. The consultants interviewed a range of stakeholders to ascertain their differing views on decisions that had been taken and relations that had developed in the reform. It was proposed that the lessons would be shared in a report and a workshop.

If the terms of reference are anything to go by, the DFID team had expected that the learning outcomes would be a set of apolitical and generalized lessons on public-sector reform, and a set of recommendations for easy-to-implement learning mechanisms for the future (DFID, 2001). But the picture of difficult relationships that emerged turned out to be highly sensitive and context specific. Recommendations for bringing the reform back on line depended upon improving relationships and addressing power structures. The study did result in significant changes as people and organizations gained a new view of their own position and that of others, and it stimulated moves to create new structures for communication and decision-making. It demonstrated an approach to learning in the unstable domain of interaction, showing it to be by no means easy or apolitical.

Our small team, the organizational learning partnership, had been invited to provide support to the forest-sector learning study; but we also wanted to broaden our engagement more widely within the DFID Uganda office. Building relationships in which the national government has primary ownership was the key issue emerging from the forest-sector work, and this also appeared central to the approach of the rest of the office as it increased the levels of policy influencing and direct budget support to the Ugandan government. The partnership put together a proposal describing an action research process, arguing how it could help staff to reflect and act. However, demand from those who had initially expressed an interest never consolidated. The office was busy, our team was unknown and our suggestions lacked persuasion.

The partnership also investigated other links with DFID offices and facilitated a number of short learning events. We explored a range of options, including collaborations in Bangladesh and elsewhere, and learned a lot about DFID; but things were progressing slowly and the small flames that we were lighting were not yet building up into any substantial fires. Relationships with potential partners were not developing as we had hoped. We all felt frustrated, and this impacted upon internal team relationships. We started to get angry with one another. Eventually, around nine months into the project, our morale dipped. We paused, took a step back, and realized that we needed to do what we had been suggesting everyone else should do: reflect on our relationships and adjust.

We tested out some learning tools and methods, including organizing a peer assist (see Box 5.1), presenting our work to a group involved in facilitating learning in another development organization, and finally sharing our experiences with a process improvement facilitator with wide experience from private, NGO and government sectors. These processes helped us to question the assumptions upon which we had based our work, as well as to analyse the motivations of others to enter into a relationship with us. We realized that we had failed to do the groundwork in terms of stakeholder analysis. We had imagined that people would find the idea of learning about relationships attractive and that our own approach could thus be quite simple.

It is axiomatic that one learns most from one's own experience. Of all the cases of reflection, our own gave us the greatest insight because it was not just an observation or a theory, it was visceral. We were failing and we knew it. We began to blame each other, the DFID and the world for being obtuse. Then we stopped, reflected on our approach and relationships and changed direction. When we say with conviction that internal and external relationships become more productive if reflected upon and that more productive relationships deliver the outputs you want, it is because we felt it in practice. We took the new lessons on board and invested more time and effort in developing our next relationship, which was

BOX 5.1 PEER ASSIST

Peer assist is a process adopted by staff in British Petroleum (BP) as an early stage in any work activity (Collison and Parcell, 2001). Before embarking on a new undertaking, knowledgeable colleagues from outside the project team are brought together to share their lessons from experience and to offer relevant insights and ideas in relation to the new proposal. This ensures that existing knowledge within (and, where appropriate, beyond) the organization is drawn upon, and that a wide range of perspectives can inform the work. Someone may know where similar work has been carried out already. It also helps to establish a support network that may last into the future.

with DFID Brazil, and in gauging where our project could best add value to its work.

In 2003, DFID Brazil put considerable emphasis on partnerships as a means of influencing pro-poor change in Brazil and the Latin American region as a whole – it considered partnerships to be central to its way of working. As such, it, like other DFID offices working in middle-income countries, had much to offer the rest of DFID in terms of innovations in partnership management.

Early in the year, Ana Christina Guimarães and Emily Larbi-Jones carried out three case studies to understand the elements of partner relations and to test a methodology for monitoring them (Guimarães and Larbi-Jones, 2005). They proposed to reflect with three sets of partners on their relationship with DFID and its impact on their work. Successful aspects of the reflection approach could later be broadened and institutionalized into DFID Brazil monitoring and evaluation procedures. One case related to a trilateral partnership, in which DFID facilitated exchange between the governments of Brazil and Russia of experiences with HIV/AIDS prevention and treatment. A second looked at how DFID developed a relationship with municipal government, which led to an increase in pro-poor influence at state level. A third reported on how DFID facilitated relations between civil society, state government and an international financial institution.

Larbi-Jones and her team worked with each partner to construct a history of their relationship with DFID. They identified the highs and lows of their engagements and shared the pressures they faced and the challenges that these posed, and went on to make substantial recommendations. Some of the things they said were surprising to DFID:

> DFID's projects talk about participation; but this is rarely put into practice. DFID's unilateral and imposed decisions often undermine participation and empowerment.
>
> Cooperation with TCOs [technical cooperation officers][1] and advisers is usually very good. However, with the Brasilia and London offices, this relationship tends to be weaker. Projects have many times been marginalized without a concrete basis. Some projects have more credibility than others, and this is usually based on personal preferences.

Some comments were less surprising, but no less difficult to deal with:

> The instability of DFID's commitment to national partners causes concern. We also have commitments to our own partners that depend on DFID's resources.

We facilitated an office in-day in Brasilia to share and analyse lessons from the case studies, along with other experiences of office staff with respect to partnerships. We discussed implications for internal working relationships. Finally, we organized a Latin America-wide workshop with DFID Brazil to consolidate thinking and experiences around its approach to influencing and partnerships more broadly.

These exercises not only contributed to clearer (if not better) relations between the participants in Brazil and in DFID Latin America, but provided the basis for procedural innovations for more consistent and continual learning about and within relationships.

The irony of all this was that DFID Brazil staff, having instigated the partnership enquiries to improve relations, then found themselves forced to arbitrarily curtail their funding relationships. In late 2003, the country office budget was drastically reduced. With a considerable effort, the team made use of their relationship work to weather what was, by any measure, a very stormy time:

> *Communications were confusing and incomplete. Information coming from the centre was vague and DFID Brazil felt it didn't have sufficient facts to share with partners... No one felt the new arrangements were fair or had been decided on with the transparency and accountability that were in the Sahy principles.[2] And although DFID Brazil had no control over the changes, it was not possible to avoid the general feeling that the Brazil office's behaviour was as unilateral as the UK's. The Brazil team admitted several times during this period that all partnership principles were being broken... DFID Brazil found its way forward in opening itself to admit failures and hear what the partners had to say. In meetings with partners, DFID staff explained the changes and exposed the criteria used to make choices about budgets and duration of projects. The team knew the decisions had been unilateral and this message was clearly conveyed to partners. By admitting that, DFID Brazil also opened the doors to negotiation of a better way to exit from bilateral projects.* (Guimarães and Larbi-Jones, 2005, p18)

Developing sustained learning

Although all these learning enterprises contributed to new structures and ideas, none of them was formally maintained as a 'relational learning' system in itself. In Chapter 2, Eyben describes the context that gives rise to this failure to solidify and sustain learning about relationships. At one level, it comes about because of the flighty politics and historical culture of aid, and because the practical and bureaucratic structures that define how things are done do not give priority to such learning. At another level, there is a simple lack of practical methods, tools and facilitation for doing relational learning consistently and well. These two levels coincide with Senge's framework described by Pasteur in Chapter 1 (Senge, 1990), which differentiates the domain of action (theory, methods, tools, infrastructure and guiding ideas) and the domain of enduring change (attitudes, skills, capabilities and sensibilities). Ironically, an element of the latter is required in order to provide the conditions for sustaining the former. The innovators stand on the threshold of an interesting idea and ask where they will get the capability and institutional support from to engage in a sustained but low-priority activity. Notwithstanding, thousands of DFID staff do engage all the time in relational learning of one sort or another, so there is a groundswell of support for interesting approaches among innovators across the organization. This willingness to take a risk, combined with an imperative to deliver aid that works, is perhaps all that is needed. What follow are some tips on how to make relational learning work and some approaches that are worth avoiding.

Opportunities to learn: The domain of methodical action

Relational learning does not come easily since it often requires a level of self-exposure for individuals and organizations. Methodologically, this entails using facilitators wisely, dealing with issues of power and providing appropriate physical and procedural space. Learning processes benefit from being well organized and having a clear procedure for dealing with issues arising. Finally, they need to lead to action.

Choosing the method

Making space among routine activities and choosing a fitting method are the first issues to be tackled. Should there be formal procedures or are *ad hoc* opportunities enough?

Having noted that no DFID procedures appeared to exist for detailed reflection on relational issues, we initially thought of using a formal action research methodology in selected DFID offices. This would have involved groups coming together regularly to reflect on a topic of common interest and to test out alternative actions to produce change (see Box 5.2). Action research, however, requires a significant commitment of time, and this proved too heavy a constraint for busy DFID staff. Furthermore, the idea of engaging with learning in new ways did not appeal to those with whom we were in touch, and may not have been incorporated easily within typical office routines. As a result, we used more common learning strategies – case studies, small meetings and workshops – and found that they worked perfectly well. We found that these could be effective for learning about relationships if facilitators invested effort in ensuring their quality and appropriateness.

Analysing the stakeholders

A crucial element of a successful relationship is the degree of, and potential for, common interest between the parties. Who would gain or lose from this interaction? How would they perceive each other? What should be done to ensure that the activity has the best chance of success? Relational learning provides opportunities to see one's organization and one's partners and interlocutors more

---

BOX 5.2 WHAT IS ACTION RESEARCH?

Action research is a methodology that pursues action (or change) and research (or understanding) at the same time. It does this through a cyclic process, alternating between action and critical reflection. It is a participatory process – working on the principle that change is easier to achieve when those affected by the change are involved.

Collective enquiry takes place through group-based reflection and sharing meetings. These help to deepen understanding and generate questions around a central, commonly agreed, theme. Between meetings, individuals undertake enquiries or experiment with new ways of working. They then bring their findings and insights to the next group meeting. As the process progresses, methods and interpretation are continually refined in the light of the understanding developed in the earlier cycles.

Source: adapted from Reason, 2001; Reason and Bradbury, 2001; Cornwall et al, 2004

---

clearly and to interact with them not only to deliver aid, but to learn together. The analysis looks at one's own organization, its policies and agendas, noting the way it looks from the outside, as well as how it perceives interlocutors. It also demands self knowledge – examining oneself as a player. Individual reflexivity can be developed in a number of ways: by having a discipline of self-review; by having time to think and reflect alone; by reading widely; by using forms of expression such as writing to explore one's own opinions and culture (Marshall, 2001; Scott-Villiers, 2004). It then requires a thorough analysis of all other stakeholders and their influences on one another and on you. This suggests some primary questions as a guide:

Awareness of self: (as an individual and an organization):

- What do we understand of ourselves and our own organization – its culture and politics?
- Who are we listening to and why? Who are we ignoring?
- What are our own motivations; are we clear about our agenda? Why have we chosen this partner?
- Who are we accountable to, for what and how does this affect our actions and attitudes?
- What are our capabilities and role?

Awareness of others:

- What do we understand of our interlocutors and the cultural, political and historical context within which the relationship is operating?
- What are their perspectives on an issue and their perceptions of 'us'?

- Do they share our agenda? Why (not)? Why have they chosen this relationship with us?
- What other pressures are they facing? To whom are they accountable?
- What is their role?

Agreement and trust

Reflection and learning can be helped by openness, which relies on a level of trust in the 'contract' between the parties. To create an environment in which people feel happy to share and build on (often) sensitive experiences or opinions, attention needs to be paid to building understanding and agreement around the purpose and rules of the reflection, as well as to how lessons will be shared or acted upon. The more players involved, the more numerous the unspoken assumptions and the more complex the initial negotiation.

In Brazil an earlier effort to engage with partners around the quality of the relationship had failed to produce useful results. The adviser had asked partners directly: what makes a good partnership? What do you think of us? She got superficial and polite answers. Partners, given their dependence upon DFID resources, were not forthcoming. Larbi-Jones offered a less threatening environment, pointing out that she was only a temporary member of the DFID Brazil team. She allayed their fears by explaining the purpose, implications and exact products of the work, exploring the potential benefits in improving the relationship with DFID and reaching agreement on how the information would be used. Her process started with detailed negotiation, both within the DFID office and with the partners involved. The partners wanted to know why it had been suggested that they review partnerships together, what would be done with the results and what their rights were. Larbi-Jones explained that DFID's idea was to learn together and therefore improve the relationship and DFID's ability to play its part well.

The reviews that Larbi-Jones conducted with partners became an integral part of the relationships themselves, in each case strengthening the next stages of interaction (whether continuation or withdrawal). They allowed a systematic clarification of the learning that had been continuously generated in managing the relationships themselves.

Like DFID Brazil, the DFID Uganda team also employed a method of mediated reflection with stakeholders. This time the facilitation team was entirely external to DFID. The team was, however, known and, importantly, well respected, particularly by government forestry staff. Much attention was paid to assuring participants that their views would be treated with respect and sensitivity. The case study process provided an opportunity for people to express any frustrations and anger with relative security.

Difficulties arose for Kazoora's team, however, when they wished to disseminate the findings. They had promised to be diplomatic in dealing with the material, and yet the most useful lessons from the process related to this sensitive input. How could they share it without causing offence? In the final report, many of the key relational lessons were merely alluded to rather than substantially discussed. Nevertheless, the overall result was that the issues were addressed. It was enough to have brought them to the surface in conversation.

Facilitation

Both the Uganda and the Brazil processes were facilitated by people who were not directly and continually involved in the partnerships themselves. They did not bring DFID and other partners together to learn and resolve challenges face to face. Instead, they extracted the lessons and communicated them to the relevant counterparts in the relationship. This approach has certain advantages of creating an opportunity for people to share issues that they could not do face to face with the partners themselves. It avoids confrontations and, in cases where relationships are fraught, is probably the best option. However, the downside is that many of the lessons end up in the heads of the mediators; as already noted, passing those lessons on is often difficult. A mediated learning strategy should perhaps be followed by further learning where partners come together directly.

Getting the right people at the right time

DFID Brazil organized a three-day regional workshop on partnership and influencing for DFID Latin America advisers. They were bound by a strong common interest in illustrating to DFID more widely the value of lessons from the region. There was also a sense of urgency to the task, as budgets for DFID's work in middle-income countries were under increasing pressure from competing requirements in poorer countries. It was important to show that pro-poor work in the middle-income countries could also generate invaluable learning for often more difficult partnership situations in poorer countries. This provided a strong incentive to reflect together.

An effective space

Providing a physical and mental space was important, away from the usual demands of the office, setting good questions for deliberation and making space for being informal, as well as formal. Several conscious preparatory steps were taken to ensure appropriate expectations, a positive environment for working and reflecting, and an effective process for sharing views, but also developing practical action outcomes (see Box 5.3).

The feedback was good: many participants noted that it felt unusually productive (see Box 5.4). After the event there was an unusual amount of follow-up action despite the intangible subject matter, and a number of participants used frameworks and ideas from the workshop in their subsequent missions and projects. There were plenty of areas that could have worked better at the event;

BOX 5.3 THE KEY INGREDIENTS FOR A SUCCESSFUL WORKSHOP

Preparatory steps taken to provide a positive working environment, as well as to ensure practical action outcomes, included the following:

- The *participants* were carefully chosen.
- The facilitators and hosts spent time together *clarifying the context* of the workshop and participants. This included understanding the needs of the Brazil office and conducting a stakeholder analysis of participant and organizational interests. These were considered in developing the agenda.
- A *clear purpose and broad but flexible agenda* were circulated before the event so that participants knew what to expect and what was expected of them.
- External resource people gave *intellectual* input to challenge participants, highlight useful questions and stimulate more fruitful conceptual discussions. There were also opportunities for *telling relevant stories*.
- Time was dedicated to *developing actionable strategies*. These drew on both the intellectual discussion and detailed contextual analysis, including a stakeholder mapping of potential allies.
- *Facilitators were external* to DFID; thus, they did not have an internal agenda to push. They were also able to *limit unhelpful norms of behaviour* – for example, domination of discussions by the more confident, participants not building on previous contributions, poor time management, or jumping to unrealistic actions.
- The workshop was held in *pleasant surroundings*, and the timetable incorporated options for daytime relaxation and networking within a realistic time schedule.
- A *workshop report* and summary were produced in a consultative and timely manner, and there has been *follow-up* on the event to encourage participants to carry through proposed actions.

BOX 5.4 SOME FEEDBACK FROM THE DFID BRAZIL WORKSHOP PARTICIPANTS

Our department's workshops are usually awful – the power dynamic between London and the region is played out.

The flexibility of the agenda was a bit strange at the start – but then I realized it was a tool.

Just the location has been very positive, and the structure was very good. I have never done a workshop like this before.

but this case demonstrates a way in which a traditional form of reflection can be made more effective by increasing the quality of its management and the skills of its delivery (including preparation and follow-up), creating an environment in which productive relationships could be developed.

Emotional intelligence

In learning about relationships, people are dealing with issues that are intangible, political and sometimes painful. Experiences and concepts pertaining to relationships will tend to be shared through stories and anecdotes, and will thus involve high levels of ambiguity, as well as emotion. Relationships involve power and feelings as well as rational negotiation. They occur in informal and irregular spaces, as well as the more formal. They grow and change over time, and their dynamics and products are not easily captured. They may be chaotic, uncharted and iterative. Much of the iteration in a relationship is based on conversation, assumption and the power relations between the parties. Creating opportunities for productive negotiation and learning, and making the most of them, requires sensitivity to individual perceptions and behaviours, and to group and organizational dynamics based on self-awareness, empathy and social skills. These competences have been called emotional intelligence (Goleman, 2001).

Emotional intelligence is needed in order to define appropriate questions and interpret what is going on in relationships; at the same time, it is necessary to be able to handle the results of relationship enquiries. The irony is that emotional intelligence itself can really only be learned in action. A more turbulent, dynamic and competitive environment makes emotional intelligence both more important, but also more difficult to nurture: 'The development of emotional intelligence needs sustained reflection and learning... Only the most emotionally intelligent have the insight and determination to do so' (Cherniss, 2001, p11).

Particularly if a project or programme is not felt to be going well, reflecting on its relationships may be embarrassing instead of encouraging, and the exercise may shut down communication rather than stimulate it. One's sense of identity and worth may come under threat; anger and defensiveness can be typical responses. This requires a skilled hand at preparing for and containing the reflection and involves a fair degree of emotional intelligence. The more emotional intelligence that is present in the participants, the less will be the need for a mediator.

All the case study enquiries dealt with emotions. In the Uganda case, it became very clear that how upset or happy people were at a given interaction had strong and usually unrecognized effects on the reform. The enquiry raised the emotional temperature yet further, but paradoxically also helped to cool it. Our own experience raised the challenges of emotions and how they can constrain learning. We were under pressure to show results on a project that we had all fought for, so our meetings were highly charged. It was challenging, even in our small team, to be open with one another and reflect honestly, admitting when things were not going well. The facilitator whom we brought in for a number of sessions helped us to maintain focus on our goals and sort out our processes. But investment in reflection, as opposed to more productive action, felt counter-cultural. These reflection meetings took time and had financial implications, although they were very useful to later activities and final output.

Skilful conversation

What sorts of questions should be asked and how can a conclusion be built? In each of our cases, the players asked questions in order to look below the surface of their own actions and those of their interlocutors. They questioned their underlying assumptions and examined the context in which the relationships were developing from several angles.

The DFID Brazil enquiry used an approach that looked through various 'systemic windows' (Flood, 1999; see also Chapter 1). Using a detailed timeline, partners plotted processes and events in the history of their partnership with DFID, identifying the effect that each event had on those who followed it. They were asked about *interpretation and emotion* in order to describe how they felt about the relationship at each of these moments and the effect of these perceptions on actions and outcomes. They considered the effects of different stakeholders' *power and knowledge* on validating particular groups or ideas. They identified the *structures and procedures* of communication, contracting and accountability that both caused and were the result of the other two systemic areas. Finally, they looked at the whole for patterns and turning points and drew out insights and proposed activities.

The team drew up a list of questions suitable for a single conversation or a lengthy process of interactive learning:

- Delimiting the reflection: *what are the relationships to be investigated?* This establishes the purpose and parameters of the reflection, identifying how it will link to action and agreeing clear rules of interaction.
- Stakeholder analysis: *who are the players; what are their interests, interpretations, powers and interactions? What are their accountabilities outside the reflection?* These questions allow insight into enthusiasms, biases and barriers. Once an individual or a group of people recognize and deal with relational forces, the capacity for creative and clear reflection is enormously increased.
- Mapping the terrain: *what are the key events and ideas? When and where do things happen? What patterns are showing up?* These questions bring to the table what is already known or believed and illustrate the complexity and interconnections of the themes under investigation.
- Gathering inputs: *what are other innovators thinking about these sorts of relationships? What examples are there from other places?* Outsiders are invited to share their thinking, experience and research. Alternative views provide opportunities for comparison that can call into question existing paradigms and approaches.
- Analysis: *what meaning can be drawn?* Having laid out existing knowledge and ideas, this stage starts by standing back and looking for patterns, then digs deeper and asks difficult questions. It is useful to ask 'why?' several times. Detailed reconstructions of small but significant events can also be very powerful in producing new understandings.
- Experiential and emotional perspectives: *what were the experiences and how did people feel at the time? What is happening here and now?* It is useful to see people's

emotive actions as logical and skilful responses to situations in which they are embedded.

- Analysis: *what summary can be made?* This pulls together threads from all the previous questions to arrive at a new view of the relationships being analysed.
- Practical questions: *what is a new goal or purpose that incorporates the insights from this reflection? What would have to change? Who would be involved and what would they gain or lose? What roles would they play? How would these be negotiated? What is the first actionable step?* Reflection needs to result in action. Actions are often agreed to; but to ensure that they are carried out, practical steps need to be agreed upon.

Implications for organizational change

The previous section used real cases to illustrate methods, skills and ideas of relational learning. Where things went well, it was because we, and others, were working to improve existing learning procedures, recognizing the effect of perceptions, ensuring good physical and mental space, making clear agreements with participants, ensuring that they felt safe, actively following up, bringing in facilitators where necessary, and not trying to mediate relationships that were beyond our capacity. However, all these activities were short-term. They may have briefly demonstrated the value of relational learning, but they did not necessarily generate a lasting momentum because other more fundamental issues are at stake. These lie in Senge's (1990) 'domain of enduring change' (see Chapter 1), where skills, attitudes, capabilities and sensibilities become embedded as organizational norms. What behaviours, procedures and opportunities could donor organizations introduce that would sustain reflection on relationships?

A key starting point is with *individual appraisal and incentives*: without an incentive to act on relationships, there will be no incentive to learn about them. What kind of actions does a development professional think that he or she is rewarded for? All too frequently, the bottom line is disbursement of funds, and other aspects of the aid delivery process, such as understanding the working context and building relationships, are secondary. Staff investment in forging useful and skilful relations with government, multilateral, bilateral and civil society actors needs to be given its due. Furthermore, lessons learned from difficulties, or even failures, need to be made good use of rather than hidden. This implies rewarding honest learning and supporting the resulting innovations.

Team-working and relational skills are amongst the key competences for which DFID recruits. However, once inside the organization, a strong culture of competition and independence, and a failure to actively reward relationship-building may undermine these capacities. Change towards an organizational culture that strongly values relationship skills alongside other necessary competencies will be driven, in part, by innovations in practice, but also requires leadership and *management backing*. Leaders are crucial in providing guidance and models to staff to get their relationships right, and in ensuring that time invested in learning about them is recognized and rewarded. They will be needed to defend this type of investment of development funds. Experimentation with learning about relationships in country offices – such as the cases documented here – can be stifled if managers do not value such activities.

Contradictions of *accountability* were found to be a major barrier to learning in our case studies. Country office officials are under pressure to prove high levels of efficiency and effectiveness, principally in getting money well spent, which they must report upwards in order to prove the impact of government spending and to secure further funding. Although the impact of development assistance is long-term, indirect and difficult to measure, the demand is for rapid, attributed and accurate reports of positive results. This means that relationships, particularly between donor and recipient, can often be completely false, with partners literally lying to one another or at least avoiding certain unpalatable truths. While the procedures for learning and accountability are often one and the same, their aims can be at cross-purposes. People should be held accountable; but this should not suppress their willingness to take intelligent risks, for the good of pro-poor outcomes; or their ability to admit to problems, share them and seek solutions; or their willingness to understand their work in new ways. Upward accountability must be balanced by horizontal and downward accountability – that is, people also need to know how they are doing in the eyes of recipients and partners and should build systems to respond (see Chapter 7). They need to build sufficient trust to be able to give and receive honest feedback even where hierarchy and resource dependence influences what people are willing to say (Hobley, 2003).

The *procedures and processes* that make space for learning are a further arena for change. Could existing learning and accountability formats, such as output to purpose reviews, evaluations and other forms of appraisal, be improved to put more weight on the issue of development relationships? How could opportunities for reflection on relationships become more routine without becoming ineffective, meaningless or coercive? It is important to clearly separate the moments of evaluation, upon which funding and other benefits depend, from moments of off-the-record review, upon which relationships depend. Could hitherto less recognized forms of learning, such as communities of practice, action research and action learning,[3] be incorporated within standard office practice (Pedler and Boutall, 1992)? The key to successful institutionalization of any of these strategies is ensuring that they are adequately funded, well supported and well executed.

A number of development agencies have experimented with new approaches, some of which are detailed in this volume. The Swedish International Development Agency (Sida), for example, tested participatory learning groups (another variant of action research/action learning), where staff explored organizational policies in a series of facilitated meetings interspersed with investigation within the agency and with partners (see Chapter 4). ActionAid abolished some of its unnecessary upward reporting requirements in favour of more flexible downward reporting, which encourages reflection on, and transparency in, relationships with partners. This has begun to revolutionize the way in which the agency learns and what it considers important (see Chapter 7). The process was neither simple nor swift to translate into accepted practice. Building systems and culture takes time. Moving from isolated instances of innovative learning to an organization-wide imperative is a grand endeavour; but it will prove its worth if development decisions are swifter and more appropriate.

Conclusion

In the cases we describe, it was through introducing quality, variety and depth to ordinary meetings that unusual conversations were seeded, differences of perception revealed, knowledge bases interrogated, and insight and action stimulated. All the cases were seeking, and found, shifts in the patterns of conversation – in other words, learning happened.

The result of attention to *methods* as much as to *incentives* for relational learning would be an increase in the quality of each individual's engagement in every part of the day-to-day processes that make up the work of development agencies. Efforts to improve the quality of interaction of every staff member with one another and with partners, collaborators and detractors would thus have a significant payoff. New knowledge is actively created only when it is used, and this happens mostly in dialogue and cooperation with others; therefore, a more acute appreciation of the nuances of relationship would have enormous implications for development. Donor organizations, with their enormous mission to fulfil lofty development goals, need to recognize, learn from and act on relationships.

Notes

1 Technical cooperation officers is the term used by DFID for the specialists that it recruits to work on aid programmes.
2 A set of principles for relationships based on empowerment, accountability and learning, which were validated at a DFID workshop held in Sahy, Brazil, May 2003.
3 Action learning is slightly different from action research. It involves a group of peer learners in cycles of reflection and action in which each group member brings their own particular issue to the group, and the group assists resolution through asking useful questions. The practice is quite widely used for learning in organizations, including at senior levels of the UK government.

References

Chambers, R., Pettit, J. and Scott-Villiers, P. (2001) *The New Dynamics of Aid: Power, Procedures and Relationships*, IDS Policy Briefing, Institute of Development Studies, Brighton
Cherniss, C. (2001) 'Emotional intelligence and organizational effectiveness', in Cherniss, C. and Goleman, D. (eds) *The Emotionally Intelligent Workplace: How to Select For,*

Measure and Improve Emotional Intelligence in Individuals, Groups, and Organizations, Jossey-Bass, San Francisco

Collison, C. and Parcell, G. (2001) *Learning to Fly: Practical Lessons from One of the World's Leading Knowledge Companies,* Capstone Publishing, Oxford

Cornwall, A., Pratt, G. and Scott-Villiers, P. (2004) *Participatory Learning Groups in an Aid Bureaucracy,* Lessons for Change in Police and Organisations no 11, Institute of Development Studies, Brighton

DFID (UK Department for International Development) (2001) *Terms of Reference: Learning from the Experience of Policy and Institutional Change in the Uganda Forest Sector,* DFID, Kampala

Flood, R. L. (1999) *Rethinking the Fifth Discipline: Learning within the Unknowable,* Routledge, London

Goleman, D. (2001) 'Emotional intelligence: Issues in paradigm building', in Cherniss, C. and Goleman, D. (eds) *The Emotionally Intelligent Workplace: How to Select For, Measure and Improve Emotional Intelligence in Individuals, Groups, and Organizations,* Jossey-Bass, San Francisco

Guimarães, A. C. and Larbi-Jones, E. (2005) *Working for Pro-poor Change in Brazil: Influencing Partnerships?* Lessons for Change in Policy and Organisations, no 10 Institute of Development Studies, Brighton

Hobley, M. (2003) *Workshop Report: Partnership and Influencing Workshop,* DFID Brazil, Sao Paulo

Kazoora, C., Sekabanja, F. and Ijuka-Kabumba (2002) *Learning from the Experiences of Policy and Institutional Change in the Uganda Forest Sector,* Draft Report, Sustainable Development Centre, Kampala

Marshall, J. (2001) 'Self-reflective inquiry practices', in Reason, P. and Bradbury, H. (eds) *Handbook of Action Research: Participative Enquiry and Practice,* Sage, London

Pedler, M. and Boutall, J. (1992) *Action Learning for Change: A Resource Book for Managers and Other Professionals,* National Health Service Training Directorate, Bristol

Reason, P. (2001) 'Learning and change through action research', in Henry, J. (ed) *Creative Management,* Sage, London

Reason, P. and Bradbury, H. (eds) (2001) *Handbook of Action Research: Participative Enquiry and Practice,* Sage, London

Scott-Villiers, P. (2004) 'Personal change and responsible wellbeing', in Groves, L. and Hinton, R. (eds) *Inclusive Aid: Changing Power and Relationships in International Development,* Earthscan, London

Senge, P. (1990) *The Fifth Discipline: The Art and Practice of the Learning Organization,* Doubleday, New York

Part 3

ORGANIZATIONAL LEARNING THROUGH VALUE-BASED RELATIONSHIPS: POSSIBILITIES AND CHALLENGES

6

Supporting Rights and Nurturing Networks: The Case of the UK Department for International Development (DFID) in Peru

Fiona Wilson and Rosalind Eyben[1]

Introduction

Shaping this chapter on the UK Department for International Development's (DFID's) experiences in Peru are questions concerning an aid agency's practice when it seeks to make relationship-building the principal means of promoting a rights-based approach to social change. Are there possible contradictions between the means and the end, and how can these be managed? By focusing on rights, DFID broke ranks and came to stand apart from other bilateral and multilateral donors in Peru. For the DFID office, this was by no means simply a matter of applying policy dictated from above or of treating rights as an approach carved in stone. Issues of rights had to be addressed in dialogue with Peruvian activists, pursued through trial and error, and claimed before a periodically recalcitrant and oppositional state. As Cornwall and Nyamu-Musembi (2004, p1415) reflect, far from being a single approach, 'there are plural rights-based approaches, with different starting points and rather different implications for development practice'. What kind of thinking about rights lay behind the actions of DFID in Peru, and what can be learned from this experience about the risks/dangers and possibilities/ benefits when donors join forces with local social actors to make rights central to aid practice?

Answering these questions means asking how donors manage their organizational and relational work. With whom does an agency establish contact and alliances; on what basis are partners selected; what is the nature of the arrangement; how durable are alliances expected to be? To look at it from another angle, which groups in society have been interested (and successful) in bringing international donors into their activities and securing funds from this source? To what extent are donors recruited – maybe even co-opted – by activists into supporting a group's own political project? Has this become an important aspect of political entrepreneurship? One can suggest at the outset that this leads to different kinds of networks with different results than when bilateral donors channel most resources through official institutions. From mid 2000, DFID in Peru invested far more energy and resources in supporting relationships, networks and social processes outside the state; and its emphasis was other than securing technical and measurable outcomes. To understand more about this we need to take a fresh look at relational work – a donor's alliance-building and networking activity.

As Henry, Mohan and Yanacopulos (2004, p839) argue, the network has 'become one of the hallmarks of the development industry and is central to its discourses and self-image'. One finds increasing reference to 'alliance-building' and 'networking' in development documentation, where these terms are taken as indicating 'a more flexible, flat and non-hierarchic means of exchange and interaction' (Henry et al, 2004). In other words, all sorts of relationships are now labelled as networks and thereby given an egalitarian gloss; networking has become a potent self-image, but one that may obscure how relations and alliances actually work in practice, for they tend to leave out of account the matrices and landscapes of power that underpin all aid relationships.[2] One therefore needs to critically explore what lies beneath the surface – how networks as an organizational form are structured not only by good intentions and goodwill but also by power relations, hierarchy and exclusivity. There are bound to be distinctions between who 'nets' and who 'works'. Thus, one key question becomes whether power can be recognized and mediated by a bilateral agency that is also an actor. A second is whether a strong relational and networking approach of the kind adopted by DFID in Peru to promote the realization of rights at the same time runs the risk of contradicting some of the foundational principles that DFID was also advocating, such as transparency and accountability.

In this chapter we explore how donors cultivate and work through networks when engaged in promoting societal change in complex political environments. Drawing on the limited case material available to us concerning DFID's role in Peru in helping to shift policy and practice in the area of health, we point to some of the less well-recognized implications of working through networks rather than formalized institutional and organizational structures.

The Peruvian context

Peru, like the rest of Latin America, is characterized by extreme social inequalities. Nevertheless, it is designated by international aid agenda-setters as a 'middle-income country' because of having an average annual income of US$2100. Yet, one half of all Peruvians live in income poverty (less than US$730 per annum) and one fifth in extreme income poverty (less than US$365). In the rural areas, not only do more than 50 per cent live in extreme poverty, they are subject to multiple exclusions stemming from deep-seated racism and social discrimination that are reflected in poor access to state services and ineffective political representation. Citizen/subjects unable to read and write in Spanish (mostly female and indigenous) only won the right to vote in 1979. Broadly speaking, the darker your skin, the lower your position in the social hierarchy and the more limited your rights as a citizen with claims on the state.

During the 1980s, Peru experienced both political violence and serious economic dislocation as a result of the debt crisis. This created insecurity at all levels of society and brought the established political order to its knees. The guerrilla war waged against the state by the Maoist political party, *Sendero Luminoso* (Shining Path), from 1980, was one of the most violent episodes of Peru's history. A consequence of these crises was the emergence of an authoritarian regime that ruled with strong military backing. Elected in 1990, Alberto Fujimori built up a centralized system of power over the next decade and managed to overcome economic and political dislocation. Seeking to perpetuate itself indefinitely, the regime was shored up through manipulation of the media and social policies that used clientelism and government handouts to win popular support. Fujimori skilfully made use of factionalism and public distrust in the country's political parties to boost his own political fortunes. But it was his attempt in 2000 to secure a third term in office on the basis of overt fraud that led to his eventual fall from power. The governments that replaced Fujimori, the interim government of Valentín Paniagua and elected government of Alejandro Toledo that took office in July 2001, found themselves faced with monumental tasks of post-conflict recovery, severe income and social inequalities and building up an institutional framework to sustain a process towards democracy. It was in this context that DFID in Peru decided to focus on rights.

DFID in Peru

Within the overall policy approach set by London, DFID country offices are charged with identifying how to most make a difference in a particular country context. This results in a country assistance plan, initiated by the local office and approved in London, that includes not only how DFID's money will be spent, but also the partners and associates with whom DFID intends to work. Partners may comprise institutions and bodies within the recipient government and civil society, as well as other international aid agencies.

Until 2000, there had been no country office in Peru. British aid had been managed from London; but by the late 1990s, the Labour government's aim to be a global player in eradicating world poverty led to a decision to increase the aid budget to Latin America and improve project quality by placing more staff 'in the field'. The head of the new Peru office was someone who, long familiar with DFID's rules, procedures and processes, was in a good position to explore more innovative channels for aid intervention than had been the case when the programme had been managed from London.

The amount of money directly managed by DFID's Peru office was proportionately a very small sum compared with overall current bilateral assistance to Peru. However, as DFID in Peru argued, the small budget did not necessarily constitute a major hindrance. It was the *way* in which the money was spent that mattered. DFID claimed to have achieved significantly higher socially sustainable returns for Peru than if it had invested in conventional development projects.

The office opened in March 2000 six months prior to Fujimori's downfall. At the outset, the office questioned the wisdom of continuing to support a (by then) notoriously corrupt and authoritarian regime. So DFID quickly moved towards establishing a new set of alliances that brought together non-state actors working on civil and political rights, and on human development and poverty reduction, with support to specific interest groups in civil society, helping local organizations to scale up their activities in demanding rights and services, and strengthening civil society organizations that were attempting to hold the Fujimori government to account for its political use of service provision to the poor. After Fujimori had gone, an effervescent 'democratic spring' accompanied the transitional government, opening up new opportunities for DFID. Now, not only did it appear a promising time to renew relations with the state, but the climate of the times led to much open debate about democratic reform and, within DFID, to a consolidation of its focus on rights, participation and governance, with the effect of giving greater emphasis to alliance-building and networking in civil society. But what can be learned from comparative experiences where donors 'broke ranks' and opened up to alliance-building and networking with civil society? We find two contrasting scenarios.

Networks: A response to emergent change

'Networks' have long been a central concept in the social sciences and their theorization is found in a number of disciplinary strands. Social network analysis focuses on the density and types of connections between individuals; in organizational and business studies, the concern has been with inter-organizational relationships; and political science has been interested in policy networks and advocacy coalitions (Robinson et al, 2000; Hajer and Wagennar, 2003; Berry et al, 2004). Recently, drawing on ideas from complexity theory, self-organizing networks are being understood as a key element in societal change (see Chapter 2). While the DFID staff had not consciously engaged with network or complexity theory, it was responsive to the potentials that self-organizing networks represented for aid practice. In nurturing these processes, the head of office saw himself as a 'development diplomat'. Such an approach sees change as emergent rather than pre-planned in terms of the usual goal-setting undertaken by hierarchical organizations that generally 'problematize' along the bureaucratic rational lines of cause and effect. The assumption in the latter case is that effective aid means getting the policy right in relation to a single diagnosis of the problem and, once that is established, putting policy into practice through an administrative command structure, whereby messages flow from top management down to be carried out by frontline workers. Through regular monitoring and evaluation, the model can be adjusted, but only within certain parameters that do not challenge the essential model.

Thus, the DFID *Country Assistance Plan* for Peru is a remarkable document for a donor agency in that it offers several diagnoses, rather than a single one. There is an interesting disjuncture between this open-ended 'messy' approach to diagnosis and the logical framework 'blueprint' requirements of the later section of the plan that defines objectives and activities. The logical framework way of thinking, if rigorously applied, tends to penalize rather than reward spontaneity, creativity and experimentation. It discourages approaches that support investing in relationships and networks without being certain of the outcome or where the path will lead. When interviewed, the head of the DFID's Peru office recognized that the logical framework with its 'embedded linear logic' had 'its limitations for dealing with the complex process that many of our initiatives have supported' (Lewis and Sagasti, 2005, p168).

The involvement of official aid agencies (as distinct from international NGOs) in supporting networks and processes of emergent change has been remarkably under-researched. But Wedel's (2001) account of aid to Eastern Europe following the collapse of communism gives some provocative pointers on this. Wedel notes how partners found each other in a context where donors were new arrivals with no knowledge or experience of working in the region, and discovered they were entering a world of cliques and intrigue in which local actors, too, though having little information about the aid world, were 'quick studies in manoeuvring the situation to their advantage' (Wedel, 2001, p94). She argues that donor support of one group to the exclusion of others helped to build up certain elites so that those with enough clout and contacts to get foreign money gained steadily, while others with equally strong claims and local constituencies but less visibility lost ground. For donors to overcome this dilemma, Wedel comments, would have required an in-depth knowledge of the histories and politics of the many local groups. Arguably, DFID in Peru was placed in a less vulnerable position than counterparts in Eastern Europe some ten years earlier. Even so, can one suggest that some of the same tendencies were being induced?

DFID's Peru programme (had it continued) may have incurred comparable risks despite its longer historical presence and serious effort to understand the complexities of the local political scene. As with Eastern Europe after communism, so DFID in Peru also took advantage of 'the democratic spring' to reach out to existing groups who had been 'in resistance' under the previous authoritarian regime. In both contexts, we can note the prevalence of what one might call 'submerged networks' or, following Wedel (who, in turn, draws on Boissevain), 'cliques' – namely, clusters of persons, all of whom are linked to each other by overlapping ties of education, profession and political affiliation, and who remain conscious of their common identity (Wedel, 2001, pp105–106). With the crumbling of state institutions, Central and Eastern European educated cliques from the elite and middle classes tended to pursue their own personal and group agendas. They were 'institutional nomads' who moved between state and civil society institutions and whose primary loyalty remained with their own group.

However, an opposing case can also be made. In exploring how donors can best support reform processes, Fox (2005) argues for the importance of understanding how informal power resources and relationships operate within and between state institutions, and also stretch across the state–society divide. Research in Mexico has looked at how reformers in the federal government (with World Bank and other support) created regional economic development councils with elected representatives of indigenous producer organizations. Fox compares this experience with a number of other rural development programmes in terms of the willingness of state government officials to share power with civil society. In all cases, he notes that power-sharing depended heavily upon the presence of a faction within the state institution that was willing to enter into partnership with autonomous social organizations. Since he is interested in understanding how state institutions can most effectively work with civil society, he concludes that pro-poor change is most likely to occur when coalitions are formed between state and society actors who share a common reform agenda and apply simultaneously top-down and bottom-up pressures to neutralize resistance from established rural (and other) elites. He emphasizes the need for donors to support reformers with progressive track records and to continue supporting them when they move from one institution to another. In other words, the implication here is that 'institutional nomadism' is more effective than when the reform-minded stay concentrated within a single institution, while other institutions are without or drained of their reformers.

Comparing the two accounts, Wedel (2001) sounds much the more cautious note. Her account of how the US Agency for International Development (USAID) supported a network of self-proclaimed reformers in the former Soviet Union highlights the potential dangers of promoting change through investing in 'irresponsible' partners and relationships. For Fox (2005), it was the possibility of donors' practice of supporting local actors engaged in pro-poor consensus-building across state and civil society that enthralled him. The latter scenario lay behind the stance taken by DFID in Peru. But, clearly, complex political situations can never be defined in terms of 'black and white'. There is a danger that donors by 'interfering' may undermine or distort the evolution of a robust democracy by selecting and dismissing particular factions in civil society. In a presentation to DFID staff in the Latin American region in 2002, the head of office stressed the risks that accompany this explicitly political agenda and, thus, the importance of doing thorough groundwork before embarking on new alliances and relationships. This would include making a detailed analysis of the political context and actors involved in arenas which DFID wanted to enter.

DFID's approach to rights and networks

DFID in Peru took rights-based approaches as far, if not further, than any other DFID country programme (Piron and Watkins, 2004). The Peru team began to use rights as a benchmark for informing choices and taking decisions, as set out in the following principles:

- A rights-based approach for donors frames action within the international human rights agreements.
- Poor people are perceived as citizens, rather than clients or beneficiaries.
- There is a principle of mutual accountability, responsiveness and transparency between donors and partners.
- Partners are encouraged to practice similar rules of engagement with their fellow citizens/members.
- The donor works with government and civil society to help citizens acquire voice and knowledge to improve their lives and participate in decision-making spaces.
- Decisions are shaped by values, concepts and analysis, while recognizing that in the real world choices are usually difficult and outcomes unpredictable.

But the emphasis on poor people's rights when directing practice was soon seen as possessing weaknesses as well as strengths. By placing the rights of excluded and marginalized people at the centre of its work, DFID laid itself open to criticisms from Peruvian partners who recognized how the label of poverty could be demeaning to people at the centre of DFID's programmes. A poverty focus taken on its own was insufficient in that it concentrates on insufficiencies and problems, rather than on resources and capabilities, and discourages a fruitful, open-ended discussion about what people value and want to keep and what they want to change (Buell and Eyben, 2004).

While DFID's rights-based approach did not underplay the significance of working to strengthen formal institutions and structures of the state (Crabtree, 2005), it adopted a citizen-based approach to strengthening state–society relations. This meant there was no *a priori* necessity to work through state structures, even after democratic government was formally resumed. Rather, it saw alliances and networks with civil society as the prime means of pressing for the transformation of state structures so that statutory human rights could be extended to include all the country's citizens.

One way to visualize DFID's way of working with rights is to conceive of DFID as an actor located within a series of arenas of debate and consensus-making. From debates at the global level, DFID picked up on the shift in aid discourse, and the way in which issues of rights and citizenship were more firmly established in public debate. In this, DFID became recognized as one of very few bilateral donors (the Swedish International Development Agency, or Sida, being another) to have developed a strong policy on rights, although the extent to which the policy was fully internalized is debatable (Cornwall and Nyamu-Musembi, 2005; Piron, 2005). Moving down scale, we come to the DFID country office as an organizational arena. The DFID team was constantly engaged in making sense, translating and mediating between broad international debates about rights and citizenship, guidelines from the London office, the swings and intricacies of Lima politics and the complex, often unpredictable, situations in the highlands where many of the projects were located. At this level, in close association with the country office in Bolivia, DFID in Peru was able to pioneer a pro-poor, rights-based approach. The office was the site from which DFID, the bridge-builder, engaged with networks. Advisory staff members were active in a welter of other arenas where they argued for the centrality of rights and tried to influence the policy and practice of others. Then one comes to the project level: the alliances and networks built up with local actors in relation to specific issues. In this chapter, we focus on one of these: DFID's support to health-sector reform.

Making health policy inclusive of, and responsive to, the country's poorest citizens was summed up in a DFID paper, 'Improving the health of the poor: A rights based approach' (DFID, 2000a), which rested on three broad strategies that reflected DFID's overall policy paper on human rights (DFID, 2000b):

1   *strengthening participation* to develop a greater understanding of Peru's cultural diversity and to enhance participation in health policy decision-making and standard-setting;
2   *strengthening inclusion*: working with healthcare providers to support their efforts to respond to the healthcare priorities and needs of the poor and excluded;
3   *fulfilling obligations*: developing an understanding of international and national frameworks of conventions, laws and constitutional protections intended to provide Peru's citizenry with rights to health and healthcare, and assessment of the effectiveness of the current framework of health-related rights.

Our argument is that DFID's rights-based approach would not have added up to much in practice had it not been for the existence of a network of policy analysts and health professionals in Peru who were already thinking along the lines of democratization, decentralization and inclusion/participation, and who could take up DFID thinking on rights and run with it. Thus, it was decisively important that rethinking and trajectories of change taking place within DFID intersected with the rethinking and analysis in Peru with respect to health-sector reform. The centrality of this kind of foundational alliance tends to get forgotten or brushed aside in aid agencies' documentation, which often gives misleading impressions of unbounded and unmediated donor influence or of aid practice as technical and apolitical.

The networks of health-sector reform

With respect to the health sector, the first alliance the DFID office entered into was with the Economic and Social Research Consortium (CIES) under the leadership of the flamboyant Carlos Aramburú. CIES is an umbrella research organization, founded during the late 1980s, which has been successful in attracting long-term donor support, especially from the Canadian International Development

Agency (CIDA). The consortium is itself a network of institutions, comprising 35 members, including the most prominent universities and research centres in Lima and a scatter of institutions in the provinces. Donor funds channelled through CIES allow the academic community 'to produce and disseminate knowledge that is useful for analysts and decision-makers in the public sector, civil society and academia' and, thus, to fulfil CIES's overall mission 'to contribute to the development of Peru, raising the level of national debate on key options of economic and social policy'. For DFID, wanting to engage with health rights and with those working towards the democratic reform of the health sector, CIES was a good place to start. CIES affiliates spoke the same language of democracy, reform and citizenship, and its leader was well practised in the art of mediating between academics/consultants and international donor interests. Through its alliance with CIES, DFID agreed to fund an investigation into health policy reform that would not only contribute to public debate, but help define the parameters for DFID's future support to the health sector.

The CIES–DFID project did investigative groundwork for 'the generation of spaces and consensus for a new health policy'. Known as Consalud, its first phase ran from March 2000 to July 2001, and a second phase from August 2001 to July 2002. In the first phase, eight health professionals were brought together under the coordination of Pedro Francke, a senior economist working on social policy at the Catholic University and Universidad Peruana Cayetano Heredia in Lima,[3] to write chapters on different aspects of health-sector reform.[4] They were an interdisciplinary group, although most held a Masters degree in public health, were connected with the Universidad Peruana Cayetano Heredia and shared a political background on the left. Some had worked in the Ministry of Health (Ministerio de Salud, or Minsa), others with NGOs, and several had experience as consultants working directly for international donors.

The investigation started in the final months of the Fujimori government and soon encountered opposition in that Minsa refused to collaborate with the specialist charged with investigating health financing. But then the political context dramatically changed. After Fujimori fled, the new interim President Paniagua appealed to the Colegio Médico and to health professionals for their help in reorganizing the health sector. Suddenly, after years of political repression and submerged resistance, democratic reform could be openly debated. The findings of the CIES team took on new urgency in that Minsa members could now work from the 'inside' to bring about democratic reform. Two documents on the future directions of health-sector reform were produced: one, *Proposals for a Health Policy, 2001–2006*' (published in July 2001), stemmed from the CIES–DFID investigation, while a similar set of proposals was produced by the ministry.

The arguments made in the CIES–DFID document were as follows. Despite the notable expansion in the provision of health services during the 1990s, little had, in fact, been achieved with respect to a democratic transformation of the health system to meet objectives of equity, efficiency and quality. Health-sector reform was one of the most pressing tasks now facing Peru. Attempts at earlier reform had fallen short partly because the different stakeholders had not been brought into the picture. There was a need to take stock of lessons learned and to propose a reformulation of health policy. But there did not exist any forum where open discussion could take place. This was because of the strident differences dominating the national political scene, distorting the discussion of new approaches to health-sector reform. Symptomatic was a lack of dialogue between planners and academics exacerbating Peru's characteristic debilities: policy incoherence and improvisation. The CIES–DFID publication was hailed as articulating demands coming from civil society to participate fully in public debate. Working towards 'good governance' was no longer solely a matter of state management: democratic transition also had to be undertaken in the broad arena of the health service.

As Pedro Francke noted in his overview, a new vision of health policy was needed, a new '*norte*' (magnetic north), and this meant establishing health as a universal right. This, in turn, entailed democratizing the state, prioritizing basic health services to reach the rural poor and reorganizing the health system. Establishing health as a right necessitated a new social pact among Peruvians and a new relationship between people and the state 'that would give place to citizenship in health'. While not all authors thought in terms of rights, there was consensus on the need for a new forum for public debate. The chapter on relations between government and civil society by Juan Arroyo, a sociologist and planner who headed the Department of Health and Social Sciences in the Faculty of Public Health at the Universidad Cayetano Heredia, spelled out the need to resuscitate the old National Health Council that had fallen into disuse. It was imperative for those engaged in the health sector from civil society to have a new space where they could meet and debate proposals for democratic reform. Such a space had to be open to new representatives of civil society (namely NGOs and community-based organizations). Thus, while working on Consalud, the CIES health team, along with DFID, pushed ahead with these plans. The result was ForoSalud.

ForoSalud: A networked organization of civil society

Foro de la Sociedad Civil en Salud, known as ForoSalud was formally established through the signatures of 12 people representing four institutions: CIES, the Colegio Médico del Perú, the Asociación National de Centros, and the NGO Centro de la Mujer Peruana Flora Tristán. Funds to get this new body on its feet came from DFID. Only later, when the organization had grown to some 100 affiliated institutions and 300 affiliated health professionals did other donors (USAID, the Ford Foundation, Spain and the European Community) become interested in offering financial support. ForoSalud was hailed by its founders as a body working towards a new conception of citizenship rights and responsibilities; a pluralistic movement in civil society; a network of networks; and a national umbrella to open up new spaces for dialogue and to foster greater public involvement in health issues, especially amongst the poor. DFID's initial support was acknowledged as crucial to its success. ForoSalud was clearly an achievement; but it had been one among several proposals tabled at the time. We need to look at ForoSalud in the light of this context and go back in time.

Looking back at the effervescent 'Lima spring' when Forosalud was launched, Juan Arroyo, the first national coordinator, provided an illuminating commentary on its background.[5] Members of the CIES–DFID health group, those behind both Consalud and Forosalud, had been meeting regularly since 1997 to discuss health reform, thus marking the resurgence of 'civil society in the health sector'. The group came together to oppose Fujimori's re-election plans and the continued autocratic management of the health sector by a small clique running Minsa since the early 1990s. Joining this movement of resistance were health professionals from NGOs, leaders of the medical profession, researchers, consultants, university teachers and organizers of women's and youth groups. After the fall of Fujimori, the clandestine health reform movement abandoned its 'identity of resistance' to take on an 'identity of project' – as Arroyo noted, quoting the terminology made famous by Manuel Castells (1997).

Through a flurry of seminars and workshops, health-sector reform was brought to the forefront of public attention. The old 'oficialista' line of modernization in Minsa that had involved applying foreign models and following World Bank dictates was now openly under attack. According to Arroyo, at least nine proposals for new health policy reform were now tabled. Apart from that of the CIES–DFID health group, proposals were prepared by the Colegio Médico, the Peruvian Health Academy and Minsa, as well as by political parties: Agenda Perú, Alianza Popular Revolucionaria Americana (APRA), Unidad Nacional, Perú Posible and Solidaridad Nacional. Since DFID already collaborated with the CIES health group, there was no question of the agency backing another horse. But other options had been on offer, and ForoSalud was not the only possible outcome. Most striking was the apparent division between proposals emanating from political parties and from 'civil society' (although the latter identification was tricky, as we shall discuss below). A bilateral donor was bound, in practice, to support either the state or a group calling itself 'civil society'. Channelling support to a political party (whether the 'old' APRA or the 'new' Perú Posible[6]) was out of the question. But donor support to 'non-party' 'civil society' organizations could cumulatively undermine processes of institutionalization in Peru's political parties and political system and thus inadvertently prolong party fragility, division and irresponsibility. If they were to access donor funds, political entrepreneurs needed NGOs, and this made the political landscape more complicated and unpredictable and the donor relationship more problematic.

During the transitional government, there was a sudden loosening up of positions. In projecting their goals and visions for a democratically reformed health sector, social actors could either integrate with political parties campaigning in the forthcoming national elections to promote processes of democratization inside the political system and the state, or remain on the 'outside' in 'civil society'. But this duality was made less sharp on account of the networks of social actors linking civil society and the state that offered greater chances of collaboration. In this situation, social actors who had chosen to stay clear of party politics founded ForoSalud as a new organization representing civil society.

In the view of ForoSalud's organizers, what was needed in Peru was an independent body that could secure and protect a political space to take up the language of rights, ensure inclusion and help find consensus among the widely differing interests in civil society. ForoSalud was set up to act as a kind of mini-parliament to achieve unity out of diversity and to be strong enough to promote civil society's collective interests in front of the state. However, despite these aspirations, it was difficult for ForoSalud to escape being identified as overwhelmingly middle class, intellectual and based in Lima.

At first, the political conditions for establishing ForoSalud as sparring partner to Minsa had seemed propitious. But as the Toledo government (in power from July 2002) wore on, conservative groups (including the Catholic sect Opus Dei) came to take a leading position in Minsa. Some of those openly campaigning for democratic reform inside the ministry were forced to leave; others got on with putting reforms into practice and kept a low political profile. ForoSalud was accused of being too outspoken and critical of ministry policy and performance, and the tensions became particularly acute around key issues of reproductive rights and abortion. This conflict came to a head when the ministry refused to sign a DFID health project document and demanded that DFID act like it used to: hand over funds for supporting health in Peru directly to the ministry. Official disapproval, in turn, weakened internal cohesion within ForoSalud – it became more difficult to achieve consensus among a plethora of organizations which, despite belonging to 'civil society', nevertheless depended for their survival upon state (and donor) funding. Soon, ForoSalud was in serious confrontation with Minsa, and this reflected back on DFID. For supporting declared opponents of the Ministry and formulating a health programme that included reproductive rights (an anathema to the conservative faction in power in the Ministry), DFID risked being thrown out of the country. This experience highlights the tensions provoked when adopting a rights-based approach in the turbulent period of post-authoritarian rule.

When the conservative faction lost control of Minsa, the prospects for ForoSalud brightened. In 2004, a minister of health who was committed to rights and keen to re-establish more supportive, cordial relations with this national organization was appointed. Now ForoSalud moved to centre stage, in charge of organizing a National Health Conference attended by some 2000 delegates and presided over by the minister herself. With health policy proposals based on a rights approach presented and discussed, Forosalud had managed to gain a leading position in health-sector reform.

An important lesson for DFID was that selecting, supporting and thereby privileging particular groups and networks in civil society, and working across the civil society–state divide, proved more tricky and contradictory than the rhetoric of a rights-based approach admitted. The success of a civil society forum, ForoSalud, still hinged on political will within a ministry; but in a highly personalized, non-institutionalized political culture, this could not be taken for granted and could shift abruptly. By allying with a network known to be challenging official claims, DFID was intervening and engaging politically. As a bilateral donor, it was laying itself open to the charge of being partisan. This would have been even more risky had DFID not built up legitimacy and credibility from its earlier phases of support and been well informed on the backgrounds and political positions of the people with whom the agency worked. The possibilities for a rights-based approach had been strong in the 'Lima spring', but afterwards had faltered due to a reassertion of old patterns of power and privilege, including a conservative backlash in the ministries. It was impossible for DFID to remain on good terms with both sides.

Political pasts

Since 2000, DFID had given consistent backing to a network of health professionals who shared a past vision and were working on health-sector reform largely outside the state. But could this group be categorized in a meaningful way as belonging to 'civil' as opposed to 'political' society? This is the question to which we now turn.

Peru has long been an intensely 'political' society. One indication of this has been the number of political parties. The first emerged during the 1870s, and between 1928 – when José Carlos Mariátegui founded the Partido Socialista del Perú (that changed its name to the Partido Comunista Peruano in 1930) – and the end of the century (1999), more than 100 parties had been officially registered. Radical political activity went in waves when political ideologies of the left fused with widespread popular opposition. Most recently, during the 1960s and 1970s, communist factions (both Marxist and Maoist) had dominated left-wing politics.

Students entering the universities during the 1970s encountered an intense underground opposition to military rule (1969–1980) and internecine struggles between different political factions, each claiming to be the true revolutionary line and Mariátegui's rightful heir. While some retained intense dogmatism, a rhetoric of violence and rigid party discipline, the intelligentsia increasingly favoured a more open and moderate interpretation of Maoism that led to a 'new left'. Preparing for a return to democracy during the years after military rule in 1980 brought a dilemma for the radical groups: whether to continue in clandestine activities and engage in armed struggle (as did Sendero Luminoso and the Movimiento Revolucionario Tupac Amaru (MRTA)), or to reconstitute themselves as democratic political parties, take part in elections and fight for political change through the ballot box. Several attempts were made to bring radical factions into united fronts, although only the party Izquierda Unida survived. But the political immaturity of the leaders and a host of doctrinal (and personal) differences meant that the left failed to gain in the presidential elections of 1980 and 1985. With the violent Maoist party, Sendero Luminoso, occupying central political space, disillusion with party politics and the dissolution of the left, political commitment was channelled away from doctrinal issues and into other fields, including the NGO sector of civil society.

Many of those who campaigned for the democratization of the health sector, for a health system that could reach the poor and increasingly for health as a human right, had shared a past in the politicized universities of the 1970s and 1980s, where they had been associated with parties of the 'new left'. The membership of ForoSalud's executive committee seems to bear this out, especially the presence of the distinguished political figure Julio Castro Gómez. Julio Castro started his political life as a doctor in Cusco and became regional and later national leader of the health workers within the powerful Comité Intersectoral de Trabajadores Estatales (CITE). He, like many others of the group, had belonged to a party of the Maoist 'new left', which later joined forces with Izquierda Unida (United Left). Under the presidency of Alan García (1985–1990), he continued to lead the health workers and was elected member of congress. In 2004, he was joint founder of a new political party, the Partido Democrático Decentralista, and will fight the presidential elections of 2006. Others shared this political background, but had subsequently moved away from formal political activity.

Thus, represented in the health-sector reform network were activists committed to working for democratization and rights inside state and non-state institutions receiving donor funds. They knew the health field intimately and worked to channel donor support to pro-poor change. Included were public health professionals and policy analysts who had taken Masters degrees abroad, spoke fluent English, and were familiar with the language and political culture of international development cooperation. They now constituted a stratum of committed intermediaries who could form links of trust with donors coming to Peru and could mediate between them, national and regional NGOs and the state, as well as take on posts as field officers in donor country offices. The relational work of DFID in Peru had depended upon these social actors, and their political understandings and networks; DFID's rights-based approach had resonated with them. In turn, donor support had given the health reform group a new lease of life. The network could change its tone and language by moving from the political to the professional; by being flexible and responding to the opportunities for discussion and debate that DFID had provided (along with financial support), the network's bonds and broad political commitment could be developed once more.

Discussion: Advantages and challenges of supporting networks

DFID's evolving interpretation and response to changing political and institutional contexts in Peru was shaped by the dynamic interaction of a number of factors. These included close association from the outset with radical groups eager to think through policy reform for a post-Fujimori Peru; deepening knowledge of the DFID team that shaped thinking about the agency's role – knowledge gained both by learning from active engagement in Peruvian political processes and by commissioning analytical studies; investment of staff time in conceptual debate and reflection about social and political change and the role of donors in this process; and organizational alliances and personal relationships created along the way in connection with the activities that DFID was supporting, which, in turn, influenced the perspectives of the DFID team.

In the case of its support to health reform, DFID's presence in the sector for many years had made it both known and respected prior to its decision to make a radical shift in approach. After this, one finds that assistance to a network of policy analysts and health professionals helped to institutionalize a new public space for policy debate (with ForoSalud), as well as to bring about new university training courses linking rights to public health management (at the Universidad Peruana Cayetano Heredia). The nature of the networks coming into play in the 'new' reform period cannot be disassociated from Peru's political past. They corresponded to political positions formed outside and in opposition to the formal institutionalized political sphere. But they were able to transform themselves from Maoism to working towards democratic and participatory policy alternatives in order to replace an intensely hated authoritarian political culture. The strength of these networks by the end of the 1990s lay in their being partly outside the system, yet committed to reforming it. Among the bilateral donors, DFID led the way in understanding the potential that such networks possessed, gave them encouragement and support, and let them take the lead. However, over time there was also a danger. Small 'exclusive' networks could come to represent the interests of only a minority, they could become a new political clique, while extensive 'inclusive' networks could fail to attract attention and become sufficiently institutionalized so as to carry on working without donor support.

While DFID in Peru labelled most of its activities as 'projects', they were very different from how these have been classically understood. These projects tended to be more responsive, flexible and built around relationships that had often started experimentally with a small grant made for a time-bound specific purpose. As mutual trust developed, so DFID became ready to invest more financial resources in supporting organizations and networks so that they could pursue their evolving agendas. What many appreciated from their relationship with DFID was not the money, but the intellectual input and the accompaniment (Crabtree, 2005). Key to this was the country team whose Peruvian members brought with them their own commitment, knowledge and networks.

Arguably, in pursuing this approach DFID ran the risk of being co-opted by agendas that might have been in discordance with DFID's own aims: less well-informed foreigners in the country team might not have been aware of what was happening and found themselves overly influenced by their more connected and knowledgeable local colleagues. On the other hand, it is possible that an over-reliance on certain networks that had a political past, presence and programme (behind the blanket epithet of 'civil society') led DFID to becoming too involved in domestic politics and subterranean political rivalries. It could also mean that DFID overlooked other possibilities and social actors with less experience in dealing with donors or in expressing themselves in a language that resonated with the donors and which they could understand and empathize with. If the office had not been closed, this should have been a key issue to explore in any evaluation of DFID's work in Peru.

DFID's approach to engaging with networks as a means of promoting rights and deepening democracy chimes with much of the current literature on policy processes in Organisation for Economic Co-operation and Development (OECD) countries concerning the advantages of networks in tackling complex public management problems and coordinating state and society actors in pursuit of common goals (Innes and Booher, 2003). Noting this point, the concept of the 'dark network' has been introduced (Raab and Milward, 2003); but here the concern is for mafia-like drug rings and other illegal and illicit networks. More interesting and relevant for donors such as DFID is the extent to which progressive networks are themselves political actors and, thus, also run the risk of developing a dark or shadow side to them in countries where the institutional practice of transparency and accountability is challenged by the informal ties of patronage that permeate the structures of governance.

Thus, an emphasis on relationships and networks points to the need for a donor country office to be regularly testing the quality of these relationships through iterative feedback, reflection and change. It also requires a balance of international and national professional staff working together to ensure that support to networks does not shore up informal and exclusionary systems of social relations that are maintained more to the mutual advantage of their members than to deepening democracy. Finally, in order to check whether the supported networks are relevant for agency priorities in particular situations, staff need to stay in touch with the grassroots through frequent visits and immersions with the ultimate intended beneficiaries of the agency's assistance (see Chapter 3).

Notes

1   The material for this chapter is based on work that DFID Peru commissioned from the two authors in autumn 2004 and that appears as Chapters 1 and 3 in a book published by DFID to capture its experience before its closure in early 2005 (DFID, 2005). The office was closed because of DFID's decision to prioritize its resources for low-income countries and the rehabilitation of Iraq. The authors wish to thank members of DFID Peru and ForoSalud for sharing their knowledge and thoughts with us, as well as Patricia Oliart, University of Newcastle, for her perceptive comments on an earlier draft.

2   As Gould (2004, p1) comments, involved in aid relationships are 'matrices of rhetoric, ritual, power and material transactions euphemistically termed "development cooperation" between rich and poor countries'.

3   Francke had also been employed for many years in the Banco Central de Reserva, and in the Ministries of Health (1998–1999), Economy and Finance (1999) and Labour with The National Fund for Compensation and Social Development in Peru (FONCODES) (2000–2002), and had worked with NGOs dedicated to labour issues and human rights.

4   Chapters were devoted to the function of government and civil society in health reform; institutional reform; decentralization; inequalities in health coverage; primary healthcare, especially in the rural areas; hospital services and human resources in the health sector.
5   The second publication set out proposals on more specific aspects of health-sector reform and was published as *Peruvian Health in the 21st Century* (July 2002). In this second phase, the 'Policy Project' (part of USAID) was a joint sponsor with DFID.
6   APRA, founded in 1930 by Victor Raúl Haya de la Torre, first formed a government in 1985–1990 under Alan García; Perú Posible is a new party led by Alejandro Toledo.

References

Berry, F. S., Brower, R. S., Choi, S. O., Xinfang Goa, W., Jang, H., Kwon, M. and Word, J. (2004) 'Three traditions of network research: What the public management research agenda can learn from other research communities', *Public Administration Review*, September/October, vol 64, no 5, pp539–552

Buell, B. and Eyben, R. (2004) *Review of the DFID–Oxfam Human Rights Programme in Peru: Derechos, Inclusión y Desarrollo*, Unpublished report, January, DFID and Oxfam

Castells, M. (1997) *The Power of Identity, vol 2: The Information Age: Economy, Society and Culture*, Blackwell Publishers, Oxford

Comisión de la Verdad y Reconciliación (2003) *Los Partidos de Izquierda*, vol 3, Los Actores Politicos e Institucionales, Chapter 2, www.cverdad.org.pe

Cornwall, A. and Nyamu-Musembi, C. (2004) 'Putting the "rights-based approach" to development into perspective', *Third World Quarterly*, vol 25, no 8, pp1415–1437

Crabtree, J. (2005) 'Supporting institutions for political inclusion', in DFID (ed) *Alliances Against Poverty: DFID's Experiences in Peru 2000–2005*, DFID, London

De Landa, M. (2000) *A Thousand Years of Non-Linear History*, Swerve Editions, New York

DFID (UK Department for International Development) (2000a) 'Improving the health of the poor: A rights-based approach', DFID, London

DFID (2000b) 'Realizing poor people's rights', DFID, London

DFID (2005) 'Alliances against poverty. DFID's experience in Peru 2000–2005', DFID, London

Fox, J. (2005) 'Empowerment and institutional change: Mapping virtuous circles of state–society interaction', in Alsop, R. (ed) *Power, Rights and Poverty, Concepts and Connections*, World Bank, Washington, DC

Gould, J. (2004) 'Introducing aidnography', in Gould, J. and Secher Marcussen, H. (eds) *Ethnographies of Aid: Exploring Development Texts and Encounters*, International Development Studies Occasional Paper no 24, Roskilde University, Roskilde, Denmark, pp1–13

Hajer, M. and Wagennar, H. (eds) (2003) *Deliberative Policy Analysis, Governance in the Network Society*, Cambridge University Press, Cambridge

Henry, L., Mohan, G. and Yanacopulos, H. (2004) 'Networks as transnational agents of development', *Third World Quarterly*, vol 25, no 5, pp839–855

Hinojosa, I. (1998) 'On poor relations and the nouveau riche: Shining Path and the radical Peruvian left', in Stern, D. (ed) *Shining Path and Other Paths: War and Society in Peru, 1980–1995*, Duke University Press, Durham, pp128–157

Innes, J. and Booher, D. (2003) 'Collaborative policy making: Governance through dialogue', in Hajer, M. and Wagennar, H. (eds) (2003) *Deliberative Policy Analysis, Governance in the Network Society*, Cambridge University Press, Cambridge, pp33–59

Kabeer, N. (2005) 'The search for inclusive citizenship: Meanings and expressions in an interconnected world', in Kabeer, N. (ed) *Inclusive Citizenship*, Zed Books, London and New York

Lewis, F. and Sagasti, M. (2005) 'For those of you attempting this at home', in DFID (ed) *Alliances Against Poverty: DFID's Experiences in Peru 2000–2005*, DFID, London

Piron, L.-H. (2005) 'Rights-based approaches and bilateral aid agencies: More than a metaphor?', *Developing Rights, IDS Bulletin*, vol 36, no 1, pp9–18

Piron, L.-H. and Watkins, F. (2004) *DFID Human Rights Review: A Review of How DFID Has Integrated Human Rights into Its Work*, Overseas Development Institute, July, London

Raab, J. and Milward, J. (2003) 'Dark networks as problems', *Journal of Public Administration Research and Theory*, vol 13, no 4, pp413–440

Robinson, D., Hewitt, T. and Harriss, J. (eds) (2000) *Managing Development: Understanding Inter-Organizational Relationships*, Sage Publications in association with the Open University, London

Wedel, J. (2001) *Collision and Collusion: The Strange Case of Western Aid to Eastern Europe*, Palgrave, New York

7

Bringing Systems into Line with Values: The Practice of the Accountability, Learning and Planning System (ALPS)[1]

Rosalind David, Antonella Mancini and Irene Guijt

Introduction

Organizational change is born of tension and succeeds best when it aims for alignment of purpose and action and attunement of the internal and external environment. It is impossible to avoid conflict, inertia and confusion in this process; the only option is to make use of these forces by being aware of their potential. If a development organization makes it possible for its staff and partners to thrive on change, then it will be, in essence, a learning organization. (Scott-Villiers, 2002)

I have been inspired by learning more of the ActionAid (ALPS) journey. The readiness to admit how difficult and flawed it has been, and the admission that it is very far from perfect, has not in any way diminished my appreciation for it, or my ability to learn from it. On the contrary, it feels like something real and honest and worthy of my attention and respect. Perhaps this is the power of vulnerability at work? (James Taylor, 2004)[2]

This is a story of trying to change organizational systems so that they facilitate, rather than hinder, good development practice. It describes the rethinking of ActionAid's internal planning and reporting system – trying to institutionalize organizational changes so that poor people and their organizations are given the space to be centrally involved in initiating, monitoring and evaluating their own development process. The story gives a personal perspective. Rosalind David and

Antonella Mancini were both members of ActionAid's Impact Assessment Unit (IAU) and from that position contributed to the development and introduction of this new, organization-wide Accountability, Learning and Planning System (ALPS). The aim is to give an honest insight into organizational change, sharing with others the difficulties involved and the problems encountered.

Change is never smooth, nor is it easy. It requires politically strong champions and it takes a long time. This chapter explores the introduction of ALPS, what it symbolized and the implications that it has had on ActionAid's work and ActionAid's relationships with its partners. It discusses the contradictions and difficulties that adherence to the principles underlying ALPS posed within the organization. It explores some of the pressures and problems faced in negotiations with donors. Finally, it outlines some of the future challenges that ActionAid faces in protecting the valuable essence of ALPS, while rapidly undergoing current processes of change.

In 2004, ActionAid invited Irene Guijt to undertake an independent review of ALPS. In a postscript to this chapter (see Postscript, p148), Guijt highlights the salient findings of that review, reflecting on the challenges of switching to an approach that strives for greater accountability to the people whom the organization exists to support.

ALPS was part of wider organizational change processes

Over the last six years, ActionAid has undergone substantial transformation. In 1999, a new strategy – *Fighting Poverty Together* – set a new direction. Between 1999 and 2005, a process of organizational change began. The UK offices were downsized and its functions and power were decentralized to regional programmes. In 2003, ActionAid embarked upon a process of 'internationalization'. ActionAid's headquarters were relocated to South Africa, new staff were recruited and a new international board (composed of members from the North and South) was formed. The commitment to 'internationalize' ActionAid is at the core of *Fighting Poverty Together*. Internationalization is a key part of the attempt to distribute power in a more equitable manner within the organization and, in the longer haul, between ActionAid and poor people.

ActionAid has undergone wide-scale change. It has become bolder, more outspoken and much clearer about its principles and values. As an organization, it has become much more effective in its work with partners in tackling social injustice.

One important aspect of ActionAid's organizational change has been the rethinking of its accountability, planning and evaluation systems. In 2000, ActionAid took a fresh and principled approach by introducing the Accountability, Learning and Planning System (ALPS). This system had widespread implications for ActionAid's work right across the world. It has also attracted much attention within the international development community.

The origins of ALPS

There are many factors that, together, enabled ActionAid to take a fresh look at its internal accountability, planning and evaluation systems. Among them were: widespread staff frustration with internal bureaucracy; a bold new organizational strategy that set a clear agenda: new leadership across the organization; a hard-hitting external review of its programmes; and the active involvement of key trustees.

ActionAid's (1999) new organization-wide strategy – *Fighting Poverty Together* (FPT) – refocused ActionAid's work from delivering services to addressing the fundamental causes of social injustice and poverty. From being a slightly cautious UK charity raising funds through child sponsorship, ActionAid was now to link with others (partners, networks, trade unions and social movements) to reinforce the global anti-poverty movements. The clear articulation of organizational goals – and, particularly, principles – in FPT only served to highlight the disjuncture between ActionAid's vision and the management systems that were supposed to facilitate organizational performance. It became abundantly clear that internal systems had to change in line with its strategy. The most obvious system requiring revision was the internal accountability, planning and reporting system.

During the mid 1990s, ActionAid, like many of its peers, equated accountability and reporting with central systems and bureaucracy. The instruction manuals were long and detailed and the thinking inherently linear, the assumption being that certain activities lead to certain outcomes which bring about positive change in people's lives. Both ActionAid staff and local partners were frustrated. Everyone was complaining of spending so much time on project planning and reporting. The paradoxes were many. At the time, ActionAid was known for its pioneering work on participation; yet, somehow values of involvement had not permeated into its systems. While considerable staff effort was spent on reporting, the organization knew little about the lasting affects that its work had bought about in people's lives. Large, wordy reports tended to describe project activities in great detail. Far less emphasis was given to the wider impacts and changes perceived by the groups of people living in poverty with whom ActionAid and ActionAid's partners worked.

Initial attempts to rethink the internal accountability and planning system were mired in confusion and struggles to retain power, and it was hard to see how we would move forward. However, a major impetus came through a highly critical external review in 1999 of ActionAid's work, *Taking Stock* (Dichter, 1999). The reviewers were blunt. ActionAid was not transparent. It was not accountable to its partners or to poor people and its planning and reporting system was bureaucratic and burdensome.

The *Taking Stock* review accelerated the changing power dynamics within the organization. In particular, the ways of raising money would change, decreasing the proportion of 'tied money' raised through child sponsorship and increasing unearmarked funds raised through new funding mechanisms. The reassertion of the paramount importance of programme work influencing support functions, rather than *vice versa*, had a dramatic effect. With the support of some key trustees, the chief executive officer (CEO) and the international directors received the mandate to revise ActionAid's accountability, planning and reporting system. The aim was to develop internal reporting systems that would be in line with the principles and values of the organization as outlined in the new strategy *Fighting Poverty Together* (ActionAid, 1999).

The Accountability, Learning and Planning System

What was developed was, and remains, challenging. A long process of internal dialogue and discussion led to the design of the new system: the ActionAid Accountability, Learning and Planning System.

On the face of it, ALPS is no different from many other international NGO accountability systems. Core requirements include programme, project, country and regional appraisals; strategies; three-year rolling plans (with annual updates); annual reports; and strategic reviews (see Figure 7.1).

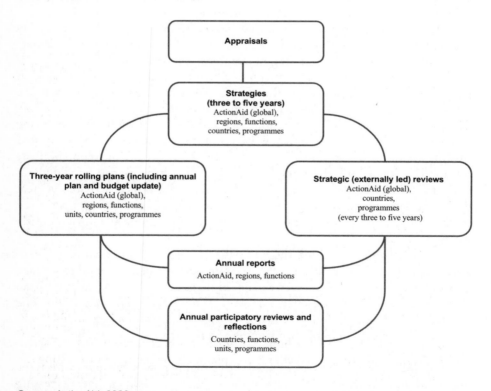

Source: ActionAid, 2000

Figure 7.1 *Core elements of the Accountability, Learning and Planning System (ALPS)*

However, ALPS was and remains quite different. At the time, it represented a complete paradigm shift. It starts with the belief that poor people and their own organizations are capable of – and should be involved in – managing their own development processes. While ALPS called for core documentation (for the purposes of statutory upward accountability), it recognizes the importance of downward accountability to local stakeholders, particularly the poor. Indeed, without their central involvement in development planning, monitoring and assessment, upward reporting was perfunctory. What use is it to know how many kilometres of road or how many health centres were built without knowing what (if any) difference this made to the lives of the poor? Indeed, was building the roads and health centres the best way to tackle poverty?

ALPS supports the view that poor people and their organizations should be given the space to negotiate their own position and have the opportunity to do so at local, national and international levels. It requires a belief that the international NGO's role is to support development initiatives, initiated and led by poor people (and their organizations) themselves.

Three quintessential elements of ALPS render it different and (to some) quite radical:

1 First, the system puts heavy emphasis on the principles and attitudes that drive ActionAid's work. ALPS recognizes these, and the ways in which we do things, as more important than functional planning and reporting. It emphasizes the principles of transparency, participation, learning, awareness of gender and power and, above all, accountability to primary stakeholders: poor people. ALPS outlines the importance of process and encourages adherence to the above principles in all that we do.
2 Second, in its very essence, ALPS went against the flow. It digresses from logical thinking by recognizing that social development, rights and justice cannot be planned, managed and delivered in a linear fashion. To carry out *Fighting Poverty Together* (ActionAid, 1999), ActionAid needed to create the space to reflect and work in different ways with its partners and with poor people. In order to provide space for partners and staff to respond appropriately to changing situations and contexts, ActionAid needed to become a reflective and reflexive organization.
3 Finally, while many international NGOs have responded to the demands of greater accountability by increasing reporting to central offices, ALPS tried to do the opposite by reducing the number of reports (written in English) going to London, and emphasizing, instead, greater accountability to the community groups and partners with whom ActionAid works. It encouraged the active involvement of primary stakeholders in planning, budgeting and assessing the value of interventions. More decision-making was decentralized from London, and greater decision-making power was given to national teams running their own programmes in countries across the world. The power balance had significantly shifted to primary stakeholders. ALPS was not designed to feed the insatiable desire for upward reporting.

New elements introduced by ALPS

Although the core elements of ALPS were similar to many other international NGO accountability systems, two aspects of ALPS were new and, at the time, innovative:

1   The first was the introduction of the annual participatory review and reflection processes (PRRPs). These were to happen once a year at each level (in programmes, countries, across the functions and globally). The overall purpose was to learn and share experiences from achievements and failures to improve programme quality, with the aim of involving stakeholders – particularly the poor, but also partners, donors and peers – in the analysis of what has worked and what has not. By welcoming criticism and creating the space for honest dialogue about programme expenditure, plans and initiatives, ActionAid hoped to create the possibility for stakeholders to give critical feedback and to actively influence ActionAid's agenda.

2   The second was the decision not to require a formal annual report from country programmes. The emphasis of ALPS was to improve the quality and impact of work carried out by ActionAid country programme teams. When ALPs was designed, there was a strong body of opinion against asking ActionAid country directors to produce annual reports, the argument being that the organizational emphasis should be placed on developing the integrity of the participatory review and reflection processes. Instead of annual reports, ActionAid country directors were asked (in the spirit of organizational learning) to share rough notes from the PRRP processes, lessons and outcomes on the global intranet. These might include matrices, photographs and diagrams, as well as text.

Thus, ALPS broke new ground. Embedded in each of the core requirements of ALPS is the emphasis on process, the aim being to gradually transform the way ActionAid carries out its work. ALPS, as a system, opened up the space for programme work to change in line with the political and conceptual understanding of development work as outlined in *Fighting Poverty Together* (ActionAid, 1999).

The challenge of changing behaviour and practice

In 2001, when the then CEO Salil Shetty launched ALPS, he wrote: 'We can now say with some certainty and pride that we have a planning and review system that is as passionate and rigorous as *Fighting Poverty Together*. We are all aware that it is much easier to change the system then changing behaviours and practice'. Indeed, he was right.

On the face of it, ALPS simply tried to support the adherence to often-repeated international NGO principles. In practice, the adherence to those principles had enormous and far-reaching implications across ActionAid. ALPS – the principles, attitudes and importance of involving stakeholders in its work – was applicable to all parts of the organization, to teams based in the UK, Brussels, Italy and Washington, as well as teams based in the South. ALPS required ActionAid staff to be creative. It required a political shift and a shift in consciousness across the whole of the organization.

At the individual level, ALPS had implications for attitude and awareness. It required a heightened awareness of power and the ways in which we relate to others – especially the less powerful. Staff in many parts of the world (and especially 'front line' staff who were at the cutting edge of our development practice) were required to give up old ways of working and to learn – or hone – certain skills: those of facilitation, participation, listening, and gender and power analysis.

At the organizational level, ALPS had implications for every aspect of ActionAid's work. Staff were now required to reflect and work together in ways that challenged deep-rooted divisions and hierarchies that existed between programmes, policy and support staff. Human resource and organizational development (HR/OD) teams were required to somehow facilitate the development of new skills and align organizational incentives to support ALPS. As an organization, ActionAid needed to develop tools to support an understanding of the philosophy (as well as the mechanisms) of ALPS. It needed to clearly articulate what was meant by the principles and behaviours set out in ALPS and to support an understanding of these across the organization. In addition, the organization needed to ensure that an understanding of ALPS and the recognition of changed behaviours became embedded in formal induction and appraisal processes.

ALPS also had far-reaching implications for finance staff. Finance coordinators in country programmes were required to develop skills to share financial information with partners and primary stakeholders in ways that were meaningful to laypeople. In practice, this meant, in some cases, developing ways of sharing key financial data with people who were semi-literate, or totally illiterate.[3] Finance staff were also required to work with their 'development colleagues' (and *vice versa*) in a totally different way. ALPS emphasized the importance of comparing the costs of work with an analysis of the benefit of the work from the perspective of the poor and our partners. The deep-rooted divide between finance and programme disciplines had to be transcended.

In addition, ALPS brought about significant changes for the marketing teams. As with finance, marketing staff were required to work more closely with programme staff. Sponsorship staff in country programmes were expected to use the annual PRRP processes as the primary source of information for reporting to sponsors. ActionAid fundraisers suddenly had to explain (and 'sell') ALPS to their donors, along with its projects and programmes. This became increasingly difficult in a context where donors were becoming obsessed with logframes and 'measurable' outcomes. It is even harder when you are dealing with Northern-based desk staff whose main concern is to tick the boxes – and yet harder when Northern staff members have no practical understanding of what ALPS means.

Country programmes made ALPS a reality

ALPS therefore required changes on many fronts. The organization was on a steep learning curve. At this stage, it was the work of a small number of country programme teams that made ALPS amount to more than words on paper. To some country programme teams, ALPS made complete sense. Like ActionAid's organizational strategy *Fighting Poverty Together,* ALPS had to be understood at an intuitive or political level. At its core, ALPS is based on sets of beliefs and principles around the rights of the poor to criticize and influence poverty eradication efforts. While turning the conventional 'charitable' perspective on its head, ALPS offered little guidance and few rules. ALPS mainly opened up the space for creativity and provided a loose framework for country programmes to experiment with ways of improving development practice.

Many of the country directors who welcomed ALPS had fought long and hard against ActionAid bureaucracy. For years they had questioned the necessity of 'sign off' by ActionAid UK. They wanted to support their country teams in order to respond in flexible imaginative ways to changing contexts in their own countries without feeling the bond of rules, procedures and straitjackets from the UK. For them, the involvement of partners and community groups, in all that they did, was already important. ALPS merely gave 'permission' to push the boundaries – to extend and formalize participatory processes of accountability and to break new ground in increasing transparency.

At the other end of the scale, some ActionAid country programmes floundered. A number of country directors were struggling to maintain large service delivery programmes, which had no place for, let alone understanding of, ideas of accountability to the poor. Here, the contradictions between ActionAid's inspirational words and the reality of these programmes were too great. Indeed, the culture of some ActionAid country programmes was (and, in some cases, no doubt remains) quite at odds with both ALPS and FPT. Some programmes were characterized by a donor–recipient relationship with 'partners', centralized monitoring systems based on endless indicators and procedures, and strong internal hierarchical systems of power. The fundamental relationship with partners and particularly with the poor was one of charitable giving. Political and cultural leaps would be necessary.

Although countries were expected to lead on the change process, demands for support were still received by the IAU in London. Recognizing the absence of country programme support, the international directors asked the IAU team to produce a manual of 'best practice'. In June 2001, we published *Notes to Accompany ALPS* (ActionAid, 2001a). These guidance notes were intended to help ActionAid staff think through the practical implications of ALPS. The notes provided examples (many from ActionAid country programmes) to stimulate ideas. Printed at the top of each page was 'Health warning: Ideas and options only – innovate and learn'. The onus was on country programmes to explore the implications and possibilities of ALPS themselves.

Work was needed in the Northern fundraising countries

While work to internalize ALPS was going on in country programmes, there was a constant need for the championing of ALPS in the North. Although many Southern country programmes had invested enormous amounts of time and effort in understanding ALPS and in internalizing its implications, little had happened in the Northern affiliates, particularly the UK.

There are many reasons. Constant organizational change was a main factor. Others were lack of time and the difficulties of peer review in a Northern context (where ActionAid is competing for funding and profile). Underlying these issues was, arguably, an anxiety about initiating difficult change processes in the UK. The dominant tendency among the (then) international director's team was for action rather than process. Many had little time for internal processes and analysis. This was particularly true in the London headquarters, which was about to be radically restructured.

An added problem was that there were significant gaps in terms of what was expected in Northern countries. At the time of writing ALPS, the focus and impetus had been on Southern country programmes. While the system was intended to include the whole of ActionAid, the ALPS document had not clearly articulated what this might mean for teams based, for example, in London, Brussels and Washington.

Between 2001 and 2003, the IAU made successive attempts to initiate and support stakeholder involvement in annual PRRPs in the UK. Although this initiative had the full backing of the CEO, the unit struggled. There was a long way to go. ActionAid internal teams in the UK were markedly separate. At this time, London-based staff rarely discussed problems, learning and achievements between teams in the same division – let alone between divisions. Involving external stakeholders and peers in this process would be another major step.

High staff turnover in the UK made working on ALPS increasingly difficult. The restructuring processes unsettled many. Staff were coming and going at all levels of the organization. For a number of years, the HR/OD team was primarily concerned with restructuring or recruiting. It began to weaken in numbers and resolve. A strong induction process explaining the philosophy and thinking behind ALPS was vital. This was never given priority – a major mistake. With each new staff member, there was a tendency for 'normal professional behaviours' to return (Chambers, 1993). Those country programme teams that had invested the most time and effort in internalizing ALPS resented the lack of work in the UK.

Much of the difficulties that ActionAid experienced in translating ALPS into reality was to do with control over resources and activities – not wanting to let go of control, and fear of what would happen if we did. One of the main contradictions was a dominant desire to understand overall progress made in the goals set out in *Fighting Poverty Together*. The international directors wanted to have efficient systems for monitoring progress of FPT, as well as to develop an effective Management Information System (MIS). The tensions between providing adequate information for upward accountability, while emphasizing downward accountability to partners, networks and the people with whom the organization worked on the ground, were huge.

The global progress report

ActionAid's aim in producing annual global reports on progress, lessons and problems was considered an important way of increasing transparency. ActionAid was working in more than 30 countries across three continents; but, essentially, it was one organization. It had one widely accepted organizational strategy and a considerable amount of organizational coherence. There was a valid need to share lessons across the organization. There was also a compelling need to know if our work was worthwhile.

During late 2001, the international directors with the support of the IAU produced a framework for monitoring *Fighting Poverty Together*. The production of the 'FPT framework' (as it became known) caused internal controversy. Unfortunately, sharing the framework was badly managed. ActionAid country teams received it through email and misinterpreted its significance. The confusion was great. To country programme teams engaged in the mammoth task of developing processes for increasing transparency and downward accountability, the framework presented huge contradictions. It typified upward reporting and linear thinking. It seemed to undermine all that was espoused in ALPS.

The tensions between downward accountability and upward accountability remain to this day. Across the organization, an attempt was made to put the FPT framework firmly in context. The international directors never intended the framework to be used by country programmes. Nor did they expect country programmes to feel constricted by the 'expected outcomes' in the framework. Furthermore, they also recognized that without the solid effort in country programmes to work with partners and poor people in understanding the processes of change, there was little point in an overall global analysis. The groundwork had to be right. ActionAid partners and stakeholders had to be part of the analysis of what progress (or lack of it) it was making. Priority had to be given to the integrity of processes at the grassroots level.

A key issue in the upward/downward debate was whether country programmes ought to produce an annual country report. Each year the organization vacillated. In 2000, no country reports were required. In 2001, a country annual progress report was requested. In 2002 (after lengthy discussions at an international directors meeting in the UK), the annual country reports were again waived. The argument that the production of an annual country report discourages open, honest and transparent discussions of change in the country programme PRRPs won the day. Emphasis was again placed on adhering to the principles and values in the ALPS.

Some may wonder how ActionAid managed to produce global progress reports without annual country reports. The answer is that PRRP notes/reports, from country programmes, contained lessons, contradictions, progress and, above all, an honest and corroborated analysis of change. These raw documents provided the basis for an overall understanding of progress. In addition to these PRRPs, there were cross-organizational thematic reviews (both internally and externally led), formal country reviews (carried out during the year and led by external consultants) and, most important of all, the analysis and reflection by the international directors and ActionAid's peers.

The writing of the global annual progress report proved unexpectedly rewarding. First, the distillation and analysis of overall change and impact were challenging. Second, the international directors gave licence for incredible transparency. It was immensely cathartic to write honestly about the challenges and the problems that ActionAid faced as an organization in trying to achieve its goals. Finally, in working so closely with the international directors through the annual cycles, the IAU was able to help emphasize the importance of lessons from participatory review processes influencing budgetary allocations. ActionAid's global progress reports were warmly welcomed by peer organizations and supporters who found it inspiring that such a large international NGO could both distil some meaningful sense of annual progress against its organizational goals and write so honestly about its challenges.

External pressures for 'business as usual'

External pressure – especially from donors – to carry out 'business as usual' was (and remains) enormous. There were many contradictions. While ActionAid was getting frequent requests from NGOs and bilateral and multilateral organizations to talk about ALPS, at the same time ActionAid's funding departments were pressured to conform to 'normal practice'. A case in point was ActionAid's negotiations with the UK's Department for International Development (DFID) over a Programme Partnership Agreement (PPA). PPAs are strategic-level agreements between DFID and an organization, typically an international NGO that is financed on the basis of this agreement. These agreements set out clear outcomes which DFID and partners have agreed.

ActionAid's DFID colleagues could understand the difficulties of 'measurements' and sympathize with our reluctance to produce quantitative indicators that would create incentive systems at odds with ActionAid's principles. However, they frequently returned to the same point. They had to fulfil organizational requirements. Boxes had to be ticked. There had to be measurable, fixed indicators to satisfy senior managers. The challenges were not simple. They were not about reporting or not reporting, about monitoring or not monitoring (we all believed in light, effective monitoring that informed learning), but about a credible way of assessing progress and accountability, and, most importantly, about *who* defined and controlled the process.

What happened with the DFID over the PPA continues to occur each time ActionAid seeks donor funding. Since ActionAid has deliberately followed a policy of diversifying its funding base (away from child sponsorship), this was a frequent occurrence. While the IAU – with the support of the policy director and the CEO – is able to argue the point, most fundraisers and members of marketing teams are not. Fundraisers have targets to reach and donor reporting requirements to meet. Poor induction processes often mean that they receive no training or support that would enable them to either understand or adequately explain ALPS. Many give up and simply conform to donor requirements. Every time this happens, the contradictions build up within ActionAid. Internal incentive systems become confused and messages are blurred.

What difference has ALPS made?

This chapter would be incomplete without an assessment of what bearing (if any) the ALPS system has had on the organization's contribution to social justice and anti-poverty work across the world. In this section, we outline some of the progress that has been made as a result of ALPS and some of the challenges that remain. ALPS has made a difference; but that difference is patchy and there is considerable space for improvement. Change takes a long time; there are no shortcuts and the contradictions are many. Guijt's postscript to this chapter (see Postscript, p148) offers her perspective. For our part, we suggest that three areas of progress stand out: strong internalization of ALPS; recognizing and sharing power; and participatory review and reflection processes.

Strong internalization of ALPS

Perhaps the most important change has been the strong acceptance and internalization of ALPS and what it stands for. Along with the ActionAid (1999) global strategy *Fighting Poverty Together,* ALPS is seen as a key reference document throughout the organization. It is something that the organization aspires to achieve. Indeed, ActionAid staff commonly describe processes or actions as 'out of keeping' or 'in keeping' with the spirit of ALPS. ALPS – and particularly the attitudes, behaviours and principles that it espouses – are entering ActionAid's lifeblood.

Recognizing and sharing power

A second achievement is that ALPS has induced a growing recognition of the importance of analysing and understanding power dynamics in our work. As a large international NGO, ActionAid has huge power vis-à-vis many of its partners, many of whom rely upon it as a donor. As such, there are inherent contradictions when ActionAid is trying to open up space for honest feedback and criticism. These have to be recognized and tackled if ActionAid is to do more than pay lip-service to participation and downwards accountability. ActionAid has to be proactive in creating an environment where its partners are confident enough to make honest criticisms. A quote from a partner in Kenya amply illustrates this issue: 'We can only respond to the questions raised if you can promise that you will not victimize us by cancelling our project.'[4]

Many country programme teams have recognized the power differentials and have begun experimenting with a variety of methods to create trust. Even so, ActionAid has been criticized for occasionally appearing inflexible in expecting partners and communities to follow ActionAid definitions and understanding. It is unclear to many staff when they should expect partners to learn the new 'ActionAid approach' and when they should negotiate to reach shared perspectives.

ActionAid's internal power dynamics are also an issue. Over the last three years, some effort has gone into empowering staff at all levels to take responsibility and decisions relevant for their work, supported by the requirement in ALPS that all reports are signed off only one level up the hierarchy. ActionAid Uganda, in particular, has put a lot of work into organizational development processes to encourage staff to take greater responsibility.[5] Despite the principles codified in ALPS, however, the way in which power is used in country programmes remains largely up to the personal styles of country directors.

Participatory review and reflection processes: Catalysts for change

Third, where it has been understood, ALPS has provided space in ActionAid country programmes: space to learn and work with others to improve the quality of development efforts. A key element of this change has been the success of the innovative annual reflection process, greeted in many country programmes with enthusiasm. It provided the creative space to challenge old ways of working. The participatory review and reflections processes have been the catalysts for change with regard to principles, attitudes and behaviours.

While the picture is by no means homogeneous across the organization, the majority of country programmes have invested time and effort in the review processes – and feel proud of the changes these processes have engendered. Four areas stand out. The annual reflection processes are beginning to induce more learning, altered accountability, more transparency and enhanced organizational understanding of change and impact.

There is evidence from many country programmes that the annual reflections are influencing the nature of ActionAid's work. This is true at all levels. Country programme teams were asked to explicitly show how future plans had been affected by stakeholder feedback. Furthermore, at the international director level, PRRP analysis and feedback from peers and other stakeholders explicitly influenced organization-wide annual budgetary decisions.

The PRRPs are also beginning to affect ActionAid's accountability to partners and poor people. Achieving greater accountability to poor people has not always been unproblematic. In some cases, ActionAid's motivation for this has been mistrusted, with partners perceiving the involvement of local communities in the review process as a form of policing their own activities. However, from India, for example, it was reported that in due course the partners understood the real reasons and saw the potential of the PRRPs to help them better understand the issues facing the community. On the other hand, while it is relatively easy to ensure that poor people, women and the socially marginalized are represented in reflection and review sessions, it is harder to make certain that their voices are heard.

The PRRPs have engendered a little more transparency in the ways in which ActionAid works.

In Kenya, for example, local-level reviews have included community-based organizations (CBOs), local NGOs, provincial administration, elected local government councillors and government officials from various departments. At these meetings, ActionAid staff have presented reports on financial plans and budgets, showing the actual annual expenditure on different sectors. Participants are then able to ask questions and assess the progress made by ActionAid in implementing the plans for that year. Subsequently, the management of each CBO, in turn, facilitated a similar process with their respective members to assess the progress that they had made in implementing their planned activities and in teasing out lessons from their performance.

In some cases, this has resulted in partner CBOs challenging ActionAid to be more frugal in its use of resources. For example, in one area of Kenya, CBOs questioned why training sessions were held in large hotels outside the local area. Consequently, training is now mostly carried out locally. Similarly, during discussions on the capacity-building costs, some participants recommended that exposure visits involve smaller teams. In another instance, open financial discussions led to ActionAid modifying its policy of contracting firms to implement water projects. ActionAid now includes community representatives in the selection process of firms.

Finally, the introduction of PRRP processes has led to a shift in the way that ActionAid documents its work. Previously, ActionAid programme reports concentrated on 'activities' (basically detailing ActionAid's work). Now, because of stakeholders' involvement in the reviews, there is a growing tendency for reports to give more emphasis to the changes that its work (and its partners' work) has brought about in people's lives. Involving stakeholders in many review processes has led to a refocused analysis of what is important in people's lives.

New challenges on the horizon

ALPS has created a dynamic of cultural change within ActionAid and in the countries where ActionAid is working. However, it has not necessarily led to the abandonment of older systems or old ways of working. ALPS cannot be seen in isolation from other ActionAid systems. While some of ActionAid's systems have undergone changes over the past few years, there is still a need to clearly identify some of the practices and policies in place that are currently undermining ActionAid's changing agenda.

The expectations in ALPS depend upon attitudes, behaviours and the skills needed to carry out key change processes. This requires a huge investment in building staff and partner capacities, and in reviewing current human resource and organizational development policies and procedures. ActionAid has not yet built up the personnel and expertise required to give such support right across its programmes. Where intensive processes have happened (for example, in Uganda), the results of this work have been transforming. However across the board, ActionAid has a huge amount of work to do to address the challenge of changing attitudes and behaviours in line with ALPS. In addition, there is much to do in developing induction processes, which introduce not only the mechanisms of ALPS, but also the thinking, ideas and philosophy that underlie it.

As an organization, ActionAid still needs to challenge some of the linear thinking associated with management tools and to have the courage to communicate the (often slow) reality of trying to promote social change. This is change that is rarely clear-cut, is not always positive, occurs for a variety of reasons, and needs to be supported in ways that recognize context and cultural specificity. Promoting social development, rights or social justice cannot be planned for, managed or delivered in a linear fashion. Attempting to do so distorts and perverts the reality on the ground and closes off appropriate responses to contextual changes. ActionAid needs to challenge its own internal tendency to apply management-centred 'logical' and 'linear' thinking, as well as thinking imposed from outside.

ActionAid still has also much to do in communicating effectively with donors on how it wants to monitor and assess the value of its work with partners and with its primary stakeholders: the poor. Some of ActionAid's difficulty in challenging its donors arises from latent confusion in a few country programmes. Indeed, in some ActionAid country programmes, the enthusiasm for PRRPs has led to the abandonment of 'old' monitoring and evaluation processes – neglecting previous bureaucratic systems while not replacing them with simple methods for data collection, analysis and use. The absence of basic monitoring has led to difficulties when providing necessary information for management decisions and reporting to donors. The international directors need to cajole and support country directors and thematic leaders in order to put in place coherent monitoring systems (that are light, simple and non-bureaucratic), as well as to ensure commitment to following basic ALPS guidelines. After all, it will only be through ensuring high standards of internal practice that ActionAid will be able to convince its donors of the benefits of ALPS.

Conclusion

Real change takes time, determination and the commitment to see the process through. We have described how ActionAid is still learning, rethinking and reacting to the introduction of ALPS. Its application in country programmes is modifying and changing the ALPS system. ActionAid is seeking ongoing feedback from its major stakeholders on how to keep ALPS processes authentic and honest. ActionAid has a huge amount of work to do in fostering a true relationship with its partners where partners can openly and clearly articulate criticism and share vulnerabilities regarding the difficulties of promoting social change.

In any international NGO, it is easy to dream up plans; but these will fail if they are not adopted and prioritized by country programmes. Without the solid hard work carried out by country programme teams, ALPS would have remained words on paper. It was the determination of ActionAid country programme teams – in countries such as Uganda, Brazil, Haiti/Dominican Republic, Ethiopia, Nigeria, India, Burundi and Kenya – who actually worked with the space provided by ALPS and, in doing so, gave it substance and made it meaningful. They repeatedly reminded the organization that ActionAid really can do things differently, and demonstrated this by pushing the boundaries and developing new practice.

At the directors' level, the support of the CEO, policy director, finance director and Asia director was vital, as was the commitment of Robert Chambers as a trustee.

Despite the many champions, the reactionary forces to change are very strong. As this chapter illustrates, it takes a long time to create change on a large scale. It requires trust, effort, focus and will. It also takes unwavering commitment and visionary leadership from those in power. At the same time, applying this kind of willpower actually begins to create immediate, if subtle, changes. It is these subtle changes that may eventually result in whole systems change. It is early days yet; but we hope so.

Postscript

Through external eyes: ALPS in ActionAid four years on

Irene Guijt

In the spirit of the Accountability, Learning and Planning System (ALPS), an external review[6] was commissioned by the Impact Assessment Unit in 2004 to see what had happened with ALPS within the organization four years on. I interviewed staff and partners in five countries (Kenya, India, Brazil, Italy and the UK) to identify successes and ideas for strengthening the ongoing organizational journey of change that ALPS has come to symbolize.

ALPS is, in many ways, alive and kicking. Methods of dealing with 'balanced multiple accountabilities' have received particular attention, and within that, the financial area in particular. Overall, the need for planning with the people who are to live with the changes is well understood, and community-level plans are created with considerable investment by ActionAid to bring together diverse voices through inclusive methodologies, notably through the participatory review and reflection process (PRRP). There is increased evidence of learning and, certainly, of more reflection, at least at the operational level and, in some places, at the strategic level. Clearly, there is no lack of change. Much attention is given to the continual questioning of ActionAid's core strategies and practices through PRRPs, partner meetings, thematic assessments and function assessments, and performance appraisals. ALPS-related processes are themselves also subject to reviews and improvements in some countries and at certain levels.

The emergence of ALPS within ActionAid is, on balance, a remarkable journey of a large organization that was sincere and courageous in wanting to align its procedures with its mandate. To date, it remains unique among international NGOs and, indeed, development organizations in general, in this respect.

The review also identified several key areas for further adopting and strengthening ALPS as ActionAid continues to evolve, particularly in the wake of the recent internationalization process. Many of the recommendations echoed concerns raised by ActionAid staff members, with some initiatives already under way to address these. Four reflections are offered here as pointers for the next stage of work in the ever-changing organization that is ActionAid.

Now that the core requirements are, in general, being followed, and most principles and attitudes are being taken up in various ways in field offices and various core functions, ActionAid can *extend the uptake of ALPS* into hitherto ignored or resistant areas. In particular, the Northern country programmes will need to examine more closely how they will implement the intention of PRRPs and integrate ALPS principles and attitudes within organizational culture and functions. This is valid for all European offices, where aspects of ALPS have been tried, but have not yet taken root. In part, this is due to an orientation in the first ALPS guidelines towards field programmes, but also due to the internationalization of ActionAid that has required far-reaching changes in the mandate of European offices and in their relationships with field offices. A specific example of the latter is the relationship between marketing/fundraising that mainly takes place in Europe and in field programmes. The intention of ALPS urges that field programmes shape priorities that are then supported by all functions, including marketing, through the principle 'Bring the concerns and aspirations of poor people into the centre of our decision-making'. However, at times, marketing was still observed to operate from its own sense of priority. One painful incident that highlights this occurred between a European office and a field office, in which the field office innovated by sending video updates rather than written updates to the sponsors of children. The first time round, this was accepted; but the second time round it led to tensions as the Northern office simply sent the bill for costs incurred to the field office. There was no discussion on how to deal with marketing requirements in ways that also respected local needs for reducing the reporting burden and making communication more 'real'.

Another important uptake gap requiring attention is that of governance at the highest level – the newly existing national boards and the international board, which remain outside the ALPS embrace. More questions than answers exist. How will boards be composed in ways that embody ALPS? How will ActionAid ensure that trustees are proactive champions of ALPS when many new trustees come from the business sector and may be more interested in results than process? And what does 'downward accountability' mean for the national and international boards?

After giving meaning to ALPS internally, it is now time to embody ALPS more clearly in *relationships with partners*. Partners and ALPS are a complex topic for ActionAid. Initially focusing on service delivery, ActionAid now largely operates through diverse partnerships at all levels. In the ALPS tradition, organizations with which ActionAid undertakes joint work are supposed to be equal partners. But, at the same time, the quality of work must be maintained, forcing the question of what is non-negotiable and what is flexible. Yet, each partnership represents different power relationships (from strong to vulnerable) and offers different degrees of freedom with respect to implementing ALPS. Furthermore, staff members have different understandings of what ALPS is supposed to mean for partners. Not surprisingly, the link between ALPS and the partners is extremely varied. Where ActionAid is one of many members of an alliance, ActionAid staff members can only model ALPS through their own behaviour and may, at best, push for some kind of learned initiatives. Where ActionAid is funding the effort, ALPS may be more prominent. For some, ALPS was supposed to be ActionAid internal – if ALPS 'rubbed off', then that was fine, but certainly not necessary. Others give partners copies of the ALPS notes and expect ALPS to shape the quality of the work. In many cases, however, ALPS is part and parcel of the organizational strengthening work that ActionAid undertakes with its partners (for example, with local NGOs and CBOs in Brazil, Kenya and India). Added to this is the growing diversity of ActionAid's funding arrangements, which includes other funding agencies and *their* accountability and learning standards. The combined challenge of negotiating ALPS with donors and (potential) partners requires strong leadership and clarity for staff to be able to negotiate.

A third area for development relates to the *quality of ALPS*. The initial focus of the IAU was to stimulate innovation from which lessons and experiences could be shared. Setting standards too early on – and tracking them – could have risked creating the very procedural rigidity that ALPS was trying to shake off. Nevertheless, now it is time to reconsider the need for minimum quality criteria for the different ALPS processes that are not yet clearly defined or tracked. 'Financial accountability' is increasingly clear about what it deems good quality. For planning processes, the guidelines provide some help with stipulating the type of information required, while the principles and attitudes and behaviours should embody the standards followed. These latter aspects are, however, worded in general terms and leave much to the individual ActionAid staff member's imagination when it comes to implementation.

The need for greater clarity also extends to the need to clarify what 'learning' means in ActionAid and how this is best implemented. Many ActionAid staff seemed to describe changes when asked about what had been learned. Yet, change can happen via non-learning routes – by accident, crisis, imposition, etc. How, then, does ActionAid know when 'good-quality' learning is happening? Quality checklists could be developed to help ActionAid staff and partners scrutinize with greater care – for example, 'Is learning distributed equally between partners,

ActionAid and beneficiaries?' or 'How does a gender perspective or the quality of rights-based approach (RBA) work undertaken inform the focus of the partner meetings, the performance appraisals or the fundraising efforts?'.

An achievement of ALPS is that, by letting go of obligatory formats and reporting requirements, mental space was freed up to reflect more on practice. There is certainly considerable evidence of reflection and learning in the organization. For example, the IAU annually absorbs a range of reports and observations from the field and translates these into a global report. This is subsequently discussed by global directors and used for rethinking strategies and signalling problem areas. However, in other aspects, learning processes in ActionAid can still be improved, including:

- more effort for assessing the effectiveness of policy/advocacy strategies and processes, in terms not only of what worked but especially what made it possible;
- more consolidation of processes for organization-wide learning, particularly more horizontal dialogue across regions and country programmes, but also from local field offices to national offices – and, in particular, checking if the processes in place are actually being implemented across the organization;
- creating mechanisms to identify shared learning needs – for example, on 'networks as partners' or 'how to work on gender relations, not just with women';
- ensuring that communication flows so that field experiences inform policy – especially in larger country offices, such as India where a hiring freeze has led to an explosion in contract staff (almost four times the regular staff) who do not attend the staff retreats that are invaluable for policy review and reorientation.

Finally, there is a variable track record in *internalizing ALPS principles* despite the presentation of the eight principles as equal. For example, the principle of 'increased accountability to poor people, partners and other key stakeholders' is clearly visible throughout ActionAid via various innovations, notably the PRRP. This principle was given more prominence and represents a significant achievement for the organization. Most other international NGOs have not (yet) accepted or understood what 'downward accountability' could mean, not to mention trying to practice it. On the other hand, the principle of 'reducing burdensome reporting' is hampered by the trend in ActionAid to diversify funding, which has led to more/new donors, each with their own funding formats. Importantly, the principle of 'strengthening ... analysis of power and gender', while improved, also needs much more investment if it is to take hold in organizational practice. The variation in adopting the principles is partly a result of some being easier to implement than others, but also indicates variable perspectives within ActionAid. Considerably more work has been undertaken in terms of methodological innovation and capacity-building – for example, of the accountability and transparency principles – than in those relating to power/gender analysis and devolved decision-making. It would be inspiring if, yet again, ActionAid could lead the way amongst large global NGOs in translating this principle more concretely into improved development practice.

Notes

1 Changes that have taken place in ActionAid since 2004 are not described here.
2 James Taylor, Facilitator's reflection on a workshop exploring developmental planning and monitoring in Härnösand, Sweden, November 2004.
3 For example, through the use of pie charts, simple diagrams and participatory rural appraisal (PRA) processes.
4 Concerns expressed by a CBO member during ActionAid Kenya PRRP 2001.
5 See Wallace and Kaplan (2003).
6 The full review is available at www.actionaid.org.uk/wps/content/documents/ALPSReview.pdf.

References

ActionAid (1999) *Fighting Poverty Together: ActionAid's Strategy 1999–2005*, ActionAid, London
ActionAid (2000) *Accountability, Learning and Planning System*, ActionAid, London
ActionAid (2001a) *Notes to Accompany ALPS*, ActionAid, London
ActionAid (2001b) *IA Exchanges Special: Learning from ALPS*, ActionAid, London
ActionAid (2002) *IA Exchanges Special: Lessons from ActionAid's Review and Reflection Process*, ActionAid, London
ActionAid (2003) *Making a Difference in a Difficult World: Global Progress Report 2002*, ActionAid, London, www.actionaid.org/resources/general/general.shtml
Chambers, R. (1993) 'Normal professionalism, new paradigms and development', in Chambers, R., *Challenging the Professions: Frontiers for Rural Development*, IT Publications, London, pp1–14
Chapman, J., David, R. and Mancini, A. (2004) 'Transforming practice in ActionAid: Experiences and challenges in rethinking learning, accountability systems', in Earle, L. (ed.) *Creativity and Constraint: Grassroots Monitoring and Evaluation and the International Aid Arena*, INTRAC, Oxford
Cornwall, A. (2001) *Appropriating ALPS: Strategies for Improving Accountability, Planning and Learning in ActionAid Brazil*, ActionAid, London, June
David, R. and Mancini, A. (2003) 'Transforming development practice – the journey in the quest to develop planning, monitoring and evaluation systems that facilitate (rather than hinder) development', ActionAid paper for DAC Conference, March 2003
David, R. and Owusu, C. (2001) 'Monitoring empowerment within ActionAid: A partial view', in Oakley, P. (ed) *Evaluating Empowerment*, INTRAC, Oxford
Dichter, T. (1999) 'ActionAid taking stock summary report', ActionAid, London
Framer, N., Dub, F., Osewe G. and Enfield, S. (2002) 'To develop a monitoring and evaluation plan for SIPAA, ActionAid and SIPAA', DFID, London, December
Gatigwa, S. (2001) *Sharing our Finances: IA Exchanges Special 2001*, ActionAid, London

Guijt, I. (2004) 'ALPS in action: A review of the shift in ActionAid towards a new Accountability, Learning and Planning System', Report written for ActionAid International

Scott-Villiers, P. (2002) 'The struggle for organizational change: How the ActionAid ALPS system emerged', *Development in Practice*, vol 12, nos 3 and 4, August

Wallace, T. and Kaplan, A. (2003) *The Taking of the Horizon: Lessons from ActionAid Uganda's Experience of Changes in Development Practice*, ActionAid, London

8

Money Matters in Aid Relationships[1]

Cathy Shutt

Introduction

A complex chain of relationships and mechanisms is required to transport international aid from donor countries in the 'North' to the poor and marginalized in the 'South'. In order for money or technical expertise to be passed from one organization to another, links need to be established between the two parts of the aid chain – links commonly referred to as 'partnerships' in the current development paradigm. Most partnerships that involve an aid transfer are managed by a set of rules and procedures that make the 'partner' – that is, the recipient – lower down the chain directly accountable to the organization that handed over the aid, usually referred to as a 'donor'[2] by the recipient. As the amount of aid decreases on its way down the chain, the rules and conditions that donors use to ensure that money is spent in ways that *they* believe will achieve expected impacts tend to increase.

Many argue that mutual dependency is implicit in donor–recipient relationships (Lister, 1997, p9; Hudock, 1999; Fowler, 2000; Ebrahim, 2005, p52). Recipients require financial resources to pursue their missions and donors need recipients to facilitate development interventions and produce information that demonstrates their success – information that donors can use to claim legitimacy. Fowler[3] and Hudock both contend that despite the implicit interdependency in donor–recipient relationships, few merit the description 'partnership' since donors rarely share mutual responsibility for outcomes. In practice, recipients usually feel that the partner who has control of financial resources has the upper hand and is the more powerful party in the relationship. Organizations that hand over money are still considered as donors rather than partners, whether they are international non-governmental organizations (INGOs) or official donors. The rules and procedures that make recipients financially accountable to these donors are symbols and, indeed, instruments of the power inequity perceived by recipients in aid relationships.

This chapter considers how these rules and procedures that accompany donor funding can affect learning within recipient organizations, particularly those that receive aid from several donors, each with distinct financial rules and procedures. The method is a reflection of ten years' experience working as a development practitioner for Southern-based development organizations. During this time my roles involved working with colleagues in recipient organizations to interpret the financial and programmatic procedural requirements of different donors to accomplish several simultaneous goals: a truly participatory approach to development interventions; donor accountability; organizational sustainability; and job security for friends and colleagues.

Two of these organizations, which I shall refer to as 'Enabling Development' and 'Good Neighbours', refused to be labelled as 'international' or 'local' development organizations. They chose, instead, ambiguous identities in efforts to maximize funding options and to minimize the possibility of being made ineligible by donor conditions that privileged either 'international' or 'local'[4] legal identities. This illustrates the heterogeneous nature of organizations working in development that will be referred to as development organizations (DOs) throughout this chapter.[5] The writing is also informed by findings from research with smaller 'local' DOs in Cambodia. While I appreciate donors' motives for establishing means that allow them to demonstrate accountability to taxpayers in donor countries, I also empathize with recipient DOs that genuinely want to be accountable, but struggle with accountability mechanisms that they feel have negative effects on their practice.[6]

This chapter is organized around a central financial management theme in an effort to increase the awareness of programme practitioners about how the minutiae of financial rules and procedures can affect *inter-* and *intra*-organizational relationships and learning within organizations. The attention to detail reflects my belief that it is necessary for programme practitioners to gain a more nuanced understanding of financial management issues in order to achieve the kind of 'double-loop' learning discussed below that will lead to improved relationships and mutual accountability between programme and finance staff at the same level of the aid chain. This is based on the personal conviction that improved *inter*-organizational relationships are as important and necessary as enhancing *intra*-organizational relationships between donors and recipients in learning how to make more effective use of international aid.

The chapter begins by considering how donor rules and procedures can pose challenges to the organizational learning aspirations discussed in Chapter 1. It then goes on to consider how they shape recipient learning agendas so that recipients favour learning about how to appear accountable to donors and, very much related, learning how to survive. The conclusion suggests alternative theoretical concepts to assist donors and recipients with more transformative learning that might lead to shifts in power relations so that motives for learning become driven by efforts to improve development practice through being more accountable to people who are vulnerable and poor.

Learning within inequitable aid relationships

Earlier chapters in this book are testament to the growing recognition that organizational learning is crucial if aid organizations are to develop and improve their practice. Although the term 'organizational learning' is contested, it is generally understood to go beyond merely increasing knowledge and to involve reflection, action and change. In Chapter 1, Pasteur suggests that organizational learning requires time and space for cyclical processes that allow personal and collaborative critical reflection, leading to changes in actions. Her chapter emphasizes the importance of posing the question 'why?' in iterative processes that aim to achieve deeper levels of understanding of underlying issues. This leads to double-loop learning, allowing organizational members to question values, beliefs and assumptions that might lead to fundamental change in the way they go about their business.

As a practitioner with an interest in learning and improving practice, I had conceptualized rather naive mechanisms and processes by which such learning might occur. Monitoring and evaluation exercises were scheduled procedures within the project management cycle framework. I had assumed that these would provide cyclical learning processes for both individuals and groups of staff – who were often defined in terms of staff working on a particular donor-funded project – to reflect and learn from their experiences. I imagined that lessons or issues emerging from individual projects and programmes could then be discussed in wider spaces, such as annual organizational retreats and planning meetings, stimulating the kind of analysis that would lead to organizational learning.

My expectations proved somewhat unrealistic. There was, of course, some learning by individuals and project teams who worked closely together; but monitoring and evaluation concepts were introduced to recipients as add-ons that seemed peripheral rather than integral to normal development practice. Thus, they were not perceived as an opportunity for learning, but more as a set of procedures to be used to demonstrate accountability to donors who controlled decisions over resources upon which the recipients' survival depended. As these organizations seemed to continually experience financial problems, evaluations were conducted in situations where staff members were anxious – fearful about what might happen in the event of unfavourable evaluation outcomes. There was little incentive to identify weaknesses, nor much need. Monitoring and evaluation frameworks that placed emphasis on quantitative results failed to solicit qualitative descriptions of what was happening, a necessary precondition for probing 'why?' questions that are essential for double-loop learning. I found myself compiling impressive statistics for donor monitoring reports, frequently asking myself 'so what?'.

It was something of a relief, to return to study and discover that my experience was not exceptional. Development literature suggests that the project cycle management framework has failed to achieve many of its learning aspirations (Biggs and White, 2003). Ebrahim (2005) presents case-study evidence that demonstrates how donor monitoring and reporting requirements that emphasize financial and quantitative output indicators, typical of the management-by-results framework discussed by Eyben in Chapter 2, influence DO staff understanding of what constitutes successful development practice. 'Success' becomes equated with quantitative outputs.

Ebrahim (2005), like this present volume, argues that the positivist, bureaucratic theoretical model used by donors assumes that development is a linear process and is a fundamental obstacle to learning and improving development practice. Such a model suggests that links between parts of the aid chain are connecting impersonal organizational structures. It also ignores the fact that learning takes place in the context of social relationships and is mediated by power and emotion (Vince, 2001) – a point less often recognized.

Several contributions to this volume suggest that there is reason for cautious optimism. A growing number of people working in aid organizations have an increased awareness of power inequities in relationships and realize the limitations of learning within linear, positivist, logical frameworks. They are seeking more reflective and holistic ways to learn. Despite these encouraging developments, DOs that rely on project or programme funding from different donors may still find it challenging to convert knowledge and lessons from individual projects to double-loop organizational learning. This is due to the various rules and procedures of their different donors, which affect organizational structures, decisions about staffing and incentives, as well as inter-organizational relationships.

A reliance on project and programme funding had considerable effects on the structure and organizational layout of Good Neighbours. Programme staff funded by different donor projects and programmes were organized into a 'division' that shared an open-plan office. An analogy of 'smoke stacks' was used by some senior managers to describe the lack of interaction between the different programmes and projects within the division, perhaps evidence of the 'silo' mentality that Pasteur notes as a typical barrier to communication and learning in aid organizations (see Chapter 1).

The organization's leadership recognized that the 'smoke stacks' were a problem and tried to arrange regular meetings between staff, designed to build team spirit and encourage the sharing of information between groups of people working on different projects. Many staff members attended grudgingly as they experienced tensions between being good organizational citizens and fulfilling commitments to ambitious donor-funded projects that were sometimes executed under extreme time pressures due to donors' annual funding cycles. Some staff who were fully funded by a donor project seemed to view themselves as primarily responsible to the donor, rather than to the organization. Many left meetings frustrated as information exchanges tended to revolve around diary activities as a means of improving overall coordination, rather than asking probing questions about the quality and effects of our work. Pasteur (see Chapter 1) identifies a number of conditions that are conducive to critical reflection, which include the creation of an enabling environment and appropriate organizational culture – conditions that are dependent upon strong organizational leadership. In the case of Good Neighbours, organizational leaders failed to create this type of culture, perhaps symptomatic of how difficult it is for powerful leaders to critically reflect and admit weakness. It could be argued that if donors shared responsibilities for partnership outcomes, as suggested by Fowler (2000), reflective practice by powerful individuals within recipient organizations may become easier.

Even if Good Neighbours' leaders had been able to admit weakness, a reliance on restricted project financing would still have made organizational learning an uphill struggle. It proved difficult to persuade staff to reflect and learn from their work in the context of organizational strategic goals and objectives when they were accustomed to being evaluated by their donors within the confines of management-by-results project objectives, in isolation of the overall organization that employed them. A reliance on short-term unpredictable project and programme funding meant that organization managers were also confronted by difficult decisions about the terms and conditions of employment for their staff. Should staff be employed on contracts that were permanent or on terms that were co-terminus with the end of donor funding cycles? The latter was the financially pragmatic decision suggested by a bureaucratic approach to managing aid, casting staff as impersonal variable costs, however, it tended to be resisted for emotional reasons. In organizations with strong social cultures, frequently using a family metaphor to describe themselves, employers wanted to offer their employees long-term employment.

Financial pragmatism was not only unattractive for emotional reasons. Making staff employment co-terminus with projects or programme funding had significant implications for the recipients' ability to learn. Good Neighbours experienced vast inefficiency in the start-up of the second phase of a European Commission (EC)-funded programme, 13 months after the end of the first phase. All the original team had left the organization, taking the knowledge and learning from the first phase of the project with them. Despite the new programme staff being appointed from within the organization, they had to start from scratch, building relationships within the project team while simultaneously trying to glean lessons from reading project documents, as well as working hard at establishing relationships with partners further down the chain.

Once programme staff understand the philosophy and aims of the DO that employs them and have developed experience while employed on a donor-funded project, they become valuable assets that give the organization technical capabilities and opportunities to learn. Defining some of these competencies as 'core' or 'fixed' costs enhances the organization's ability to develop programmes, rather than projects, and to provide training and consultancy capabilities in specific technical areas. As organizational reputations are often built on the strength of the capabilities of individuals, retaining valuable people as part of core competencies increases the ability of the organization to attract funding and enables efficient start-ups to new project or programme activities that hiring on a basis that is simultaneous with donor funding cycles does not. This is particularly true when working in long-term partnerships with organizations lower down the aid chain which require relationships built on trust that can lead to greater impact (Chambers and Pettit, 2004).

A DO's decision to aim for programmatic cohesion and retain programme capabilities as core staff is desirable. These staff can be made available to different projects and programmes that can encourage learning and cross-fertilization of experience across different parts of the organization. However, the unpredictability of funding makes this difficult to manage logistically and it may involve financial risk. Temporarily assigning 100 per cent of a core programme staff member's time to one donor project or programme, and perhaps allowing them higher compensation levels for insecure tenure, is an attractive financial management tactic even though this might result in reluctance to participate in the kind of organization learning activities discussed earlier.

Given the uncertainty surrounding the success of competitive funding applications, differences in donor fiscal periods and unpredictable lags between donor approval and cash disbursements, DOs may need to negotiate a number of proposals simultaneously to maximize the possibilities of funding such staff. Situations can arise where several proposals are successful, meaning individual staff members are doubly funded for some periods and not funded for others. The restrictive nature of funding and inflexibility in donor grant and contract periods, a result of pressure for donors to spend money by fiscal deadlines, makes it difficult to maintain a stable salary structure without appearing to have committed fraud. The policies of various donors regarding the personnel costs that they are prepared to cover can contribute to inequity within recipient incentive structures. This can cause staff to devote significant amounts of time and emotional energy to trying to make sense of their relationships with other organizational members while questioning organizational politics (MacLachlan and Carr, 2005, p6) – time and energy that might be better applied to reflection on the strengths and weaknesses of relationships with partners lower down the aid chain.

Clearly, financial rules and procedures pose a number of obstacles to recipients achieving organizational learning aspirations; but does this disjuncture between the learning theory presented in Chapter 1 and practice mean that DOs do not learn? On the contrary, despite apparent barriers, recipients with financial problems experienced partly as a result of donors' procedures do, indeed, learn. Those I worked with lived on 'white waters', existing in uncertain contexts, learning and adapting to change (Vaill, 1996, cited in Chapter 1). However, what was learned, and the ways in which we adapted, seemed to be driven more by desire for financial survival and the effects of more powerful donors' financial procedures than interests of improving development practice and, thus, accountability to those whom we were employed to serve.

Learning to survive

During the mid 1990s, Enabling Development was struggling with the challenge of developing strategies that would lead to financial sustainability, a notion that was gaining currency and being promoted by donors at the time. Even though the term financial sustainability was ill defined, it resonated with colleagues who wanted the organization to be driven by the needs of its partners further down the aid chain rather than by its donors. Sustainability notions were also popular with staff who had become accustomed to the insecurity that came with working for an organization that appeared to exist in a state of paradox. Despite appearing financially healthy in public annual reports, the organization continually seemed to be in a situation of financial crisis. Sarcastic jokes from disaffected staff provided a thin veneer that disguised a highly emotional organizational climate. The management was not trusted by many, and if they were believed, were blamed by staff for not doing enough to generate new resources. Why did the organization appear to be financially healthy but still struggle to pay regular expenses? Why was job security of staff so difficult to guarantee?

The apparent discrepancy between the organization's financial situation presented in annual accounts and the reality of everyday life could largely be explained by accounting conventions and financial dependency upon donor grants[7] accompanied by rules and procedures that restricted the use of money. The statutory principles used for the preparation of annual accounts for financial auditors meant that cash inflows or grant revenues[8] were not shown in the same period as the expenses they were meant to cover;[9] thus, revenue did not synchronize with expenditure. While gross revenues received by the organization seemed to cover gross expenses, a closer examination of the financial situation revealed that much of the money was restricted through donor rules and could not be used to cover many of the expenses involved in managing the organization and retaining the staff vital to having a credible core capability.[10] Paradoxically, it was possible for gross revenues to exceed gross expenditures in a period when the organization did not generate enough money that could be legitimately used to cover core costs, with the organization effectively experiencing a financial deficit.

It appeared that Enabling Development had several distinct but related problems that needed to be tackled simultaneously, thus taking up vast amounts of staff time. Learning how to develop a financial management information system capable of providing improved information to different types of users, particularly internal managers to help them better understand the financial situation, became an organizational imperative. We also desperately needed to learn how to generate more unrestricted revenue and to ensure that the revenue raised was sufficient to allow us to 'balance the books'; cost management was a necessary condition for achieving our financial sustainability goal. I have since discovered that these are common challenges for DOs, although how they are experienced depends upon the organization's specific context and its relative position in the aid chain.

Learning to account: The challenge of multiple bottom lines

It is not unusual to see the words 'weak financial management' on flipcharts during internal or external assessments of the strengths and weaknesses of recipient DOs, yet, little time seems to be devoted to qualifying what the term 'financial management' means to different actors within the aid system. My own understanding is that financial management describes the organizational activities required to ensure that sufficient unrestricted and restricted funds are on hand to meet all the costs and contracted obligations of an organization, both in the current time period and for some predefined future period.[11] Financial management activities would thus include establishing long-term financing strategies; budgeting and accounting systems for shorter-term planning; monitoring and control measures to ensure financial accountability; and reporting functionality that supports analysis and decision-making.

The understanding of financial management by staff in many recipient organizations seems to rely on what they have learned through their experience with particular donors. Those that have had relationships with donors that have placed significant emphasis on this aspect of organizational development may have quite a sophisticated idea of what financial management is about, while others seem to have developed an understanding based on learning disciplinary rules that enable them to demonstrate accountability to their donors. This type of disciplinary learning is described by Vince (2001) as 'regressive', providing more sophisticated processes for compliance and control. The potentially damaging effects of regressive learning encouraged by power inequity in aid relationships are exemplified in a publication entitled *Learning for Transformation: A Study of the Relationship between Culture, Values, Experience and Development Practice in Cambodia* (O'Leary and Meas Nee, 2001). Findings from research that sought to establish why efforts to build the capacity of local DOs (LDOs) had achieved so little impact suggest that while much attention had been spent on helping these LDOs to develop management skills that would enable them to comply with donor rules and procedures, the developmental learning needs of frontline workers interacting with the poor had largely been neglected.

Many donors tend to restrict their financial reporting requirements to the financial transactions that they directly finance, seeming somewhat uninterested in learning how their financial contributions complement money made available from other donors. Developing the means to report to a single donor is a relatively straightforward task; but as many recipients receive money from several donors, each with their own financial definitions and reporting procedures, donor reporting becomes a far more complex business, requiring a significant amount of time being devoted to its study.

Some donors do require recipients to produce a more consolidated picture of organizational accounts. However, the latter demand results in the production of audited organizational financial accounts that comply with statutory financial accounting[12] principles and fail to provide the kind of management accounting information required to manage DOs on a day-to-day basis, something particularly important for larger DOs with complex donor portfolios. Prioritizing compliance with the demands of multiple donors who use different reporting conventions can influence the structure of organizational financial management information systems (Fowler, 1997, p130). Such systems become incapable of producing internal management reports required for organization managers to learn and analyse finances and to take action that might lead to positive change in organizational financial situations. DOs experience tensions when trying to develop monitoring systems that meet both the information needs of funders and their own practical requirements (Ebrahim, 2005, p91). The power inequity that exists within these relationships means that learning how to account to donors and meet their information needs is usually prioritized over learning how to be accountable to organizational members and those to whom the DO should be primarily responsible: people living in poverty.

The distinct financial management information needs of different stakeholders – donors, auditors, internal managers, staff and partners further down the aid chain – justify the term 'the law of non-profit complexity' coined by Anheier (2000, pp6–8). Anheier argues that it is inappropriate for non-profits to rationalize operations in terms of corporate accounting since their goals are quite different: 'Money is the means and not the end for non-profits.' He points out that it is not the absence of a bottom line that is the problem, but the fact that there are several bottom lines:

> A non-profit organization has several bottom lines because no price mechanisms are in place that can aggregate the interests of clients, staff, volunteers and other stakeholders that can match costs to profits, supply to demand, and goals to actual achievements. (Anheier, 2000, p6)

Recognizing 'the law of non-profit complexity' and the need to develop the means to interpret the organization's financial situation and make projections for its future was a significant learning milestone for both Enabling Development and Good Neighbours. However, performing the task proved rather more complicated and required additional education.

Various donors have quite different ways of conceptualizing cost definitions and what they are prepared to fund. For example, while some donors allow costs such as finance personnel to be considered a direct cost of implementing their programmes, others seem to find this unthinkable. Billing rates – the application of a margin on top of the real costs of staff time – are accepted by some donor agencies; but others find it scandalous and tantamount to 'fraud'. Some donors, such as the EC, seem to define cost eligibility on a case-by-case basis (FM Partners Limited, 2005, p18). The rationale for donor policies supporting the costs associated with an organization managing a project or programme is confusing for many recipients who receive money from various sources. Different terminology is used to describe this magic, penultimate budget line item, which for many is an important source of 'unrestricted' money. 'Indirect costs', 'administrative costs' and 'overhead costs'[13] are just three of the line item descriptions used by donors, and they can have quite different meanings. Even in the days of sophisticated computer technology, it is challenging to come up with inexpensive standardized systems that can take account of all of these peculiarities and interpret various definitions to satisfy the information requirements of a variety of donors, auditors and the DO's board and senior management.

In larger DOs based in developing countries that have to manage relationships with multiple donors, aggregating this type of financial data to produce historical financial reports and future projections for the organization can place enormous stress on finance staff. In the cases of Enabling Development and Good Neighbours, finance staff often worked late into the night, struggling to meet all the demands made on them by diverse stakeholders. They were frequently blamed for the failure to meet deadlines by programme managers and others who viewed accounting and financial management as an accurate science and were neither aware of, nor understood, the 'law of non-profit complexity'. Volatile emotional relationships between programme and finance managers were not aided by donor behaviour, which typically separated the functions of programme monitoring and evaluation from financial monitoring and auditing. This did little to encourage the mutual learning of programme and finance managers about each other's roles and responsibilities, particularly the challenges that finance staff faced in trying to produce reports with multiple bottom lines.

Learning to balance the books

Gradual improvements to the financial management systems in both Good Neighbours and Enabling Development led to senior managers having access to more useful management accounts. My specific academic background enabled me to interpret financial information, and so it became part of my responsibility to 'educate' senior managers and programme staff so that they could learn how their actions influenced organizational financial outcomes. It was hoped that this would lead to changes in behaviour that would allow the management to have tighter control over the financial situation, which facilitated progress towards 'balancing the books'.

Trying to maximize unrestricted income from new projects, programmes or consultancy services became an organizational priority, as did the strategic use of existing restricted grants. Staff members who were responsible for negotiating budgets had to learn to use discretion and recognize the 'right kind of money'. A cost-centre approach was devised, which increased competition between divisions and led to conflict, further reducing the probability that we would be able to engage in shared reflective practice.

Entrepreneurial staff who were keen to rise to the challenge of raising more unrestricted revenue quickly realized the significance of 'indirect', 'administrative' or 'overhead' line items in budgets. At Enabling Development, canteen discussions were full of references to 'administration costs' and 'overheads', with staff celebrating achievements when budgets that they had carefully constructed to generate unrestricted money were approved. In the case of Good Neighbours, the previously reluctantly attended management meetings began to have new value as we exchanged information about donors and began to develop a more sophisticated understanding of how donor organizations and, perhaps equally importantly, the individuals who worked for them conceptualized costs.

As we learned more about the specific practices and procedures of various donors – and, in some cases, the individuals whom they employed – some donors began to appear as more attractive potential partners than others. Motives for developing organizational relationships and new programme ideas became strongly influenced by financial needs and the strength of personal relationships; programmatic consistency with organizational goals and ethical considerations became a secondary consideration. Since it stood apart from other donors in its generous conceptualization of overheads,[14] there was significant financial incentive to pursue potential partnerships with the US Agency for International Development (USAID). In my experience this is a common tactic amongst INGOs who are happy to engage in 'marriages of convenience' with the agency despite the controversy surrounding some of its programme policies. Tension can emerge in USAID recipients' relationships with those further down the chain if the spoils from relationships with the American bilateral are not equally shared, but are maintained by the 'donor' further up the chain.

Our efforts to 'balance the books' had other significant impacts on feelings of inequity within relationships that reduced aid effectiveness. It often meant that there was no money for programme development. This made it difficult to provide those 'lower down' the chain with opportunities to participate meaningfully in formulating proposals when the principal objectives, indicators of success and budget parameters associated with putting donor policy into practice are set. An evaluation of one of Good Neighbours' programmes demonstrated the damage that can be done by not inviting all project partners to participate in programme design. In this instance, the lack of involvement of government officers in initial negotiations with the bilateral donor meant that it took considerable time for Good Neighbours to nurture trusting relationships with these officers and for them to develop a real sense of programme ownership, something that was essential for successful outcomes. The donor representatives became decidedly nervous about the lack of tangible outputs about halfway through the programme and started to put pressure on programme staff to hurry up and produce results.

Good Neighbours admitted that some of the problems in programme implementation were of its own making, and went to a great deal of effort to repair damaged relationships with the donor and to maintain good relationships with the relative government departments. However, delays in implementation meant that Good Neighbours was forced to request a 'no cost' extension – an extension of the project timeframe with no additional funds being granted by the donor. While such extensions come at no extra cost to the donor, they can have serious financial impacts on recipients who have to find scarce unrestricted money to support the staff costs during the extension period as the salary component of the project budget has already been expended.

'No cost' extensions were symptomatic of other financial problems. Organizational budgets assumed that a certain rate of expenditure of restricted revenue would lead to a related level of unrestricted revenue being made available to cover core costs from 'indirect cost' allowances. Slower project implementation that gives rise to the need for 'no cost' extensions may produce less revenue to cover cores costs than anticipated in a specific time period and lead to poor financial performance against budget forecasts. Historical analysis of the reasons for the financial problems of Enabling Development revealed that 'no cost' extensions had become a normal part of aid relationships, often negotiated by programme staff who did not realize the financial implications of such practice. In the absence of effective internal management accounting systems, the problem had gone unnoticed for a substantial length of time, and the accumulated effects were responsible for significant reductions in scarce reserves.

Once this problem was recognized, management made efforts to educate organizational members to desist from such practice. Board members, executive managers and finance staff were as keen as donors for activities to proceed as planned in proposal timelines. This was the cause of yet more friction as programme staff desired flexibility that would enable them to develop trusting relationships with partners that were necessary to facilitate effective participatory processes, whether working at a macro-level with government officers to develop national development policies, or at a more micro-level, developing the capacity of village-level organizations to respond to the needs of their communities.

The squeeze on unrestricted funds resulting from unpredictable 'no cost' extensions and funding gaps was further exacerbated by the terms and conditions of donors who pay final instalments of contracts a considerable time after expenses have been incurred and paid for by the recipient. The EC is renowned for taking between six months to a year to make final payments. While a recipient DO with one such grant or contract may be able to absorb such delays in cash payments, organizations that are managing several such contracts can experience serious cash management problems as a result. They may have to resort to borrowing from other restricted funds, a practice that may be considered illegal by some in the donor community. Delays in cash remittances from donors can also lead to late salary payments and transfers to partners lower down the chain, sometimes provoking emotional responses from those affected, which compromise relationships and ultimately influences policy results. In order to avoid such situations, some DOs have to take extreme measures and learn to make do with what they have, as discussed in the following section.

Learning to make do

While learning to raise the right kind of money and to comply with highly restrictive donor rules is a significant accomplishment for recipients at the middle and the bottom of the aid chain, it may not be sufficient to enable them to balance their books. The power inequity that is inherent in aid relationships may mean that relatively weak recipients who feel unable to challenge formal power structures and who appear to accept donor terms and conditions have little other recourse than to learn to manipulate or bend rules to work in their favour in order to survive, actions that some donors and auditors may consider a breach of contract. Recipients learn to make do with what they have. This third type of learning, which Eyben calls 'resistance' learning (see Chapter 2), may ultimately jeopardize their financial sustainability if judged to be fraudulent.

While Good Neighbours was able to attract significant amounts of restricted funding, it experienced problems raising sufficient unrestricted money to cover core costs that included some essential programme capabilities. Senior managers spent considerable time learning how to manipulate donor rules and restrictions without breaking them in attempts to generate money to support these unfunded core costs. Project and programme staff were encouraged to share expertise across donor-funded programmes; thus, some individuals ended up being more than 100 per cent funded for certain periods of time. Since double funding was considered fraudulent, programme staff were expected to work large amounts of overtime so that they could legitimately and transparently charge different restricted funding sources for the amount of time that they devoted to each project. This was seen as a means of generating a surplus on their salaries that could be returned to the organization as unrestricted revenue to contribute to core costs. The tactic ultimately failed since one donor would not allow staff members who were 100 per cent employed on projects that it funded to commit time to other programme activities.

Good Neighbours continued to struggle with funding its core costs. At one point, a temporary funding gap that was partly due to delays in remittances from bilateral and multilateral donors prompted senior managers and programme staff to consider pay reductions. The costs and benefits of asking staff working on donor-funded projects to sign for salaries at their original salary levels, above amounts that they were to receive after the cut – a creative application of the billing rate principle used by some large international development organizations (IDOs) and consultancy firms – was discussed at length. The intention was to minimize indirect cost claim losses as a result of the proposed cuts and to use the 'margin' created by staff receiving less money than they had signed for as a 'donation' to the DO. This money could then be used to support their colleagues' costs. The proposal was eventually rejected as there were concerns that such action might be considered 'fraudulent' by more powerful donors and auditors. Core staff and those who were partially funded by restricted grants took pay cuts, while those who were 100 per cent funded by programmes did not. This inequity within the organization predictably led to more tension in intra-organizational relationships.

Neither of the proposals mentioned above were designed for personal gain, and there was no intention to cut corners on meeting programme objectives. However, the resistance learning was expensive: it took vast amounts of time and caused friction between staff that interfered with normal working practice. Finance staff, in particular, lived with the worry that such creative practice would be declared fraudulent by auditors and might jeopardize their individual professional reputations. The only reason the overtime tactic failed, in my opinion, is that it was done so transparently. As an auditor from a highly respected audit firm recently confirmed, such practices could easily go unnoticed under the terms of reference for some donor audit processes that confine the auditors' inspection to the project that the donor financed, ignoring the rest of the organization's accounts. Hence, it would appear that expensive upward accountability mechanisms are, on occasion, likely to be ineffective.

Learning about who counts

This chapter has demonstrated that the effects of powerful donor rules and procedures extend beyond the highly visible aspects of controlling expenditure on the specific projects or programmes that donors fund. They are pervasive and influence organizational structures, incentives and relationships, making it difficult for recipients to engage in transformative learning processes since staff are inclined to see their roles and responsibilities within the terms of specific donor projects, rather than within broader organizational strategic frameworks.

Nevertheless, despite these impediments to organizational learning, experience in this chapter suggests that recipient DOs do, indeed, learn. The problem is that learning priorities tend to be driven by the need to account to donors, prioritizing regressive learning of disciplinary rules while ignoring the need to establish the means to learn about and understand their own financial situations. This can serve to undermine accountability and trust between colleagues, placing a strain on intra-organizational relationships, particularly those between programme and finance staff. Weak systems also contribute to poor financial performance as they tend to disguise early indications of financial problems, which only become apparent when it is too late to mitigate financial crisis.

DOs that find themselves in financial crisis are likely to devote enormous energy to learning how to balance their books through better understanding of donors' rules and procedures, which can result in marriages of convenience that may divert attention from organization missions. If these efforts do not produce desired results, recipients may resort to resistance learning: bending rules in order to balance their books – actions that can lead to additional tensions in inter- and intra-organizational relationships.

It seems somewhat ironic that the rational donor rules based on the bureaucratic model discussed by Eyben (see Chapter 2) which aim to remove emotion from the frame of organizational analysis and promote efficiency seem to achieve the opposite effect. They create emotional entities where it is difficult to engage in shared reflexive practice, and large amounts of recipient DO staff time is allocated to regressive and resistance learning, which is expensive as it diverts attention and resources away from transformative learning that could lead to more significant social change.

All donors have experienced serious fraud, and the importance of accountability in the expenditure of aid is undeniable. However, it is becoming increasingly acknowledged that current accountability mechanisms used by some donors are ineffective and, as Ebrahim (2005, Chapter 6) shows, detrimental to both donors and recipients learning and improving development practice. Donor rules and procedures are powerful phenomena that seem to influence the very act of organizing in recipient DOs. In some instances, donors almost become part of the 'establishment' of recipient organizations by means of their rules and procedures. They have 'colonized' the organization (see Chapter 2). Vince (2001) suggests that organizations only really learn when they are able to identify and critically reflect on this process. If donors and the rules that they use to manage relationships are involved in creating organizational power structures, information systems and emotional climates that impede 'progressive' learning, then they need to show emotional intelligence and spend time reflecting and learning with partners in order to find means of reducing power inequity that might prevent collective learning (Chambers and Petit, 2004). There is a need to be sensitive to emotions and to create relationships that involve shared responsibility for partnership outcomes and encourage trust, cooperation, adaptability and willingness to change.

Particular problems are encountered when donors develop a relationship with recipients in terms of short-term sub-contractual relationships, rather than a broader moral relationship with the recipient organization. Evidence in this chapter suggests that aid might be used more productively if donors were better able to develop relationships with the other donors of their recipients and integrate the management of programmatic and financial aspects of their aid relationships. Increasing flexibility of aid allocations for items such as personnel costs and sharing the costs of thorough independent financial audits of entire recipient organizations are two measures that might improve aid effectiveness, provided that donor agents resist the temptation to form controlling donor cartels.

It may be useful to end by considering a serious limitation of this chapter: it fails to justify why recipient DOs should survive. A DO only deserves to survive as long as it remains relevant and of value to those whom it is intended to serve. This will remain difficult to determine if success is conceived in terms of quantitative outputs, and accountability is interpreted as learning how to 'keep donors happy'. It is time for a change of tack. Donors need to encourage DOs to focus on accountability mechanisms that encourage them to undertake double-loop learning about how to satisfy the ultimate recipients of aid, such as the social audit process explored by Eyben in Chapter 2.

Chapter 7 describes ActionAid's attempts to rise to this challenge and make radical changes to traditional reporting procedures that encourage downward accountability to those who should be doing the (ac)counting. ActionAid's efforts have been responsible for inspiring other agencies to follow their example. Mango, an IDO that provides accounting capacity-building services to DOs, launched a campaign called Who Counts? in April 2005 (www.whocounts.org). This campaign calls for DOs to be more accountable to beneficiaries and to produce financial reports that increase the participation of poor people in aid accountability mechanisms, another encouraging move towards ensuring that those whom aid is intended to benefit are the ones who really count.

Notes

1   I would like to acknowledge the many colleagues and friends whom I have had the privilege to work with during my time in South-East Asia. They are too numerous to mention by name, but our mutual learning experiences have made the writing of this chapter possible. I would also like to thank Rosalind Eyben, Alan Fowler and Alex Jacobs for some invaluable comments on an earlier draft of this chapter. However, the views reflected here are my own and may not be consistent with those of any of the aforementioned individuals.

2   In this chapter, the term donor is used in a generic sense to describe the organization handing over funds to a recipient.

3   Refer to Fowler (2000) for a detailed discussion and analysis of the different types of relationships that NGOs have with donors.

4   'Local' is used in a simplistic sense to describe organizations that are not international.

5   Dorothea Hilhorst (2003) provides a more comprehensive discussion of the use of multiple identities by DOs.

6   I am particularly grateful to Alex Jacobs for helping me develop my thinking on the negative effects that current accountability mechanisms have on development practice and drawing my attention to some relevant literature.

7   The terms 'project' and 'programme' grants are used in a generic sense throughout this chapter to refer to discrete allocations of money to DOs from donors under sector-wide programmes, projects, etc. The money can be used to finance a wide range of policy initiatives – for example, fieldwork, training programmes and advocacy programmes.

8   The term 'revenue' is used to refer to income earned in a specific period, which may differ from the period in which cash is received. The receipt of cash is referred to as cash inflow.

9   In some countries, statutory accounting provisions mean that grant commitments are recognized as income when the commitment is made by the donor. This could mean that all the money for a two-year project is shown as income during the first year and none in the second. Cash-basis accounting presents similar problems as cash inflows are often recognized in reporting periods that do not coincide with their expenditure.

10 The term capability is used as a qualitative measure to denote skills, as opposed to capacity, which I understand to be a quantitative measure.

11 A more comprehensive description of financial management, as well as practical guidelines, for NGOs can be found on Mango's website: www.mango.org.uk.

12 Financial accounting aims to provide financial information to parties outside the organization. Managerial accounting information is aimed at helping managers within the organization to make decisions.

13 No precise definitions are offered for these contested terms that often have ambiguous meanings.

14 Some donors conceive such costs as an amount to cover the additional 'administrative costs' that the recipient will incur as a result of managing the project that the donor is funding, which is not necessarily related to the overhead costs of the recipient. Others, such as USAID, base their allowance on a calculation of the recipient organization's overall overhead rate. This can result in quite a generous overhead allocation compared with similar donors.

References

Anheier, H. (2000) 'Managing non profits: Towards a new approach', *Civil Society Paper*, vol 1, www.lse.ac.uk/collections/CCS/pdf/cswp1.pdf, accessed April 2004

Biggs, S. and White, S. (2003) 'A paradox of learning in project cycle management and the role of organizational culture', *World Development*, vol 31, no 10, pp 1743–1757

Chambers, R. and Pettit, J. (2004) 'Shifting power to make a difference', in Groves, L. and Hinton, R. (eds) *Inclusive Aid: Changing Power and Relationships in International Aid*, Earthscan, London

Ebrahim, A. (2005) *NGOs and Organizational Change: Discourse, Reporting and Learning*, Cambridge University Press, New York

FM Partners Limited (2005) *Striking a Balance: Efficiency, Effectiveness and Accountability. The Impact of EU Financial Regulations on the Relationship between the European Commission and NGOs*, FM Partners Limited, on behalf of Open Society Institute, Concord, The Platform of European Social NGOs, SOLIDAR, The European Women's Lobby

Fowler, A. (1997) *Striking a Balance*, Earthscan, London

Fowler, A. (2000) 'Partnerships: Negotiating relationships – a resource for non-governmental organizations', *Occasional Paper Series No 32*, INTRAC, www.intrac.org/docs/OPS32final.pdf, accessed November 2005

Hilhorst, D. (2003) *The Real World of NGOs: Discourses, Diversity and Development*, Zed Books, London

Hudock, A. (1999) *NGOs and Civil Society: Democracy by Proxy?*, Polity Press, Cambridge

Lister, S. (1997) 'Power in partnership? An analysis of an NGO's relationships with its partners', *CVO International Working Paper No 5*, USAID, Washington, DC

MacLachlan, M. and Carr, S. (2005) 'The human dynamics of aid', *OECD Development Centre Policy Insights No 10*, www.oecd.org/dataoecd/35/56/35041556.pdf, accessed November 2005

O'Leary, M. and Meas Nee (2001) *Learning for Transformation: A Study of the Relationship Between Culture, Values, Experience and Development Practice in Cambodia*, Oxfam, Phnom Penh

Vaill, P. (1996) *Learning as a Way of Being: Strategies for Survival in a World of Permanent White Water*, Jossey-Bass, San Francisco

Vince, R. (2001) 'Power and emotion in organizational learning', *Human Relations*, vol 54, pp1325–1351

Afterword

Rosalind Eyben

Reflective aid practice concerns learning in action to effect change for the better. The cycle in Figure 1.3 in Chapter 1 shows how action is followed by reflection and questioning, leading to seeing one's action in a new light, to a reframing of problems and to a revised plan of action. The contributions in this book are part of such a cycle. In most cases, the authors' intentions were to inform their own future practice, as well as to influence the practice of their readers. This is not easy, particularly when there is more than one author involved, each with a different history of involvement in the matter discussed – and therefore a different perspective on what happened and what they learned. Relationships matter as much in the reflection and questioning stage of the cycle as in the moments of planning and action. Nevertheless, while a shared effort may be a harder undertaking, it also offers greater possibilities through learning from each other.

Writing for publication rather than just for themselves poses additional challenges. If our critical reflections of aid practice are taken in bad faith, do we put at risk the financing of development organizations that are seriously committed to transformative learning? Furthermore, a readiness to be honest not only with oneself and one's colleagues but also with a wider readership may be counterbalanced by a desire to tell a good story and, thus, to encourage others to make a difference. How can we write critically about success and failure while doing it in such a way that our readers (at least, hopefully, some of them) will be inspired to go out and change the world? I remember when I was a practitioner inside an international development agency how important it was for me to read books such as *Whose Reality Counts* (Chambers, 1997) that gave me the courage to have a go.

From this perspective, stories such as that of ActionAid's Accountability, Learning and Planning System (ALPS) or the UK Department for International Development's (DFID's) learning approach in Brazil can be considered as myths. By this, I do not mean that they are untrue. Seeking to make sense of myth in terms of fact or fiction is missing the point. They are stories that are imbued with value and purpose and that resonate emotionally. Myths are an expression of a determination to act (Sorel, 1961). They are powerful as statements of aspiration, and potential instruments for changed behaviour and attitudes. If the myths are sufficiently convincing, they may give the impression of power and relationship-sensitive practices *already* occurring inside the aid agency to a greater extent than may be the case. Thus, readers might come to believe that they are laggards and be stimulated to catch up with the (mythical) account presented.

This book's myth is that international aid agencies possess the potential to become learning organizations, staffed by reflective practitioners who name power and are capable of developing value-based relationships. When we consider the context and complexity of international aid and the historic nature of the large bureaucratic organizations that sit at the top end of the aid chain, these aspirations appear utopian. On the other hand, it can be argued that it is precisely when confronted with such a difficult goal as aid organizations set themselves that 'practical utopianism' is most needed. Utopian schemes:

> ... *must leave out for the time everything irrelevant... They must bring forward the central issues, making them look clear and limited enough to tackle... Till that clarification is done, confusion reigns and people seem faced with a gorgon which turns them to stone. They are paralysed by the mere tangle of conflicting considerations.* (Midgley, 1996, p16)

Here lies the challenge. International aid as a global project is itself a practical utopian myth: money from rich countries sent to poor countries can improve the well-being and the greater realization of rights by the people living in poverty in those countries. This book has argued that this myth is by itself not sufficient. We have proposed a further myth in which the delivery of money is complementary and secondary to reshaping relationships for greater social justice. Yet, paradoxically, the foundation for this new myth requires reflective practice that would necessarily, if honest with itself, seek to query and reframe the proposition, as for example in Chapter 6, which touches on the shadow side of a relationships approach to aid practice. Yet, the greater our preparedness to enquire and be honest with ourselves and with others, the more we are living out our myth in practice.

Believing in something can make it happen. Unless the authors of this book are entirely victims of self-deception, the empirical findings presented in this volume appear to signify that change *is* possible and *is* happening. Covert knowledge is made public and difficult issues are being aired. Contributing to global poverty reduction is probably the most challenging task that any organization can set itself. There will never be any ready-made solutions. Aid practitioners are collectively engaged in something never done before in human history. They cannot know the route because they have never travelled it before. This means that asking questions and challenging assumptions is more necessary than finding quick-fix solutions. If this book encourages the questioning of certainty and a movement among development researchers and aid practitioners towards investing in value-based relationships, it will have achieved what we set out to do.

References

Chambers, R. (1997) *Whose Reality Counts: Putting the First Last*, Intermediate Technology Publications, London

Midgley, M. (1996) *Utopias: Dolphins and Computers*, Routledge, London

Sorel, G. (1961) *Reflections on Violence*, Collier Books, New York

Index